ALEKSANDR BLOK
The Journey to Italy

Aleksandr Blok.   (Tass from Sovfoto.)

ALEKSANDR BLOK
The Journey to Italy

with English Translations
of the Poems and Prose
Sketches on Italy

by LUCY E. VOGEL

Cornell University Press

ITHACA AND LONDON

First published 1973 by Cornell University Press.
Published in the United Kingdom by Cornell University Press Ltd., 2–4 Brook Street, London W1Y 1AA.

International Standard Book Number 0–8014–0756–7
Library of Congress Catalog Number 72–12286

Printed in the United States of America by Vail-Ballou Press, Inc.

Librarians: Library of Congress cataloging information appears on the last page of the book.

To my children,
Patricia and Richard,
with love

Acknowledgments

I should like to express my gratitude to Leonid Rzhevsky of New York University for his patient guidance and continuing encouragement during the preparation of this book, and to Zoya Yurieff, also of New York University, for suggesting its theme and giving me valuable insights into Blok's poetry as well as into the Symbolist period as a whole in Russian literature. I am also deeply grateful to the late Robert Magidoff and to William Rowe, of George Washington University, for sensitive advice and criticism.

My sincere thanks go to James E. A. Woodbury for his intelligent and conscientious assistance in the task of editing Blok's poetry and essays, to Betty Rosshandler and Pat O'Brien for typing the manuscript, and to the graduate school of the State University of New York at Stony Brook for the grant that enabled me to visit all the places in Italy mentioned by Blok in his writings.

On my most recent trip to the Soviet Union, in the summer of 1968, I had the pleasure of meeting and talking with the well-known literary scholars and critics D. F. Maksimov and V. M. Zhirmunskii. I am deeply grateful to them for sharing with me some of their judgments and reminiscences of Blok's life and art.

I am also much indebted to the library staff of the Pushkin Museum in Leningrad for allowing me access to Blok's Italian albums and for their courteous help, and I deeply appreciate the assistance of Norman Jung and his efficient staff at the reference library of the State University of New York at Stony Brook in locating rare reprints and books.

L. E. V.

Contents

Illustrations

Biographical Sketch

Born in 1880 of aristocratic and talented parents, and endowed with good looks and health, Aleksandr Blok enjoyed the benefits of a happy and sheltered childhood and of an excellent education. He wrote his first verse at the age of five, and while still an adolescent won literary recognition; in his early twenties he was already widely thought of as Russia's greatest living poet. Yet despite all this good fortune, his poetry reveals the tragedy of a man whose conception of the poet's role was at odds with that of his own times; who wanted to be more than a mere "poet" to his generation, and who could not bring his art and his aspirations into harmony.

Blok's childhood and youth were spent in Shakhmatovo, a small estate between Moscow and Petersburg that belonged to his maternal grandparents. Andrei Nikolaevich Beketov, Blok's maternal grandfather, was a distinguished botanist, a writer, and the Dean of the University of St. Petersburg. His wife, Elizaveta Grigorievna, the daughter of a well-known explorer, was herself a talented writer and translator, who knew personally some of the outstanding figures of the nineteenth century, Gogol, Tolstoi, and Dostoevskii among them. The poet's mother, Aleksandra Andreevna, wrote verses for children and translated French poetry into Russian.

Blok's paternal ancestors, of German descent, included provincial governors and physicians. His father, Aleksandr Lvovich, a man of impressive erudition and talent, wrote books on jurisprudence, taught law at the University of Warsaw, and was also an accomplished musician. In 1916, at his editor's request, Blok wrote an autobiographical sketch. It is significant that only the second half of this ten-page document deals with the actual details of his own life; the first five pages record his genealogy, so great was his pride in his intellectual heritage and in the integrity and progressive views of his forefathers.

Blok's parents separated shortly before his birth. Both subsequently remarried—the father almost immediately, the mother some years later. Blok grew up in the predominantly feminine environment of the Beketov household at Shakhmatovo. An only child among adults, he was pampered by his doting mother, a highly emotional, religious, even mystically inclined woman, and by his grandparents and aunts. Shakhmatovo had an enormous impact on his life and art. The low surrounding hills, the "sweet-scented wilderness" of the countryside, the peace and rustic charm of his ancestral home, left an indelible impression on his memory. His reflections in prose and poetry on the historical and transcendental meaning of Russia were deeply rooted in his early impressions, as were his attitudes toward people and events later in life.

In 1889 Blok's mother remarried, and the family moved to Petersburg. On the whole, the liberal views that emerge in Blok's later works were not characteristic of his adolescent years. With hindsight, he would recognize omens of destruction in the smooth course of the serene and complacent life that his family had enjoyed for many generations, and in its aristocratic detachment from the social inequities all around; but at the time, he resented his commonplace, undistinguished stepfather, an officer in the regular army, and the gymnasium he was forced to attend repelled him with its plebeianism. He found its atmosphere incompatible with his thought, manners, and feelings, and after spending nine drab years there he entered the University of St. Petersburg to study law. By his third year, however, he clearly realized his lack of aptitude for the subject and decided to follow a literary vocation. He then transferred to the department of philology and history at the University, but even here he did not excel as a student. During his four years of study he was far more interested in the theater and in the philosophy of Vladimir Soloviev than he was in the prescribed academic subjects. Soloviev's mystical concept of the Eternal Feminine—Sophia, the heavenly being whom he regarded as the incarnation of love, beauty, and wisdom—and his apocalyptic predictions, were then widely discussed among young Russian intellectuals. Many regarded Soloviev as a great religious teacher and earnestly believed in the truth and importance of the mystical experiences that he described in his narrative poem, the "Three Meetings" (with the Beautiful Lady, Sophia). The philosopher's nephew Sergei and Andrei Belyi, two rising young poets of the symbolist school, saw the relevance of Soloviev's doctrine and mystical concepts to their own theory of literature, and took it upon themselves to incorporate his views into an esthetic from which symbolist writers might derive knowledge and inspiration. Ultimately, they founded a society for this purpose and named themselves symbolically the *Argonauts*. Belyi and Sergei Soloviev were among the first to discover Blok, in whom they recognized not merely a talented poet but a true disciple of the great philosopher and the prophetic voice of their own generation.

The inspiration of Blok's early poems was the Beautiful Lady, the heavenly Sophia. The poet fashions himself as Her knight; humbly, and in solitude and prayer, he awaits a sign of Her grace, hoping that She will put an end to the painful longing he experiences because of his separation from Her. Although Blok's sentiments were of a mystic and religious nature (he repeatedly emphasized his indifference to everything worldly, and his contempt for the flesh), *Poems about the Beautiful Lady* might never have been written had Blok not fallen in love with Liubov Dmitrievna Mendeleeva. Liubov, who spent her summers on the estate adjacent to Shakmatovo, shared with Blok a love of the theater; together they acted in amateur theatricals, and both aspired to a stage career. Liubov's aloofness and ethereal beauty captured Blok's imagination: he cultivated a feeling for her akin to that of Soloviev for his Sophia. He attributed a hidden meaning to her every word and gesture; her apparent indifference seemed to him a sort of occult ploy to test his devotion. So intense and complicated were his feelings that when he finally decided to propose marriage, he wrote in his diary that he intended to kill himself if his proposal was rejected. He wanted to believe that his reasons for so extreme a step were transcendental in nature and "had nothing to do with 'human' relationships." His apprehensions were unjustified, however, for Liubov consented without hesitation and the wedding took place on August 17, 1903. Those who had discerned a prophetic message in Blok's poetry regarded his marriage as predestined, a symbolic union, and they promptly elevated Liubov to the status of the Beautiful Lady. They viewed even her name— in Russian it means "love"—as additional evidence of her predestined status. In short, she became an object of veneration for them.

Blok's early poetry apostrophizing the Beautiful Lady reflected in sublimated form all the nuances of his feeling for Liubov. Right from the beginning his ecstatic adoration had been tinged by the fear that he was unworthy of grace and therefore destined not to be granted a vision of Her; he was afraid that the lady would "change her countenance"; in other words, that the ineffable moment he had so long anticipated would bring him not revelation but the disclosure of his own spiritual impotence. The *Poems about the Beautiful Lady*, which appeared in 1904, end on this note of doubt. They were well received; some critics were even enthusiastic about them. But marriage confirmed Blok's fears: the extrasensory intuition that he had sensed within himself abandoned him as soon as the object of his devotion became part of his everyday life. Blok and his wife gradually drifted apart, each to pursue their separate interests and careers. Liubov, wholeheartedly dedicated to her vocation as an actress, traveled extensively and left Blok alone in Petersburg for long periods of time. Resentful and restless, beset by problems real and imaginary, he sought comfort in taverns and brothels.

Blok did not seem to be able to objectify his personal problems, and he sought means of escape rather than solutions. Whether in search of harmony or self-oblivion, he wandered off into underground labyrinths of the self from which he emerged ever more bewildered and perplexed.

Despite their basic temperamental differences, and their flagrant infidelities, Blok and his wife displayed a remarkable tolerance and forgiveness toward one another. In their erratic lives the bond of marriage was their one constant, which both evidently held to be sacred and indissoluble. Their correspondence reveals a deep mutual affection and concern. Blok never dissociated the image of the Beautiful Lady from Liubov, and he cherished that image until the end. Even in 1914, when he was involved with another Liubov—Liubov Aleksandrovna Delmas, the opera singer—he dedicated a poem to Liubov Dmitrievna, perhaps remembering scenes from *Hamlet* that the two of them used to enact together back in the days when he was courting her:

I am Hamlet. The blood runs cold
When treachery weaves its web.
And in my heart my first love
Lives for just one person in this world.

O, Ophelia, life's coldness
Has led thee far away.
And I, a prince, perish in my own land
Pierced by a poisoned blade.

Notes of faith or optimism seldom resound in Blok's poetry in the second decade of his poetic career. Most of it is written in a minor key, ranging from melancholic to tragic. Five poems of this period, under the heading "Dances of Death" (*Pliaski smerti*), are characteristic. Man is depicted in them as a walking corpse and human life as hopeless.

But Blok's pessimism was tempered by his fatalistic outlook on human destiny and by his optimistic speculations on the future of man. The problem with the "terrible world" in which he lived was, in Blok's metaphysical view, its loss of "rhythm," a rhythm inherent in the "spirit of music" which to the poet was the inner cosmic harmony that controlled the progress of mankind. The majority of people had lost all sense of value and beauty and had become insensitive to the elemental harmonies of the "world orchestra." They understood only "historical time," events in their chronological order, but not the more important "musical time," in accord with which man may feel himself one with nature and in tune with the elemental forces of the universe. The few who could understand and who possessed the power to save the world from its forthcoming doom were either ignorant of their potential or passive. They too would be doomed with the rest in accordance with the cosmic laws of retribution. In Russia the culprits and future victims were the nobility and the intelligentsia, bearers of an ancient guilt for having tacitly accepted, generation after generation, the social inequities of the tsarist regime. Their apathy was soon to blow up in their faces. "Are we not responsible for our past?" Blok asks in his article "The Intelligentsia and the Revolution." "We are all links in a single chain. Do not the sins of our forefathers weigh upon us?"

At first Vladimir Soloviev's apocalyptic writings, and then the events in Russia at the beginning of the twentieth century (the disastrous war against Japan of 1904–1905; the revolution of 1905) played a significant part in molding Blok's political attitudes. By 1905 he had emerged from his lyrical seclusion and was lending his voice to the supporters of social and political reform; during the revolution he even carried the red flag through the streets of Petersburg. But this is as far as his actual participation went. He wrote his father on December 30, 1905: "I will never be either a revolutionary or a 'builder of life,' and not because I see no meaning in one or the other, but simply because of my nature, the character and quality of my spiritual experience." His social and political awareness, however, greatly increased as he became involved in polemic discussions with his fellow Symbolists on the present and future of Russia.

Blok regarded a major upheaval as unavoidable. With uncanny intuition he predicted the coming of the Russian Revolution. When it occurred, he welcomed it as the outset of a new musical era. He accepted its bloodshed and destruction as concomitants of a higher purpose and justified them as one might justify Christ's crucifixion in the light of the future of Christianity. In *The Twelve* (*Dvenadtsat'*), he described twelve Red soldiers drunk with their new-found power, driving through the city, spreading terror and leaving behind them death and ruin. The poem has an unexpected ending, which casts a new light over the whole. Christ suddenly appears at the head of the twelve soldiers. His very presence seems to consecrate their brutal actions.

When Blok condemned his own class and predicted its extinction he was well aware that he was foretelling his own doom. When the peasants on his estate rose up in arms and burned and destroyed his property, his response proved that he had no rancor toward the despoilers and accepted his loss almost joyfully, for the burden of guilt had at last been lifted from his soul.

After the Revolution, Blok worked for the Soviet government as a writer and editor. Reluctantly he wrote what he was told to write and sat through intérminable sessions at conferences where he was obliged to listen to the advocates of mass enlightenment condemning the decadence of symbolist poetry and championing new theories of literature. In the spring of 1920, however, he was given a more congenial task, that of editing the works of Lermontov. The critic Kornei Chukovskii recalls:

He was very happy with his new assignment, for Lermontov was his favorite poet. But suddenly, at one of the meetings, he was told that his introduction was inappropriate, that what was important about Lermontov was not that he had had certain dreams but that he was a "man of progress," a "great cultural force." Blok was urged to rewrite the introduction in a more popular, "culturally enlightening tone." Blok said nothing, but I could see that he was offended. If a "culturally enlightening tone" was what they wanted, why did they turn to him? Were there not enough literary hacks?

February 10, 1921, marked one of the last of Blok's appearances in public. Before a large audience, gathered to commemorate the anniversary of Pushkin's death, he delivered what is perhaps his most poignant speech. Having quoted the poet's famous lines, "there is no happiness on earth, but only peace and freedom," he then proceeded to make a statement that revealed the agony of his own predicament: *"Peace and freedom.* These are essential to the poet for the freeing of harmonies. But peace and freedom too are being taken away now. Not the external sort of peace, but the creative kind, not the freedom of the child or the freedom to play the liberal, but the creative freedom—the hidden freedom. And the poet dies because he can no longer breathe: life has lost its meaning."

Blok worked right up to the end of his life. He reedited some of his earlier works, attended the official meetings of the numerous organizations to which he belonged, gave talks, reviewed books and, albeit wearily, worked on *Retribution,* a long poem in which the disintegration of his own family served as a microcosm of the disintegration toward which mankind was headed. His health deteriorated steadily. He was suffering from heart and lung conditions that had been seriously aggravated by neglect and by the privations of the postrevolutionary years. A mood of gloomy resignation descended on him. A few months before his death he acknowledged the failure of his dreams: "Life has changed," he wrote in his diary, "a louse has conquered the whole world . . . and now everything can change only in the other direction, not in the direction for which we lived and loved." But despite his pessimism Blok hoped against hope that his illness might be cured, and he reluctantly consented to leave Russia to entrust himself to the skill of Finnish physicians. But on August 7, 1921, before the red tape involved in securing a passport to go abroad could be untangled, he died.

ALEKSANDR BLOK
The Journey to Italy

Introduction

Sic fluit occulte sic multos decipit aetas
Sic venit ad finem quidquid in orbe manet
Heu heu praeteritum non est revocabile tempus
Heu propius tacito mors venit ipsa pede.

(Inscription under the clock in the Church
of Santa Maria Novella in Florence) [1]

Although cultural contacts between Italy and Russia date back at least as far as the fifteenth century, the direct and tangible influence of Italian literature and art on Russian letters really begins only with the nineteenth century. One of the most memorable references to Italy appears in the work of a Russian poet whose dream of visiting that country was never fulfilled. Pushkin's longing for Italy is immortalized in his famous lines in the first chapter of *Eugene Onegin:*

O waters of the Adriatic,
O Brenta! I shall see you, know
Your witching voice and be ecstatic
With inspiration's quickened flow!
. . . . .
The nights of golden Italy,
On their delights I shall be gloating
At will; with a Venetian girl,
Her tongue now silent, now apurl.

[1] "Thus time passes secretly, thus age deceives many,/ Thus everything on earth comes to an end./ Alas, alas, time cannot be brought back;/ Alas, death with its silent step draws near." This inscription by Poliziano serves as an epigraph to Blok's Italian poems. I have taken the liberty of substituting "fluit" for Blok's "finit" in the first verse, for that is how the inscription actually reads.

In secret gondola be floating;
And in her arms my lips will strain
For Petrarch's and for love's refrain.[2]

The Russians pictured Italy as an earthly paradise, a country of golden nights, warm color, carefree songs, and fragrant aromas—worlds away from the drab, regimented existence of a politically backward and autocratic Russia. This romantic dream inspired verses such as:

Italy, motherland of inspiration!
A time will come when I shall love you
With rapturous delight
As now I love your image in my happy dreams.[3]

Educated Russians who traveled abroad found that the reality of Italy did not fall short of their expectations. In 1819, the poet Prince Petr Viazemskii, who had never been in Italy, wrote to his friend and fellow poet Konstantin Batiushkov, who was leaving for that fabled land: "It must be so beautiful there that one could even do without happiness. . . . This is what I think life in Italy must be like: to live there is to live in heaven." [4] Many years later, when Viazemskii visited Italy, he found that his intuition had not deceived him:

Here is heaven! Happy creatures,
Here people live without care:
It is as though they were not destined
To bear punishment for Adam's sin.[5]

[2] Aleksandr Pushkin, *Evgenii Onegin*, trans. by W. Arndt (New York: E. P. Dutton & Co., 1963), p. 26.

[3] Dmitrii Venevitinov, *Polnoe sobranie sochinenii* (Biblioteka poeta.; Leningrad, 1960), p. 99. All the translations of poetry in this book are the author's unless otherwise indicated.

[4] Quoted in Nina Kauchtschischwili, *L'Italia nella vita e nell'opera di P. A. Vjazemskij* (Milano, 1964), p. 8.

[5] Ibid., p. 235.

Upon returning to Russia, Viazemskii strove diligently to imbue his countrymen with an interest in all things Italian. Batiushkov's interest in Italy had been stimulated by his knowledge of the Italian language and his love of Petrarch and Tasso. His excellent translations of their poetry, enhanced by his efforts to approximate in Russian the harmonious sounds of the Italian, won the acclaim of Pushkin, who compared Batiushkov's talent to Petrarch's consummate artistry in Italian: "Italian sounds! What a magician that Batiushkov!" [6] His close contact with Italian literature developed in Batiushkov a sense of spiritual kinship with Italy: "I am all Italian," he wrote to the poet Nikolai Gnedich, "I am translating Tasso." [7]

As a consequence of this fervent immersion in Italian letters, a kind of cultural and national disorientation was not uncommon among Russian intellectuals. Stepan Shevyrev, the critic, historian and poet, who was passionately interested in classical culture, was ridiculed by an anonymous critic who noted that Shevyrev "in the course of his scholarly career had so often drawn parallels between Russia and Italy that, in the end, he began to confuse the essential qualities of the two countries." [8]

A love for Italy was instilled in Evgenii Baratynskii early in life by his Italian tutor, Giacinto Borghese.

> Sky of Italy, sky of Torquato,
> Poetic dust of ancient Rome,
> Land of delight, rich in glory,
> Will my eyes ever behold you? [9]

[6] Quoted by D. D. Blagoi in Konstantin Batiushkov, *Sochineniia* (Moscow, 1934), p. 31.

[7] Quoted in A. I. Nekrasov, *Batiushkov i Petrarka* (St. Petersburg, 1912), p. 4.

[8] Quoted in *Sovremennik* III (1860), 28.

[9] Evgenii Baratynskii, *Polnoe sobranie sochinenii* (Moscow, 1957), p. 217.

Baratynskii wrote in 1831. It was not until 1844, however, that he was able to undertake the journey, but the "spiritual rebirth" which he had anticipated in Italy was not to be, for he fell ill and died unexpectedly in Naples shortly after his arrival.

Italy had no more devoted admirer than Gogol, who lived in Rome intermittently for six years and whose ardent enthusiasm for the Eternal City's ancient and modern culture never waned. "One falls in love with Rome very slowly," he wrote to Danilevskii, "little by little—but for a lifetime. In short, all of Europe is for looking, but Italy is for living." [10]

The image of Italy appears quite frequently in the Russian poetry of the nineteenth century and is sometimes found where one would least expect it. Not all the poets who celebrated Italy—Zhukovskii, Maikov, Tiutchev, Apollon Grigoriev, Karolina Pavlova, Kozlov, Ogarev, Miatlev, Polonskii, Shcherbina, Countess Rastopchina, among others—wrote from actual experience. Some saw Italy only through the writings of their more fortunate compatriots. But those who did live abroad for any length of time usually returned only reluctantly to their native land. Blok's younger contemporary, the eminent poet Osip Mandelshtam, in his article on the philosopher Petr Chaadaev, reflects upon the effects of first-hand contact with Western culture:

Chaadaev was the first Russian to live abroad who actually absorbed the ideology of the West without rejecting that of his own country. His contemporaries felt this instinctively and valued very highly Chaadaev's presence among them.

They could point to him with the same almost religious veneration with which Dante's contemporaries had once spoken of

[10] Nikolai Gogol, *N. V. Gogol v pis'makh i vospominaniiakh*, ed. by V. Gippius (Moscow, 1931), p. 164.

him: "There is the man who was there, who saw—and came back."

But how many of us spiritually emigrated to the West! How many there are among us—who live in a subconscious duality, who are here in body, but still there in spirit! [11]

The interest in Italy, which reached its peak under the influence of the romantic world-view, began to decline in the second half of the nineteenth century. Distant, exotic lands did not have the same appeal for the "sons" as they had had for the "fathers." The new generation was far more concerned with the moral and social aspects of Russian life than with the culture of other lands. The poet Nikolai Nekrasov, after returning from Italy where he had gone to recuperate from a serious illness, sang not of Italy's salutary climate, but of Russia's "health-restoring expanses." He delighted his Slavophile readers by declaring that he "found nothing abroad":

> However warm an alien sea,
> However fair a distant shore,
> It cannot relieve our sorrow,
> Or dispel our sadness.[12]

Italy left but limited and fragmentary traces in the works of Tolstoi and Dostoevskii. Turgenev alone among the classic nineteenth-century "realists" was moved enough by Italy to make the country and its people more than a casual part of his works.[13] Although Italy appears in Chekhov's writings it never occupies a significant place in them. Chekhov's impressions of his visits to the country,[14] recorded with sensitivity

[11] Osip Mandelshtam, "Petr Chaadaev," *Apollon* VI–VII (1915), 62.
[12] From the poem "Tishina" (1857).
[13] Cf. I. Grevs, *Turgenev i Italiia* (Leningrad, 1925).
[14] Chekhov visited Italy in 1891 and 1894.

and humor in his letters, reveal an alert, even excited interest, but not a deep involvement. A rainy April proved enough to dampen his initial enthusiasm. He admitted, however, that "[Italy] is a delightful country. Were I a solitary, independent artist, I would live here in the winter. Aside from its landscape and warm climate, Italy is the only country where one is convinced that art is indeed the ruler of everything, and such a conviction raises one's spirits." [15] Chekhov's notion that art is man's highest endeavor, an idea confirmed by his Italian experience, reflected an attitude common among many Russian intellectuals of his day.

A renewed interest in Italy was stimulated in the late 1860's by the publication in the *Messenger of Europe* of an article by D. Kachenovskii, "Florence and Its Old Masters." In the 1880's, a series of art books by A. Vysheslavtsev laid the groundwork for a serious and lasting appreciation in Russia of classical and Renaissance painting. From then on, interest in Italian culture rose steadily. *The World of Art*, a lavish art journal which first began to appear in 1898, devoted many articles to Italian painting, sculpture, and architecture.

The Symbolists, newcomers to the literary scene at this time, who were seeking fresh insights and new themes to revitalize Russian letters, turned to the fertile heritage of Italian art. Their ideal of a cultural revival based on a syncretism of all the arts led them to a serious study of the Italian Renaissance, where such a syncretism had actually manifested itself. The popularity of Dmitrii Merezhkovskii's fictionalized biography of Leonardo da Vinci [16] (1901) and Akim Volynskii's scholarly biography of the great painter-inventor (1900) gave

---

[15] Anton Chekhov, *Polnoe sobranie sochinenii i pisem*, ed. by A. Egolin and N. Tikhonov, 20 vols. (Moscow, 1944–1951), XV, 185.
[16] The full title of this book is *Voskresshie bogi. Leonardo da Vinci*. It will be referred to from now on as *Leonardo da Vinci*.

evidence of these new interests at the turn of the century. Russian intellectuals envisioned in the ideal of the *uomo universale* a goal toward which they could and should strive. "Oh, Leonardo, You are the herald / Of a still unknown tomorrow," wrote Merezhkovskii in his poem "Leonardo da Vinci."

Although romantic pathos still echoed occasionally in the Symbolists' poetry about Italy, a mystical note predominated. In the first half of the nineteenth century, the Russian poets had seen Italy as the answer to their quest for a freer and emotionally richer life; its relative accessibility (travel restrictions were less stringent under the Tsarist regime than they are today in Soviet Russia) allowed cultured Russians to hope that their dreams of an Italian holiday might one day come true. "It is not the mind that needs Italy, but the heart," Baratynskii had asserted, "and not so much as a land of the past, but as a land of the present." [17] The Symbolists, on the other hand, despite their discontent with the general grayness of Russian existence, harbored no illusions that a Garden of Eden awaited them on Italy's sunnier shore. Rather, they were yearning for experiences that would open to them new areas of perception. The past of Italy was at least as important to them as its present. In their eagerness to penetrate into the spiritual essence of things, they probed beneath the shimmering, deceptive surface of Italian life for those deeper meanings that escape the casual observer. "Why is it that beneath the southern sun, amidst bright colors and flowers, among vividly wonderful forms, all I can see is ashes?" asks Valerii Briusov in his poem "Venezia." [18] Viacheslav Ivanov

[17] Quoted in P. P. Filippovich, *Zhizn' i tvorchestvo Baratynskogo* (Kiev, 1917), p. 170.
[18] Valerii Briusov, *Izbrannye sochineniia v dvukh tomakh* (Moscow, 1955), I, 181.

strips the Venetian scene of its brilliance and exposes the ominous forces that are astir within its deceptive stillness:

> Along the pale shroud of a motionless lagoon,
> Casting gloom over the peaceful sky and milky horizon,
> The shameful nakedness of trees summons slumbering
>   thunder
> And summer storms to these shores of despair.[19]

There was hardly a Russian writer in the first decade of the twentieth century who did not in one way or another express an interest in Italy. Some writers devoted only a few lines of their total *oeuvres* to that country, while others wrote entire books inspired by it. Although Aleksandr Blok's Italian poems and essays would fill only a thin volume, they afford one of the most original and complex visions of Italy in all of Russian literature. These works supply invaluable material for our understanding of the poet, and from them it transpires that his journey took place on two levels: on one level there was his actual exploration of Italian nature, art, and life; on the other, there was a symbolic pilgrimage into Italy's past, an escape from the shifting and shallow realities of day-to-day life into the stately permanence of the country's ever-present history. The purpose of this work, then, is twofold: to study Blok's immediate impressions of the Italian scene in relation to his art, and to interpret the profound impact of this journey on his thought.

In a brief autobiographical sketch written in 1915, Blok listed those events in his life that he considered most significant (VII, 7–17).[20] Among them he included a trip to

---

[19] Viacheslav Ivanov, *Kormchie zvezdy* (St. Petersburg, 1903), p. 193.

[20] References to Blok's poems and prose work are cited from A. Blok, *Sobranie sochinenii v vos'mi tomakh* (Moscow–Leningrad, 1960–1963). The volume and page numbers are given in parentheses in the text.

northern and central Italy, during which he visited Venice, Ravenna, Milan, Florence, Pisa, Perugia, and a number of other towns and villages in the province of Umbria.

Blok and his wife spent almost two months abroad. They arrived in Italy on May 1, 1909, and departed on June 21. The poet's romantic hopes and expectations were frustrated by what seemed to him the predominantly tourist-oriented and commercial spirit of the country. Irritated by the unusually sultry weather, unimpressed by the beauty of Italy's celebrated countryside, and exhausted by their crowded itinerary, Blok abandoned his plan to visit Rome and returned to Russia earlier than he had intended. So vehemently had he expressed his disappointment while still abroad, so bitter was the invective he had heaped upon the Italians, that one would expect him to have promptly dismissed the whole experience from his mind. But as the poet looked back upon his travels, distance imparted a special enchantment and a new significance to his memories. After returning home, he immersed himself in the study of Italian culture and literature, and later he recalled the summer of 1909 as one in which "Italy absorbed and dominated all [his] life and thought" (VII, 188).

Blok's observations and his complex and ambiguous sentiments about Italy are recorded in his diary, in his letters, in a cycle of twenty-three poems, and in "Lightning Flashes of Art," an unfinished series of prose sketches. Considered individually, these works provide only isolated glimpses of Blok's journey to Italy, but taken as a whole, they give a fuller, more integrated understanding of the poet's pattern of perception and thought.

Blok's immediate impressions were to a considerable extent preconditioned by his philosophy of history and by his pessimistic view of civilization and modern life. The Italian countryside, culture, and art often served as a catalyst to his imagination, prompting new reflections on old subjects. "The trip to Italy," observed a contemporary critic, "played an enormous role in Blok's creative development." [21] Distant Russia, viewed through the haze of his emotions, now appeared to Blok as an abstract vision of a nation moving toward its unique and inescapable destiny rather than the oppressive reality from which he had so often dreamed of escaping. The realization that he could not live anywhere but in his native land now strengthened his feelings of loyalty for the "unfortunate and destitute" country he had left behind and made him regard its faults and failings with greater tolerance.

Blok himself recognized the value of his Italian experience. "In Italy and Germany," he wrote to his friend Vladimir Piast, "I experienced, thought over, and discovered many things, and understood much that was new to me" (VIII, 292).

Only a year after his return from Italy, Blok was already planning to visit the country again: "I envy you, for you are in Italy," he wrote to his friend and peer the poet Andrei Belyi in 1910, "and, by the way, I might be there myself soon" (VIII, 323). But in fact he was destined never to see Italy again.

The memoirs of his contemporaries repeatedly mention the fact that Blok's thoughts often dwelt with nostalgia on his Italian journey. The poet Nadezhda Pavlovich recalls a visit he paid to her late one autumn: "It is very cold in my room. Winter is approaching . . . You can see your breath. We speak of Italy, of that piercing consciousness of art which he experienced there; and then of the ages of man, of wisdom, of Siena Cathedral . . . of an immediate, almost physical per-

---

[21] Viktor Goltsev, "Tvorcheskii put' Bloka," *Sobranie sochinenii A. Bloka* (Moscow–Leningrad, 1929), p. xxvi.

ception of history.—'Italy teaches this too!' Blok exclaimed." [22]

S. M. Alianskii, the publisher, recalls in "Meetings with Blok" one of his last visits to the poet to discuss a new edition of his works. This was in the late spring of 1921. Despite his wife's admonitions to keep the meeting brief and not to become overtired (the poet was already in poor health), Blok insisted on detaining Alianskii so that he could show him his Italian albums—his "travel diaries." These albums contained picture-postcards which he had collected in Italy and had then painstakingly pasted in and arranged according to a definite plan. [23] Alianskii listened avidly to Blok's detailed reminiscences: "Blok's stories about the Italian landscape, about architecture, museums, archives and cathedrals packed with treasures of art—all this was new to me and extremely interesting. His words made such a deep impression on me that for a long time I did not want to see Italy with my own eyes; I was afraid I might not see it as he had seen it. I was afraid to lose that living image which the poet had communicated to me." [24]

Among Blok's most cherished possessions was a drawing in India ink by N. K. Rerikh, which was intended to serve as a frontispiece to the first edition of Blok's Italian poems. [25] The

[22] Nadezhda Pavlovich, "Vospominaniia ob Aleksandre Bloke," *Blokovskii sbornik* (Tartu, 1964), p. 485.

[23] One of Blok's Italian albums is preserved in his archives in Leningrad (Pushkinskii Dom, F. 654, Op. I. N. 403). It contains 290 picture postcards, of which 197 are Italian reproductions of paintings, mosaics and sculptures, coats of arms, sarcophagi, interiors of churches, views, etc. These cards are grouped according to cities and follow an order parallel to that of the Italian poems.

[24] Samuil Alianskii, "Vstrechi s Blokom," *Novyi mir* VI (June, 1967), 202.

[25] N. K. Rerikh, "K ital'ianskim stikham A. Bloka," "Literaturnyi al'manakh," *Apollon* IV (1910), 37.

landscape in this drawing, while unmistakably inspired by Italy is nonetheless a product of the artist's imagination. It depicts a medieval village perched halfway up a mountain above what appears to be a steep and rocky ravine. Below the village the mountain is gouged by deep crevices and strewn with rocks as though it had been devastated by an earthquake. The village is suspended miraculously over this precipice. The drawing suggests two distinct realities: one above the ground—peaceful and bright—the other underground—dark, mysterious, and lifeless. Blok was so fond of this picture that when Sergei Makovskii, the critic and editor of the journal *Apollon,* asked him if he could borrow it for display at an international exhibition to be held in Leipzig in the spring of 1914, Blok replied: "Rerikh's drawing has become a part of my life; it hangs right in front of me where I can see it, and it would be very hard for me to part with it, even for these [few] months. I beg you not to be too vexed with me for refusing; I hope you will understand why I feel I have to" (VIII, 436).

It was not by chance that Blok chose this picture as a frontispiece to his Italian poems. It expressed his deeply felt belief that beneath the visible and tangible phenomena of this world there exists a mystic underground where powerful and mysterious forces dwell that control all life above.[26]

Indeed, Blok's attachment to the Rerikh drawing resembled the jealously proprietary feelings he had for his Italian poems. His firm refusal to accept any editorial revisions of the latter, a stand that jeopardized the publication of the first six Italian poems in *Apollon* and also, incidentally, of Re-

---

[26] Blok's reflections on the mystical significance of the underground first appeared in "Stikhiia i kul'tura" (December, 1908), an essay inspired by the earthquake which struck Calabria and Messina. (See Ch. II.)

rikh's drawing, showed how carefully he had pondered each line in them. "If you do not agree to publish these poems just as they are," he wrote to Makovskii, "all that remains for me to do is to regret the inconvenience which I am causing you just before the publication of your next issue and my own awkward position as far as Rerikh is concerned . . . I shall do my best to smooth things over with him" (VIII, 300–301). In a subsequent letter to Makovskii, Blok compared his feeling for the poems to that of a mother for her child.

The critical reaction to the Italian poems testifies to their excellence. The poet Valerii Briusov praised some of them as "magnificent poetry." [27] The writer and critic Vladimir Kniazhnin declared that they were "the best lyrics on Italy ever written in Russian." [28] Sergei Bobrov, in an article ridiculing Blok's symbol-laden poetry, nevertheless excluded from his strictures the Italian poems which "come almost as a surprise with their superb lines and their lofty fantastic quality." [29] And recently Vladimir Orlov, the well-known authority on Blok, declared: "The 'Italian Poems' are the finest things ever written about Italy in Russian poetry. Written for the most part in 1909, the year when Blok was complaining that he 'could not write,' they prove that the concept of 'artistic order,' measure, and harmony which had always captivated him was already at that time deeply embedded in his lyrics." [30]

Very soon after the publication of the first Italian poems, Blok, who had been disturbed for some time by the indiffer-

[27] Valerii Briusov, *Izbrannye sochineniia*, 2 vols. (Moscow, 1955), II, 290.

[28] V. N. Kniazhnin, *Aleksandr Aleksandrovich Blok* (Petersburg, 1922), p. 107.

[29] Sergei Bobrov, "Simvolist Blok," in *Krasnaia Nov'* (Moscow, 1922), No. 1, p. 249.

[30] Vladimir Orlov, *Aleksandr Blok* (Moscow, 1956), p. 151.

ence of the public to his works, was able to state that they
had "brought [him] renown all over again." [31] He often read
his Italian poems at public recitals where they invariably met
with an enthusiastic response. One of his last personal appearances was at the *Studio Italiano* in Moscow in 1921.

Victor Erlich, in his article "The Concept of the Poet as a
Problem of Poetics," notes the important role of Blok's lyrical cycles "in projecting a personalized and dramatically
effective image" of the poet.[32] Erlich's comment is especially
relevant to the Italian cycle. It is this cycle which reveals
more vividly than Blok's explicit statements in his prose
works his complex and often paradoxical reactions to Italy,
and it must therefore be central to our study of the poet's
Italian journey. His essays and letters simply complement the
poems and enable one to interpret them with greater accuracy and discernment.

In his article on Henrik Ibsen, a writer whom he greatly
admired and for whom he felt a spiritual affinity, Blok expressed his belief that "every artist's style is so closely related
to the content of his soul that an expert eye can perceive the
artist's soul in his style and penetrate to the very core of this
content through an analysis of the form" (V, 315). This
statement—a Russian version of the French "*Le style c'est
l'homme même*"—is particularly applicable to Blok's own
poetry. It is therefore essential, when analyzing the Italian
poems, to give considerable attention to their formal aspects.

The journey is presented in its chronological sequence.
Such a presentation affords the reader the best possible op-

[31] *Pis'ma Aleksandra Bloka k rodnym*, ed. by M. A. Beketova, 2
vols. (Leningrad, 1927–1932), I, 277, hereafter referred to in the text
in parentheses as *Letters*.

[32] Victor Erlich, "The Concept of the Poet as a Problem of Poetics,"
Poetics (Warsaw: Polska Akademia NAUK, 1961), p. 715.

portunity to observe the progressive development of Blok's thought and attitudes. We shall follow the poet through his travels and travails from the moment when he arrived in Venice in a mood of eager anticipation, until his disenchanted departure from Milan eight weeks later.

I

Before 1909

Blok's first mention of his desire to visit Italy is found in a letter written in June 1906 to his friend Evgenii Ivanov: "Perhaps Liuba and I will take a trip to Italy this fall, although I personally doubt it. Liuba wants to go very much, and indeed life is supposed to be quite good in Venice, Rome, and Florence" (VIII, 157). The trip did not take place until three years later, however, and then it came as the result not of careful planning, but of a decision arrived at rather suddenly after a series of disappointments and misfortunes.

A brief review of some of the major events and concerns in Blok's life in the year 1907 and 1908 is necessary to supply a background and introduction to his Italian experience.

For the poet, these were restless years of inner searching. On the intellectual plane, his life was dominated by his growing anxiety about the social and political climate in Russia and about his own role and responsibility as a writer. These concerns found cogent and vigorous expression in his prose. Writing on matters of social import also had a therapeutic value for Blok: it served as an antidote against what he himself had called his "curse of abstractness," that is, his instinct to withdraw and stand apart from life which tended to obscure his perception of reality, so that, as a result, what he produced lacked "pithiness, vividness, and vitality." It was his emotional life, however, which affected him most deeply at this time, above all his turbulent love affair with the actress

Natalia Volokhova, which lasted from the winter of 1906 well into the following year. The manifold literary and social activities in which he engaged in 1907 did not succeed in filling the inner void left by this experience.[1] Only by committing to poetry his most intimate thoughts and feelings could he find temporary relief from his spiritual loneliness and intellectual unrest.

By transposing his life into writing, by lyrically externalizing his feelings and thoughts, Blok was able to bear the oppressive burden which his constant introspection imposed upon him and to see his own experiences in a new and dispassionate way. The poet Nikolai Gumilev concisely defined Blok's relationship to his art when he stated: "Usually a poet gives to the people his creative works; Blok gives himself." [2] "Blok is Blok's major theme," [3] observed the critic Iurii Tynianov, and another critic and scholar, Sergei Bondi, noted the "exceptional sincerity" and "depth of content" [4] which distinguished Blok from other poets. As it had been for the Romantics, the act of composition was for Blok a means of spiritual liberation. But it was even more. Significantly, he employed religious terminology to describe his three published volumes of poetry (1911). He called them a "trilogy of incarnation" (*trilogiia vochelovecheniia*) [5] (VIII, 344). He viewed his poems as a verbal embodiment of those inner changes which he experienced in the course of his intellectual

[1] In his poetry Blok sings of his "neradostnaia strast' " (cheerless passion) during the "bezumnyi god" (frenzied year) 1907 (II, 269).

[2] N. Gumilev, "Pis'ma o russkoi poezii," *Apollon* VIII (1912), 60.

[3] Iurii Tynianov, "Blok," *Problema stikhotvornogo iazyka* (Moscow, 1965), p. 249.

[4] Quoted by L. Dolgopolov in his "Notes" on the drama "Roza i krest" (IV, 592).

[5] "Vochelovechenie" (incarnation, humanization) in Russian has a strictly religious connotation.

and spiritual growth from youth to maturity. In the foreword to the 1911 edition of his poems, he stressed the interrelatedness of seemingly unrelated parts: "Each poem is essential to the structure of a chapter; several chapters make up a book; each book is part of the trilogy; the whole trilogy could be called a 'novel in verse': it is devoted to a complex of thoughts and feelings to which I was committed during the first twelve years of my conscious life." [6]

Blok viewed the total immersion of one's spiritual self in art as something of a baptism of fire and as a *sine qua non* for those who aspire to immortal fame. "We no longer have reason to doubt that great works of art are chosen by history only from among works of a "confessional" character. Only the confession of a writer, only the work in which he is *completely consumed*—either to be born again to create new things, or to die, can be considered truly great" (V, 278).

In January 1908, Blok wrote to his mother: "The colder and crueler this unfulfilled 'personal life' becomes . . . the more profound and wide-ranging are my artistic plans and intentions. There are so many of them that sometimes I can only throw up my hands—there is so much that has to be done: my most immediate project is a play" (VIII, 224).

The play to which Blok refers here is the "Song of Fate," an allegorical dramatization of motifs from his own life, many of which had already found expression in his earlier lyrics. At the center of this drama looms the personified image of Fate —Miss Volokhova. Although by this time Blok's passion for the actress had cooled, the memory of it still haunted him. Only by transposing his emotions into art could he rid himself of their disquieting influence. "I am going through a very

[6] Quoted in *Aleksandr Blok i Andrei Belyi. Perepiska* (Moscow, 1940), p. 262, footnote 3.

difficult period," he wrote in January 1908, "and I am laboriously writing something big. . . . I hardly ever see people or go out. I must first get rid of what has settled within me like a heavy stone" (VIII, 226). And in March: "At last my drama is almost completed. It was a harassing experience, but this one turned out better, I think, than my previous plays" (VIII, 233).

After finishing "Song of Fate," Blok gave it the following evaluation: "This is the first thing I have written in which I feel that my work rests on a firm foundation that is not merely lyrical. That is what the 'Song of Fate' means to me, and that is why I love it more than anything else I have written" (VIII, 240). In his *Notebook* he added, "It is the most significant thing I have done" (*Notebooks*, 106).[7] He read the play to friends and acquaintances and was pleased with their reaction, but it was Stanislavskii's judgment which Blok valued above all others. He sent Stanislavskii the "Song of Fate" and waited eagerly for the famous director's verdict. The latter's reply came only after many months. Although impressed by the lyricism of the play, Stanislavskii thought it lacked unity, and found its characters unconvincing (VIII, 265, 596). His unfavorable criticism, although tactfully expressed, came as a great disappointment to Blok. He laid his play aside and even in later years was reluctant to allow it to be staged.

Blok's faith in his friends was severely tried during this period. His articles published in 1908 in which he had discussed problems close to his heart—art, culture, the role of the writer, the relationship between the intelligentsia and the people—had not been well received. He had at times espoused views that differed significantly from those of his fel-

---

[7] The citations from the *Notebooks* (*Zapisnye Knizhki* [Moscow, 1965]) will be indicated in the text in parentheses as *Notebooks*, with page reference.

low Symbolists and that even conflicted with his own former symbolist positions. Some of Blok's conclusions antagonized, even enraged his fellow writers. Comments ranging in tone from light raillery to downright rudeness came from those whom Blok had viewed as kindred spirits. For instance, Merezhkovskii derided the poetic tribute paid by Blok, the "knight of the Beautiful Lady," to what he regarded as the barbaric past of Russia. "Blok," this critic wrote, "suddenly leaped straight out of a Gothic stained-glass window and plunged right into 'uncultured Russia'" (VIII, 590). Gippius, Rozanov, Struve, Briusov and others scorned what they regarded as a poet's pretentious aspiration to play the role of a literary critic. To these literati Blok addressed one of his most cynical poems, ironically entitled "To Friends." He regrets that, "We are secretly hostile, envious of, insensitive and alien to one another." Writers, he says, are "traitors to life and friendship" and "squanderers of empty words"; his own kinship with them is so distasteful that it makes him want to repudiate his own art: "Be silent, accursed books! I never wrote you!" (III, 125–26).

Perhaps the nadir of the year 1908 was Blok's dispute with Andrei Belyi. A crisis developed in their already complex relationship with the publication of Belyi's *Fourth Symphony*.[8] Blok found this book personally offensive, "not only alien, but deeply hostile in spirit." To this "friend," whom he would acknowledge three years later as the most perceptive critic of his work, Blok wrote that he had come to the "final and irrevocable conclusion that we cannot pass judgment on one another" (VIII, 238). This letter called a dramatic halt to their stormy and erratic friendship. Two months later, Blok made the following admission in his *Notebook*, presumably

[8] Cf. Vladimir Orlov, "Istoriia odnoi 'druzhby-vrazhdy,'" *Puti i sud'by* (Moscow–Leningrad, 1963), p. 446.

not without a secret ache: "Thank God! I have broken inwardly, and forever, with my best friends and 'patrons' (with
Belyi at their head). At last! (I mean the 'half-crazies'—
Belyi—and the prattlers—the Merezhkovskiis)" (*Notebooks*, 108–109).

Despondency and pessimism pervade Blok's poetry and
correspondence throughout 1908 and the early part of 1909.
He felt lonely, dissatisfied, and prematurely old. "I sit and
feel my 28 years" (VIII, 261), begins the letter he wrote to
his mother on his birthday; a few months later he lamented
that "life had roared past and left him behind" and that "the
day has burned itself out in his soul long ago" (III, 74).

Blok's marital life was also a major cause of his unhappiness. His relations with Liubov Dmitrievna, already far from
satisfactory, took a turn for the worse when she left Petersburg in February 1908 to join Meyerhold's theatrical group.
Her enigmatic letters, full of recondite allusions and an-
nouncing repeated postponements of her return, preyed on
Blok's mind and contributed to his gloom. More than ever
before, he indulged in heavy drinking. The anguish of this
period is reflected in his correspondence with her:

Just look around at the desolation and darkness that surrounds
us! Take a sober look at your theater, and at the people you
work with. I always thought that you, a woman with a lofty
soul, were not capable of sinking to the level to which I have
fallen. Help me if you can. I cannot even work, I have no goal.
And my days are all alike, one just like the other. . . . If only I
could lie down and fall asleep and forget everything. . . . Never
in my life have I experienced *such* feelings of loneliness and
rejection. (VIII, 248–249)

The poet had mixed reactions to Liubov Dmitrievna's return
in August, for during her absence she had conceived another

man's child. Nevertheless, he not only forgave her, but accepted the unborn child as his own. For a while his spirits revived and he was even cheerful. Statements such as "we are living well," "I am able to concentrate," and "I am overflowing with new plans" began to appear in his letters; positive notes of challenge and acceptance of life resounded in his poetry:

> Or is happiness really deceptive and fleeting,
> Or am I indeed weak, ailing, and old?
> No! The last embers still glow in the ashes,
> There is enough of a spark for a fire to start! (III, 169)

Zinaida Gippius gives us a unique portrait of Blok during this period: "I remember Blok as he was then—simple, human, with an unusually bright face. As a rule [when I think of him], I do not remember him smiling; if he did smile, it was quickly and imperceptibly. But it is precisely his smile that I remember from that time: it was concerned and gentle. And his voice was somewhat different and warmer. It was when he was expecting his child and especially for the first few days after the baby was born." [9] But his infant son lived only a week. Gippius noted the change in Blok's appearance: "Assiduously and in detail Blok kept on retelling and explaining why [his son] could not live and had to die. He spoke in a matter-of-fact manner, but his expression was one of bewilderment and disbelief. His face had suddenly grown darker and he looked frightened and dazed." [10] Gippius' memoirs carry the reader along to the day when the Bloks came to pay her a farewell visit before departing for Italy: "They both came to say good-bye: they were going abroad. 'We have decided to rest awhile, to see other places.' . . . Both had a disconsolate look, and their visit seemed unnecessary,

[9] Z. N. Gippius, *Zhivye litsa* (Prague, 1925), p. 39.   [10] Ibid., p. 40.

grey and dreary. Everything seemed unnecessary. A hope had been extinguished. A door which had been open slightly was slammed shut." [11]

The loss of the child deepened Blok's anxiety and bitterness. He could not with resignation accept decrees, whether human or divine, that he could not reconcile with his image of a just Providence. In a defiant mood, he wrote the poem "On the Death of a Baby":

> I shall suppress my numb bitterness,
> I shall bury my anguish in oblivion,
> Each night I shall pray
> Before the small, sacred coffin.
>
> But—to bow the knee humbly
> And give thanks to Thee as I mourn?
> No. Over my baby, *my blessed one,*
> I shall grieve without Thee. (III, 70)

Blok's depression was more intense now than it had been during the months of separation from his wife. "I have never yet experienced such a gloomy spell as in this last month— a spell of deathly desolation," he wrote to his friend, the writer Georgii Chulkov (VIII, 282).

Blok's personal unhappiness was aggravated by his growing dissatisfaction with life in Russia. He was not among those few privileged noblemen who could live comfortably on the income from their estates: his own had to be supplemented by his earnings. But to gain a livelihood as a writer at that time was difficult and frustrating. In his letters and articles he repeatedly voiced his indignation at a system which imposed enormous hardships on talented and productive people and encouraged mediocrity and conformity. He was also repelled

[11] Ibid., p. 40–41.

by the hypocrisy which he detected among the great majority of cultured Russians. They had become masters of rhetoric, they spoke vehemently and self-righteously on questions of politics, morality, and religion, but the polished surface of their verbiage and their ironic mode of expression belied their indifference, their calculating self-interest, and mutual ill-will. In a letter to his mother on April 13, his last before leaving for Italy, Blok diagnosed these ills as the product of a hypocrisy originating from and encouraged by the political system:

> What a misfortune for all of us that our native land has provided us with such a fertile soil for malice and quarrels with one another. We live behind a Chinese wall,[12] half-despising one another, and our common enemies—the Russian Government, the Church, the taverns, the treasury and the bureaucrats—hide their true face from us while they are setting us against each other. (VIII, 281)

At this point, Blok must have envisioned a trip abroad not only as a welcome escape from his oppressive social milieu, but also as holding out the promise of reviving his poetic inspiration. "A winter of idle talk," he had stated in February, "has again completely drained me, I do not have enough creative energy for four poems. I hope it will not be like this forever" (VIII, 278). A month later, however, already anticipating his trip to Italy, he wrote more optimistically: "So far no poems. But I think they will come—in Venice, Florence, Ravenna, and Rome" (*PAB*, I, 251).

The need to release his emotions in poetry was, as we have noted, vital to Blok; but since poetry depends on inspiration, the creation of verse was in a sense beyond his conscious control. When his emotional state was not conducive to creativ-

---

[12] A Russian idiom meaning "completely isolated from foreign influences."

ity, he experienced an ominous inner silence. Unable to cope with the resulting frustration, he was driven to excesses harmful to his health. He recognized the crucial role of his muse, but felt woefully unable to keep his art and life independent of each other. That is why the "sacred melodies" of his muse conveyed to him a "fatal forewarning of doom." [13]

Thus, the fear of waning creativity was not the least important of the factors that prompted Blok to seek a change of pace and environment. He hoped that in Italy, a country young in spirit and old in culture, he might be able to rejuvenate his prematurely aging soul, regain his inspiration and, enriched by new insights, muster enough spiritual strength to cope better in the future with the vexing problems of his personal life. "Every Russian," Blok wrote in his first letter from abroad, "has the right, if only for a few years, to shut out all that is Russian and see his other homeland—Europe, and in particular, Italy" (VIII, 284). It was as though he felt the need to offer a formal justification for his trip.

[13] From the poem "K muze" (III, 7).

II

Ideological Influences
Before the Journey

Blok had accompanied his mother and aunt to northern Italy at the age of three. Although the effect of that trip must remain unknown, it is noteworthy that at the age of sixteen Blok collaborated with his cousin A. A. Kublitskii-Piottukh on a play entitled "A Trip to Italy." This "heartrending drama" written for the school journal *Vestnik* (The Messenger) was never reprinted and, according to M. Beketova, Blok's aunt and biographer, with good reason: "He used to publish poems and stories in the *Vestnik* . . . and even the absurd play 'A Trip to Italy.' There was much that was silly in the play, but at least it had no pretensions. . . . It indicated his complete ignorance of ordinary human relationships." [1]

It seems likely that the Italy which Blok later encountered in no way corresponded to the country of his youthful imagination, for while he was in Italy he never mentioned his early play in his letters or his notes. And yet we know that he never forgot it; curiously enough, a few years later, in the city of Dordrecht in Holland, he thought of it again. "Dordrecht," he wrote, "is a very beautiful city . . . canals, ships, *polders*, and windmills are everywhere. . . . Everything seems to remind me of my play from the *Vestnik*—"A Trip to Italy" (VIII, 372).

[1] M. A. Beketova, *A. Blok i ego mat'* (Petersburg, 1922), p. 50.

Although we have no evidence that prior to 1909 Blok was especially interested in Italian literature, his references to it suggest more than just a casual acquaintance. His interest in classical Italian art, however, was indisputable; it may even have dated back to the days when he was courting Liubov Dmitrievna. In her memoirs she recalls their frequent visits during 1901 to the house of the painter Mikhail Botkin who owned a magnificent collection of Italian masterpieces.[2]

Sergei Soloviev, the poet and literary critic, noted the influence of Italian art on Blok's early works. In his biographical sketch of the poet he wrote: "Already in his early poems the influence of the Italian pre-Raphaelites could often be detected: the gold and blues of Fra Angelico, 'the white steed the color of cherry blossom' as on the fresco of Benozzo Bozzoli in the Palazzo Piccardi, and also something of the moist quality of Botticelli."[3]

Sharing the cultural pursuits of his intellectual circle, Blok kept abreast of publications and events in the art world. Al-

---

[2] L. D. Mendeleeva-Blok, "Tri epizoda iz vospominanii ob Aleksandre Bloke," *Den' poezii* (Leningrad, 1965), p. 317.

[3] Sergei Soloviev, "Vospominaniia ob Aleksandre Bloke," *Pis'ma A. Bloka* (Leningrad, 1925), p. 36.

Critics offer differing interpretations of Blok's selection of color epithets. Z. Mints, in her article "Poeticheskii ideal molodogo Bloka," discusses the color scheme of his early poems. According to Mints, Blok surrounds his heroine with white, red, gold, blue and other bright shades, in order to create a "beautiful" and "colorful" setting to enhance the luminous quality of her image (Z. G. Mints, *Blokovskii sbornik* [Tartu, 1964], p. 214). Another Soviet critic, L. Dolgopolov, disagrees with this interpretation, perceiving in Blok's color scheme a symbolic rather than an aesthetic rationale. For example, Dolgopolov regards the frequent recurrence of the color white as symbolic of the poet's premonition of the apocalypse (*Russkaia literatura* [1965], II, p. 187). Georgii Fedotov, the émigré critic and philosopher, on the other hand, claims that Blok associated white with purity (G. P. Fedotov, *Novyi Grad* [New York, 1952], p. 285).

though his interest was keen, he felt that his knowledge was inadequate: "I love the art of painting, although I do not really know enough about it, and that is why my judgments are probably not decisive or daring enough. In any event I am learning from antiquity, from the Renaissance and from the *World of Art* and not from *Peredvizhniki* [4] nor from academicians" (VIII, 88–89).

The aesthetic gratifications and the intrinsic merits of art were not the only factors that attracted Blok to painting. He studied especially closely the relationship between an artist and his paintings and, comparing it to that which exists between a poet and his verses, he sought to analyze the anatomy of the creative process *per se*. Plutarch's famous saying that "Painting is mute poetry, and poetry a speaking picture" expresses this relationship as Blok may have seen it. However, he did not equate painting and poetry, but believed the former to be superior to the latter because it conveyed external reality more objectively.[5] The painter's relation to his subject was, in his opinion, more direct and authentic than that of the writer, who is haunted by the "curse of abstractness," burdened by introspection and often defeated by the inadequacies of language.

In "Colors and Words," an article written in 1905, Blok in his own peculiar way had already presented some thoughts on the painter's and writer's modes of expression:

Gentle and bright colors help the artist to preserve his childlike perceptivity; but adult writers . . . "greedily guard the remnant

[4] *Peredvizhniki*, a movement in Russian art of the second half of the nineteenth century. It had a realistic and social orientation.

[5] It is significant that Blok did not regard abstract painting as art. Paradoxically, while his own poetry often seems to have only an aesthetic or symbolic purpose, Blok in his essays rejects art for art's sake and expounds social consciousness and the alliance of the beautiful and the useful (cf. "Tri voprosa" and "Vechera 'iskusstv' ").

of feeling in their souls." [6] Anxious to save precious time, they substitute the swift word for the painter's slow design; but in so doing they become blind and insensitive to visual impressions. Needless to say, there are more words than colors; but perhaps all that the polished writer or poet requires are those few words which correspond to colors, words which form an amazingly colorful, expressive and harmonious vocabulary. (V, 21)

These reflections were undoubtedly influenced by contemporary trends among the Symbolists. In *Leonardo da Vinci*, for instance, Merezhkovskii made his protagonist, in the course of a dispute with a poet on the nature of painting and poetry, proclaim the pre-eminence of painting over poetry:

The eye gives man a more perfect knowledge of nature than the ear. What we see is more reliable than what we hear. This is why painting is mute poetry, closer to exact science than poetry, which is blind painting. In verbal description there is only a sequence of separate images, following one after another; whereas in a picture all the images, all the colors, appear simultaneously, blending into one whole, just as notes blend into a melody. This makes possible a greater degree of harmony in painting and music than in poetry. And where there is no higher harmony, there is no higher beauty.[7]

In Italy, Blok's interest in art received a renewed impetus. After only a week in Venice he felt that he had gained new insights. "Here many of my thoughts about art have been clarified and confirmed. I have come to understand much about painting, and love it now no less than poetry," he wrote to his mother, and later added: "Here one would like

[6] From Lermontov's poem "Duma." Blok paraphrases this quotation in "Florence 6." For further reference see Chapter V.

[7] Dmitrii Merezhkovskii, *Leonardo da Vinci*, Book 10, Ch. X. All the quotations from this work have been translated by the author.

to be a painter, not a writer; I would draw a great deal if I knew how" (VIII, 283).

Unable to paint in oils, Blok painted with words. In the Italian cycle of poems, his precise and concise use of poetic tropes and his frequent inclusion of color epithets create the effect of visual images. Many of his poems, compact and delicate in design, are genuine vignettes. Keen thought, however, invariably underlies the poet's simple plan and seemingly casual observations. In these poems Blok drew naturally on his surroundings, and succeeded in freeing himself of that vagueness of expression which so often plagued him in earlier works. With the concreteness of a painter, he captured the essence of the scene and the moment.

Art became an absorbing passion for Blok after his return from Italy. "Art burnt me," he admitted, "it burnt me so that I began to shun modern literature and literati. . . . For this and for many other reasons, I stopped seeing almost everyone and retired into 'my own solitary ecstasies.' " [8] Kniazhnin in his biographical sketch of Blok noted the impact of Italian art on the poet:

Italian art "burnt" Aleksandr Aleksandrovich. Generally speaking, he loved art. "Architecture, perhaps, affected him more than any other art except the drama," claims Vladimir Piast. "The old masters of Italian painting were apprehended by him in all the fullness of their revelation." Almost everything of value which had emerged in the field of art in the past twenty or twenty-five years could be found in the old, dark mahogany chest in A.A.'s study. [9]

[8] "Vospominaniia A. Bloka," *Kniga o Leonide Andreeve* (Berlin, 1922), p. 59.

[9] V. N. Kniazhnin, *Aleksandr Aleksandrovich Blok* (Petersburg, 1922), pp. 106–107.

The immediate cause of Blok's interest in Italy was the earthquake at Calabria and Messina in December 1908 which took the lives of nearly 100,000 people and destroyed twenty-three towns and hundreds of villages in southern Italy.[10] People from all over the world, deeply moved by the tragedy, offered their help to the distraught survivors. Russian sailors stationed off the southern coast of Italy distinguished themselves by acts of sacrifice and valor in their efforts to bring relief to the stricken areas. In Petersburg a literary fund-raising project was undertaken: an anthology, *Italia*, was compiled by some of the foremost Russian writers, including Blok.

The earthquake, seemingly remote from Blok's immediate concerns, had an unexpected impact on him. Although he was appalled by its fateful consequences, he was less shocked by the actual destruction than by the symbolic significance of the event. He had long shared with other Symbolists the belief that Europe had started along the path to self-destruction when it fostered a materialistic, soulless civilization which alienated man from nature and hopelessly distorted his sense of values. Now the retribution of the elements was inevitable. Primordial forces, he believed, were brewing in the bowels of the earth, and soon they would be unleashed to bring chaos and destruction. The Italian earthquake loomed before him like a preview from the elemental world of an impending apocalypse. Man's inability, for all his newfangled technology, to predict or prevent this tragedy was for Blok the supreme and final irony—a sign of the ultimate failure of science in which modern man had mistakenly placed his faith.

Blok presented his own unique interpretation of the earthquake in two articles, "Culture and the Elements" (De-

[10] A death toll of 100,000 is quoted in the "Notes" to Blok's article "Gorkii i Messina" (V, 572).

cember, 1908) and "Gorkii on Messina" (October, 1909). In the latter he assessed the catastrophe as follows:

The earthquake in Sicily and Calabria is an event of universal importance. . . . No matter what people may say, however much they may try to localize its significance, it did *change* our lives. *What* changes it has wrought cannot yet be determined, but it is impossible not to believe that it reverberated and will continue to reverberate in the events of our outer and, especially, of our inner life. One must simply be spiritually blind, indifferent to the life of the cosmos and insensitive to the daily ferment of chaos to presume that the formation of the earth goes its own way independently and without influencing at all the development of the human soul or of life. (V, 380–381)

Viewing the earthquake as one of those cryptic phenomena whose true significance is clear only to a chosen few, Blok felt obliged to warn the unsuspecting public of its fateful consequences, for "it is the business, the *obligation* of the artist to see *what* has been predetermined, to listen to that music with which 'the air sundered by the wind' reverberates thunderingly" (VI, 12).

The Soviet critic V. Asmus sees Blok's reaction to the earthquake as a typical illustration of the poet's inability to analyze in conventional, realistic terms actual problems or situations. Asmus writes:

Despite Blok's aversion to every kind of estheticism as a surrogate for a worldview, he can find only esthetic solutions for the paradoxes of life. . . . In Blok's consciousness, the earthquake of Messina becomes mysteriously associated with the brewing revolutionary social storm. His feeling that a social catastrophe is about to descend on Russia and the whole world is based not on the principles of social science, but on mystic analogies with geological phenomena.[11]

[11] V. Asmus, "Filosofiia i estetika russkogo simvolizma," *Literaturnoe Nasledstvo*, Vol. 27–28 (Moscow, 1937), 52–53.

As Asmus infers in his article, Blok's theoretical premises cannot withstand scientific scrutiny. Their significance with regard to Blok's art, however, should not be underestimated. Although the poet's understanding of the historical process may have been subjective and unscientific, his view of reality was shared by a whole generation of Russian intellectuals, and directly affected their life and work. Furthermore, the beliefs and premonitions which Blok expressed in his essays provide a key to his poetry. While his mystic *Weltanschauung* can easily be discerned in his critical prose, it is less explicit in his verse, where melodiousness and pathos predominate over content, and the lyrical elements overshadow the mystical allusions. Sometimes Blok's language is so clear and direct that some of his poems at first glance seem to be free of symbolic overtones and to amount to nothing more than the product of his romantic imagination. But, as will be shown, their simplicity is deceptive. Beneath it lies a complex structure of esoteric symbolic references, and only the more factual, even if at times ambiguous, exposition of the poet's views in his prose enables one to grasp and appreciate more fully the latent meanings in his verse.

Early in his poetic career Blok recognized his own proclivities for mysticism. In a letter to his father he described himself, when he attended literary gatherings, as an "onlooker with an air of silent mysticism." He then admitted: "This [silent mysticism] does not leave me even now and, needless to say, I cherish it most deeply, seeing in it something basic, and therefore more sound than almost all the other 'criteria' of my spirit and flesh" (*Letters*, I, 80).

The Italian earthquake inspired new reflections in Blok and furnished fresh images for his poetry and prose. In his article "Culture and the Elements" (1908), Blok analyzes the causes of the rift between the masses and the intelligentsia. He likens the masses' deep, mute resentment, the product of many centuries of slavery and oppression, to the subterranean rumblings which precede an earthquake. And while the ruling classes and the intelligentsia rely complacently on their superior culture and on progress, the awakening social consciousness within the people stirs menacingly in its still barely perceptible but inexorable movement toward a fatal confrontation. Further on in the article, Blok compares the masses and the intelligentsia to two smoldering fires, and concludes prophetically with the awesome image of an erupting volcano:

We live between two fires of blazing vengeance, between two camps. That is why it is so frightening: what kind of fire is struggling to break loose from beneath the "crusted lava"? Is it like the one which ravaged Calabria, or is it a purifying fire? Whatever it may be, we are in any event living through a terrible crisis. We still do not know exactly what events await us, but *in our hearts the needle of the seismograph* is already registering disturbances. We see ourselves as though against the background of the glowing horizon, in a fragile aircraft high above the earth; below us there is a rumbling, fire-spitting mountain, down along which, behind clouds of ashes, streams of incandescent lava roll as though they had at last been set free. (V, 359)

Once again, in the poem "Retribution" (1910–1919), Blok recalls the "merciless end of Messina" as one of the most momentous events of the twentieth century, an "unmistakable portent of unheard-of changes" and "revolts" such as "had never been seen before." In "The Scythians" (1918), he accuses Europe of failing to understand the fateful meaning of earthquakes: "The destruction of Lisbon [12] and Messina was for you but a wild fairy tale" (III, 360).

When the revolution of 1917 came, it seemed to Blok to be the final act of that elemental play whose ominous preview

[12] The earthquake at Lisbon occurred in 1755.

had echoed in his ears some nine years earlier, when he had pondered the meaning of the Italian tragedy. Despite the revolution's frightful and inauspicious beginnings, this was for Blok an exhilarating moment. His prophecy had been fulfilled: with joyous anticipation he watched the crumbling of the old world, confident that a new era of freedom, prosperity and progress would follow. Kornei Chukovskii explains Blok's optimism: "Blok was firmly convinced that the 'humanoid' like creatures who survived the catastrophe would then attain true humanity: the sign presaging this tragic catharsis, this regeneration through catastrophe, was the earthquake in Calabria. His article devoted to this disaster was not sad, but joyful. This calamity showed the poet that people who are purified by a mighty storm become immortally beautiful." [13]

The prophetic stance adopted by Blok regarding the symbolic meaning of the earthquake was severely criticized by his contemporaries. The critic V. V. Rozanov, among others, accused Blok of indifference, cruelty and lack of compassion, and reproached him for "embellishing" and "estheticizing" the calamity and making it seem "apocalyptic" (V, 748). The fact that Blok's impulses were in this instance not primarily humanitarian cannot be denied. But the integrity of his convictions is unquestionable. His words of warning to his generation sprang from a sincere concern for the future of mankind, a future which he could envision only in metaphysical terms.

The train of thought which the earthquake stimulated in Blok can be detected even in certain passages where he does not mention it specifically: for example, in the following excerpt from his eulogy on Vladimir Soloviev delivered in 1910 on the tenth anniversary of the latter's death. The obscurities

[13] Kornei Chukovskii, *Aleksandr Blok kak chelovek i poet* (Petrograd, 1924), pp. 11–12.

in this passage are dispelled only when one recognizes its reference to the Italian earthquake:

> It is not in vain that during the interval since the death of Vladimir Soloviev we have experienced what others live through in a hundred years; nor has it been without meaning that we have seen the new century scattering its seeds upon the earth in the thunder and lightning of terrestrial and subterranean elements; in the flashes of this lightning all the centuries appeared before us and they made us wise with belated wisdom. (V, 453)

Blok believed that the "lightning" of revelation could throw open unexpected horizons. Only if one envisioned the universe in its entirety and grasped the interrelatedness of all existence could one begin to see the human race and its destiny in the proper perspective. Enlightened by such a vision, man could perceive the link between events and natural phenomena, between civilizations and cultures,[14] between past and future. Throughout his works Blok sees history as part and parcel of our present-day life and repeatedly reaches for those meanings that relate the familiar to the universal.

[14] Blok viewed civilization and culture as two distinct concepts. He presented his thoughts on this subject in the article "The Decline of Humanism." F. D. Reeve, in his book on Blok, summarizes the two concepts as follows: "By culture Blok means the works of the heroes proper, the best work, an age's understanding of itself, a man's understanding of himself, the fabrication of art and the apprehension of meaning. Civilization is the effective product of culture, the systematic use of tools by which men manipulate their environment and themselves. Civilization means accomplishment; culture means value." (F. D. Reeve, *Aleksandr Blok: Between Image and Idea* [New York: Columbia University Press, 1962], p. 37.) For another view on these concepts see also James B. Woodward's excellent introduction to *Selected Poems of Aleksandr Blok* (Oxford, 1968), p. 12. Blok's notion of the culture-civilization dichotomy has obvious resemblances to early twentieth-century German concepts. In this connection, the English-speaking reader will recall the relevant and lengthy passages on this topic from Spengler's *Decline of the West*.

His belief in the existence of underground forces influenced the poet's perception of Italy: Italy *is* its past, a past which he envisions buried beneath the earth and living its own everlasting life. In a landscape which he associated with Dante's visions of the nether world, and where the remains of ancient cultures are constantly being recovered from the depths of the earth, Blok contemplates the flow of history with the wonder of an archeologist and the pathos of a poet. The epithet "tragic," which he uses to describe the only Italy he acknowledges—that of the past—has an Aristotelian connotation: "One thing makes Italy tragic: the underground murmuring of its history, a history that has stormed past, never to return. In this sound the hushed voice of madness, the muttering of the ancient Sibyls, is clearly audible" (V, 390). For Blok only Italy's past, not her present, is alive. He is more attuned to the voices of bygone centuries, which he hears resounding from the labyrinths of history, than to the sounds of the modern world, more concerned with the "prophetic muttering of the ancient Sibyls," than with Italy's living language.

References in symbolic terms to the "underground" abound in Blok's Italian poetry and prose. The extent to which he felt its profound significance can be seen from the following passage in which the Russian Symbolist claims to have achieved a deeper understanding of Italy than that which he thought he discerned in the works of Byron: "In [Byron's] 'Italian adventures' there is something reminiscent, however remotely, of the English tourist who is interested in everything that can be seen or heard, but indifferent to everything inaccessible to the five senses; yet there is only one thing that makes Italy tragic: the underground murmur of her history" (V, 689).

III

Venice: The
Dreamer's Stance

Venice gave Blok a pleasant initiation into Italian life. "I am living in Venice almost as though it were my own city," he wrote to his mother after his arrival, "and the galleries, the churches, the sea, the canals and nearly all the local customs have become my very own, as though I had been living here a long time" (VIII, 283). The ease with which Blok became acclimated would seem to require no special explanation: undoubtedly he had seen pictures of Venice and knew its history. His image of the city coincided happily with its reality, and it did not take him long to familiarize himself with his new surroundings and feel comfortable in them. Yet the poet's sophisticated approach to all relationships—a trait which the reader learns to anticipate in his writings— warns one against making over-facile assumptions. A letter which Blok wrote to his wife in 1908 gives us an insight into the nature of his familiarity with a city he had never seen before. After acknowledging his ideological debt to the philosophy of Vladimir Soloviev, he makes this strange admission: "I am inspired by my deep-seated historical recollections—the *Lido*, Germany, and all that I once experienced. I am gaining much greater knowledge . . . about you in particular. I can remember you in former centuries" (VIII, 231).

The *Lido* in Venice had captured Blok's imagination long before his trip to Italy. In the poem "We came to the Lido at

1. Venice, Piazzetta di San Marco. In the foreground is the Lion's Column and the Doge's Palace; in the background is the Clock Tower. (Alinari).

the hour of dawn" (I, 304), written in 1903, he had used the name of this Italian beach to designate the shores of the Baltic Sea near Petersburg. This was no mere poetic whim but a deliberate association, revealing a preoccupation with Venice and its Lido as mystic symbols, which can be found in Blok's poetry as early as 1902:

> Centuries and countries were interwoven.
> We were going north from Venice,
> We saw the rain-filled fogs.
> We broke away—and went towards the Lido.
>
> But the shore was deserted and the horizon
> Veiled in a mesh of steady, drizzling rain.
> We will wait. We will be just children,
> As we go northward in our lively game.
>
> Thus began the spectacle of time,
> The play of the centuries! O, how dear you are!
> Countless links unfolded,
> Spray, sparks, pearls flew about.
>
> But who went past? who peered into the fogs?
> The play, the dream—who saw them from afar?
> Centuries and countries were interwoven,
> Our game unfinished, we went north. (I, 500–501)

Despite the poem's obscurities, one can detect in it in embryonic form ideas which were to concern Blok throughout his life: the interrelatedness of all existence, belief in the immortality of the self and faith in the power of poetic intuition to encompass realms inaccessible to reason. Time's relentless forward motion drives the poem on; the poet is caught in the "play of centuries," an actor without a part, a dreamer lost in the "empty spaces" of his own mystical recollections.

Intrinsic to Blok's *Weltanschauung* was his secret hope of

reincarnation. Another chance on earth seemed to have a greater appeal for him than eternal bliss in unknown realms beyond. For the poet, faith in the continuity of man's spirit and a belief that humanity was gradually evolving toward a more nearly perfect state were especially meaningful aspects of Vladimir Soloviev's mystical philosophy: "The greatest tribute we can pay to the memory of Vladimir Soloviev is to remember with joy that, since the day of creation, the essence of the world has been independent of time and space; that one can be reborn a second time and can cast off his shackles and dust" (V, 453–454).

Akin to Blok's hope for reincarnation was another of his metaphysical assumptions; his version of the myth of eternal return. He believed that great men and events had, in addition to their historical reality, an extended symbolic significance. For instance, he regarded the Russian victory at Kulikovo against the Tartars (1380) as not only an actual but a symbolic event, predestined to recur in an entirely new guise in the future. The Soviet critic Boris Soloviev recapitulates Blok's views:

The notion that "symbolic events" are fated to recur in history, and that they recur in a different guise, in a different era, in another hypostasis, while remaining essentially the same, lies at the core of many images and motifs of Blok's art (Christ, Mary Magdalene, the Unknown Lady, the Virgin Mary, the Star, and so on). The poet tries to penetrate their meaning; and the theme of the recurrence of events, both personal and historical, of their eternal *return*, is related in Blok's art to the notion that these events move along certain predetermined, primordial circles.[1]

The feeling of finding himself in familiar surroundings, which Blok experienced in Venice but in no other Italian city, may have had its roots in his uncanny sensation of hav-

[1] Boris Soloviev, *Poet i ego podvig* (Moscow, 1965), p. 285.

ing lived there in a previous incarnation. Significantly, this city, which reawakened subliminal memories of a dim past, also evoked speculations about a future life. Blok's meditations on reincarnation found expression in the third poem of the Venetian cycle.

Another reason for Blok's rapport with Venice was that he saw a peculiar resemblance between that city and his native Petersburg. "Basically, Venice is still not really Italy; it has the same relationship to Italy as Petersburg does to Russia; in other words, it does not seem to belong to it at all," one reads in "Silent Witnesses" (V, 391). In a letter to Briusov, Blok reflects on the emotional effect the city had on him, and repeats the analogy: "Venice's location is . . . unique; one can even say that it lies almost outside of Italy; one can love it in much the same way as one loves Petersburg; Venice has the same relation to Italy as Petersburg has to Russia" (VIII, 293). Blok's analogy seems to reflect primarily an emotional reaction. Undoubtedly, however, this reaction was evoked by certain curious similarities between the two cities.

Both Venice and Petersburg were built on marshland, and at a great cost in human life. Both are surrounded by water and intersected by canals and as seaports both played a vital role in the cultural and economic history of their respective countries: Venice was Italy's gateway to the Orient; Petersburg, Russia's window to the West. In its architecture and art, each city shows evidence of the creative influence of foreign cultures and the extravagance of its early rulers. Petersburg owes an impressive number of its masterpieces to the genius of the Italian artists whom Peter the Great and his successors invited to participate in the city's planning and architecture. Many of the elegant buildings of Venice, reflecting manifold styles and periods, display a brilliant and generous receptiveness to the best in art, whatever its provenance.

Notable, of course, was the influence on Venice of the Moor-
ish and Byzantine styles.

Although Blok did not depict the actual "cityscape" of Petersburg, its image is an intrinsic part of his urban lyrics. Like
Gogol and Dostoevskii, he felt the "soul" of the city, its in-
sidious hypnotic power. Hallucinatory images populate the
northern capital: intoxicated red dwarfs, little black men, invisible people. The gray mornings and the fiery sunsets, the
quaint winding side-streets with their feebly flickering lights,
the fog, the shadows, the black waters, the poor of the city,
the prostitutes, are real enough, but their symbolic essence
overshadows their reality. Here life is aimless, but filled with
an infinite longing and immense loneliness. Indeed, Petersburg can easily deceive with its sham gaiety and conjure up visions which can make one oblivious to the tedium and pain
lurking beneath its glittering surface. Any attempt to understand the reasons for the city's occult power is futile: Petersburg cannot be explained in rational terms. Blok saw it as an
ephemeral entity, a place without boundaries where "Russia
almost dissolves into a nothingness, where it is Russia and yet
not Russia at all . . . a point of departure into infinity." [2]
This city, on the borderline between reality and the unknown, was for the poet as familiar and yet as mysterious as
his own soul. Like his soul it lived a double life, harboring
within itself a *memento mori* and a hope for resurrection.

Blok admired Venice's vivid, colorful life-style, and described the city in his essay "Silent Witnesses" as the only
one in Italy "where living people and merriment can still be
found." As evidence he points to a "young Catholic girl leaving the confessional, her eyes sparkling with laughter; a red
sail in the lagoon; an ancient shawl thrown over the supple

[2] Quoted from *Literaturnye pamiatnye mesta Leningrada*, ed.
A. M. Dokusova (Leningrad, 1959), p. 446.

shoulders of a Venetian girl" (V, 391). These images reappear in the first poem of the Venetian cycle, but under the influence of Blok's gloomy poetic sensibility their brightness fades as, along with the other images in the poem, they become enveloped in the penumbra of ambiguity. Blok's muse did not respond to the luminous and picturesque side of Venice, but rather to a city made empty and mysterious by the night, a city outside a country, a place where one senses the awesome tyranny of Time.

Blok's letters from Venice reveal none of the intensity or complexity of his literary work. Their tone is exceptionally relaxed and serene: "Mother, we have been in Venice four days already, and we have been wandering about together and also separately. I feel much too lazy to write. Actually, it is quite pleasant here. Best of all are the lions, the gondolas and Bellini. I am only writing so that you won't worry. I think we shall be here for a while" (*Letters*, I, 258). In his next letter, he gives some descriptive details: "Our rooms look out on the sea, which can be seen through the flowers in our window. From the Lido [we can see] the whole northern side ringed with high snow-peaked mountains, some of which we drove through. The water is completely green. All this is well known from books, but still, it is very new—a novelty which is not startling, however, but relaxing and refreshing" (VIII, 283).

Long, leisurely walks through the city gave Blok an opportunity to admire at close range the splendid Venetian sights —the dreamy canals, the ancient bridges and black gondolas, the quaint narrow streets, the historical monuments, palaces and churches, and the celebrated blending of water and sky. Clad in a white Viennese suit and a Venetian straw hat, he spent much of his time gazing at people and houses, "playing with crabs," and collecting shells on the beach. The quiet dignity and warmth of Venetian hospitality seemed to have brightened his spirits.

One of the most attractive aspects of Venice is its unusual freedom, which was even greater in Blok's day, from jarring city noises. It is the strange and restful quiet of a city by-passed by the mechanized efficiency of modern times. Its streets are too narrow for motor vehicles; and the predominant sounds are those of voices, the water, and footsteps on cobblestones. Russian writers have praised Venice's silence almost as consistently as its beauty. The poet Viazemskii described the city as an "empire of silence." [3] Briusov, who admired Venice above all other Italian cities, gave as one of the reasons for his preference the fact that it was a town without noise and without dust.[4] Muratov, the writer and art critic, was deeply impressed by the soothing influence of its peaceful surroundings:

The narrow side streets . . . surprise one with their deep, mute expressiveness. Here the footsteps of the occasional passers-by sound as if they were coming from afar. They resound and then vanish; their rhythm lingers like an echo which carries one's thoughts into the land of recollections. . . . And the water! In a strange way it attracts and engulfs all thoughts as it does all sounds, and the deepest peace descends upon our hearts.[5]

The effect on Blok's psyche of the silence of Venice can be felt in the Venetian cycle, in the poet's lyrical reaction to the nocturnal scene.

Venice's famous art galleries and museums were for the

[3] P. A. Viazemskii, *Stikhotvoreniia* (Leningrad, 1958), p. 370.

[4] Valerii Briusov, *Zapiski proshlogo, Dnevniki 1891–1910* (Moscow, 1927), p. 120. Blok admired Briusov's Italian poems. During his stay in Italy they "resounded constantly in [his] ears—and in a completely new way" (VIII, 295).

[5] Pavel Muratov, *Obrazy Italii* (Moscow, 1912), I, 20.

poet the city's most compelling attraction. After viewing an exhibition of contemporary European art and dismissing it as trivial, Blok chose to concentrate his attention exclusively on the art of the Renaissance. However, not all Renaissance paintings pleased him. In his diary and letters, where he evaluated works of art according to his personal biases, he passed some disconcertingly superficial judgments on several renowned masters of Italian painting: he praised the art of the early Renaissance but attacked that of the late Renaissance; he gave his unqualified approval to Fra Angelico, Bellini, and Boccaccio Boccaccini but "firmly and finally rejected Titian, Tintoretto, Veronese and those like them" (VIII, 283). Blok did not feel hampered by his lack of technical knowledge or formal training in this sphere; rather he set up personal standards of excellence, on the basis of which he rendered judgments that simply reinforced his own artistic prejudices. After spending only one week visiting museums and studying paintings, he declared that his knowledge had increased considerably and that he had already gained new insights into art.

The religious paintings of the early Renaissance moved him particularly. He was fascinated above all by their spiritual quality, which he interpreted as a reflection of the pure and unwavering faith of the artists of this period who were only just emerging from the Middle Ages. Seldom, however, did he elaborate on the specific reasons for his preference for or dislike of individual paintings. His comments are often limited to such simple statements as "not young," "not fresh," "not bright," or "good," "amazing." Blok's standards in painting were apparently even more rigid than his literary standards, for only a comparatively small number of paintings pleased him in every way. Perhaps this was because he was able to appreciate wholeheartedly only works in which he recognized aspirations akin to those he had cherished in his youth. The yearning to recapture his early ideals never left him: as Briusov affirms, Blok never quite "succeeded in burying his dreams in the past." [6] His negative views on the secular art of the late Renaissance and his refusal to acknowledge the merits of modern painting led him from a pessimistic premise to a surprisingly optimistic conclusion: "Italian antiquity proves clearly that art is still terribly young and that almost nothing has yet been achieved, and if we speak of truly finished art, then absolutely nothing has been done; thus all art (great literature included) still lies ahead" (VIII, 283).

The diversions provided by his new surroundings did not prevent Blok's thoughts from drifting back to his "unfortunate country with its ridiculous government." But his haunting preoccupation with Russia's destiny lost all sense of actuality; Russia as seen from distant Venetian shores took on mythical dimensions and became the "idea" of Russia. He wrote: "Now I know that . . . what is visible to the naked eye is not Russia; and even if the Russian boors never learn not to mix art with politics, nor to start vulgar political arguments at social gatherings, and not to take an interest in the Third Duma—still Russia will remain the same for me— the Russia 'of my dreams' " (VIII, 283).

Blok did not incorporate into his Italian cycle all the poems which he wrote in Italy, but only those that were directly inspired by the Italian landscape, history and art. The influence of Italy on his work, however, is not restricted to this cycle. "To give the past immortal life," written on May 6, a week after his arrival in Venice, is especially relevant to this study because of its strikingly biographical character. An analysis of this poem affords us an opportunity to examine those histori-

[6] Cf. Valerii Briusov, *Izbrannye proizvedeniia* (Moscow, 1955), II, p. 290.

cal and esthetic concerns of Blok's that are directly related to his Italian experience.

> To give the past immortal life,
> O, I want terribly to live;
> To give the impersonal a human form,[7]
> And make things yet unrealized come true!
>
> And even if I am stifled by life's heavy sleep,
> And even if I gasp for breath in that sleep,
> Still, a brisk and cheerful voice
> Will say of me in time to come:
>
> *What if he lived by other [dreams],*[8]
> *That was not the secret force that drove him on!*
> *He was wholly a child of goodness and light,*
> *He was the very spirit of triumphant freedom!*

This poem is a microcosm of Blok's lyrical self. Obviously this epigrammatic self-portrait cannot express all the complexities, contradictions and inconsistencies in Blok's personality. It does, however, present a vivid picture of the poet; it dramatically discloses his aspirations and candidly expresses how he wished to be understood and remembered. It also displays that direct, almost naive, quality of outspokenness which was so typical of Blok. Its bold and vivid lines reveal the poet's unusually high spirits at the time of writing. Seldom in the past had Blok expressed his love of life so emphatically. Joyfully he proclaims his acceptance of all its afflic-

[7] Literally: "To incarnate (to give human form to) the impersonal." See Chapter I, footnote 5.

[8] In Russian, the adjective "other" in the neuter instrumental (*inym*) stands alone and the line therefore lends itself to more than one interpretation. In any case, the basic meaning of the first two lines is that poets should not be judged by ordinary standards.

tions and hardships, so long as he can feel confident that his poetry will outlive him and that the spirit which motivates it will be correctly understood by future generations. Indeed, this poem is an unusual statement coming as it does from one who has been described as "extremely modest and secretive in his personal life," [9] and a poet whose works more often reflect an outright rejection of banal day-to-day realities than a willingness to compromise with them.

Since the poem reveals an aspect of Blok's personality far removed from his characteristic moods of mystical longing or gloom, it is frequently quoted by critics seeking to round out their image of the poet. For instance, Kornei Chukovskii cites its first quatrain to support his assertion that Blok is "a poet of joy." For Chukovskii "joy" implies an intense sensitivity to life and art, and as such it is an essential attribute of great poetry. "Art is always an acceptance of the world, in art there is victory over irony and death," [10] affirms the critic, who maintains that beneath the surface of his gloom Blok cherished a healthy joy, a "creative appetite" (*khudozhnicheskii appetit*) for life. "Suddenly and unexpectedly, in the midst of his most somber poems," writes Chukovskii, "he would acknowledge that even the fleeting and trivial things in life were dear to him as a poet, that he delighted in the sweet sensation of his blood flowing melodiously through his veins, and that his heart rejoiced blithely over even the slightest novelty." [11]

Orlov's interpretation of "To give the past immortal life"

[9] Viktor Zhirmunskii, "Poeziia Aleksandra Bloka," in *Voprosy teorii literatury* (The Hague: Mouton, 1962), p. 191.

[10] Kornei Chukovskii, *Aleksandr Blok kak chelovek i poet* (Petrograd, 1924), p. 136.

[11] Ibid., p. 137. In this quotation Chukovskii paraphrases a passage from Blok's Italian poem, "Art is a burden on our shoulders" (Poem 20).

stresses the poem's romantic quality. Citing Blok's own words, he defines "romanticism" as a "passionate striving to live ten lives in one, an urge to create such a life." According to the Soviet critic the first quatrain is "the most precise formula of Blok's poetic ideal, the formula of his romanticism." [12]

Vengrov shares the view that the poem is an expression of Blok's passion for life, but he also finds in it a not unexpected irony: "The lines which Blok jotted down a few days after his arrival in Italy sounded like the cry of a poet who was gasping for breath in the night of reaction: they were based on a sharp contrast—the juxtaposition of a young man who is greedily in love with life with the 'heavy sleep' of life which stifles him; of bright hope for the triumph of happiness and freedom with the unbearable reality." [13] Vengrov's observation is perceptive; one must, however, take exception to one of his inferences. To conclude from the line, "And even if I gasp for breath in that sleep," that Blok was gasping in the "night of reaction" is to propose an unwarranted social interpretation of the poem. It is not inconceivable, however, that Vengrov's metaphorical association of "gasping for breath" with the "night of reaction" might have been suggested by the words uttered by Blok at a later time when, disheartened by the censorship imposed on writers after the revolution, he cried out that a poet dies when he is no longer able to breathe. For Blok this statement became a tragic reality in the years just before his death. It was then that the poet, as Iurii Annenkov recalls in his memoirs, was "gasping for breath" in what might be called a "night of reaction":

In the last years of his life, Blok's disillusionment knew no bounds. In his talks with me he was not afraid to be outspoken:

[12] Vladimir Orlov, *Aleksandr Blok* (Moscow, 1956), p. 134.
[13] Natan Vengrov, *Put' Aleksandra Bloka* (Moscow, 1963), p. 254.

—I am gasping, gasping, . . . gasping for breath—he kept repeating over and over—and I am not alone; you too, and all of us are gasping; all of us will choke. The world revolution is becoming a universal heart attack.

Or:

—I am sick of the evil smell of Marxism. I want to shell my Moscow seeds at leisure as I float in a gondola along the canals of Venice. O, Ca' D'Oro! O, Ponte dei Sospiri! [14]

Blok never published "To give the past immortal life" in its original version. He revised it several years later and used it as an introduction to "Iambs," a cycle of poems he considered one of his best. The changes he made in 1914 are slight but significant and are relevant to this analysis of his Italian journey.

> O, I want terribly to live:
> To make immortal all that exists,
> To give the impersonal a human form,
> And make things yet unrealized come true!
>
> And even if I am stifled by life's heavy sleep,
> And even if I gasp for breath in that sleep,
> Perhaps some joyful youth
> Will say of me in time to come:
>
> *We'll pardon his gloom—for surely*
> *That was not the secret force that drove him on!*
> *He was wholly a child of goodness and light,*
> *He was the very spirit of triumphant freedom!*

In the first couplet of this latter version, Blok reversed the first and second lines and substituted "all that exists" (*sush-*

---

[14] Iurii Annenkov, "Aleksandr Blok," *Dnevnik moikh vstrech* (New York, 1966), I, p. 74. Annenkov was a leading artist and illustrator. Among his best known works are his illustrations to Blok's "The Twelve."

chee) for the "past" (*proshedshee*), thereby eliminating the idea of the past which was so prominent in the first version. In 1909, in Venice—a city whose churches and palaces are like living witnesses of her glorious and dramatic history— Blok experienced that feeling which another Russian writer visiting Venice had described as a "personal, live link with the past." [15] Five years later, however, urgent personal problems, financial difficulties, and political turbulence at home and abroad had combined to diminish his interest in the past and to intensify his awareness of the present. "All that exists" emphasizes the immediacy and intensity of this awareness.

Other changes in the poem's final version show Blok striving to achieve greater concreteness and the elimination of any possible ambiguity. In line 7 the abstract synechdoche, "a brisk and cheerful voice," is replaced by the "joyful youth"; in line 9, "What if he lived by other [dreams]" becomes "We'll pardon his gloom." By substituting "gloom" for the ambiguous "other," Blok openly acknowledges here his subjection to those emotional states of depression and sullenness so often associated with him during his lifetime. With this shift in emphasis, a paradox emerges in the final quatrain of the second version:

> *We'll pardon his gloom—for surely*
> *That was not the secret force that drove him on!*
> *He was wholly a child of goodness and light,*
> *He was the very spirit of triumphant freedom!*

The "child of goodness and light" and the "very spirit of triumphant freedom" are strangely improbable epithets for a man beset by gloom. In fact, such a description seems inconsistent with Blok's pessimistic view of life and the premoni-

[15] Vasilii Rozanov, *Ital'ianskie vpechatleniia* (St. Petersburg, 1909), p. 231.

tions of doom expressed in so many of his writings. Yet, here they are, these magnificent lines in which the poet affirms that it is possible to be gloomy and light-hearted at the same time, just as one can be "stifled by life's heavy sleep" and still cherish the dream of a joyous reawakening. Chukovskii may be right after all, Blok *is* a "poet of joy," since he is able to rise above the limitations of his tormented self and view his mission as extending beyond the bounds of his present life.

Let us return now to Venice, to the first version of the poem. Here in the first quatrain, the poet's aspirations are stated with his typical symbolic concision. In his vision as an artist he seeks to encompass at one stroke the past, the impersonal, and the unrealized. Each of these concepts evokes an antithetical image: the past engenders thoughts of immortality, the impersonal of incarnation,[16] the unrealized of realization. It is not this play of concepts, however, which first strikes the reader. The immediate appeal of this stanza is not intellectual but aesthetic. The melodiousness of the verse, the flowing rhythm and easy rhyme blend with the poetic content to produce an effect that is satisfying in itself. One need not apply to the semantics of these lines the strict test of logic. Blok's assertions can be accepted as poetic truths. Archibald MacLeish's perceptive observation comes to mind here: "The structure of meanings in poetry may be not only a structure of disorder which emotion brings to order but a structure of untruth which emotion brings to truth." [17]

There is more depth and "truth" in Blok's poem, however, than is immediately apparent. Its meaning becomes clearer if the first quatrain is interpreted within the context of Blok's views on the social meaning of art. In 1919, Blok wrote an ar-

[16] See above, n. 7.
[17] Archibald MacLeish, *Poetry and Experience* (Baltimore: Penguin Books, 1964), p. 41.

ticle which was intended as an introduction to a literary project he had in mind at that time: to write a series of plays dramatizing those events in world history that he thought were of permanent significance. Unfortunately, he did not live to fulfill his plans, but we know of his intentions from the article "Historical Scenes." He wanted

to create a series of scenes from the universal history of mankind, employing all the means which science, technology, and art offer us today. These scenes must affect the imagination and will of the viewer, they must imperceptibly bring his ancestors closer and make them dearer to him, and show him that he is not alone in this world and that the blessings and curses that fall upon him are no different from those that befall the rest of mankind. (VI, 424)

Blok then proceeds to explain that the events to be depicted need not be extraordinary exploits or acts of supreme heroism, but should show man "as he is," recounting "not only his loftiest flights but also his descents, and thus convey a truly objective picture of human life" (VI, 424). The scenes in these plays should engage the spectator totally, awaken in him a keen feeling of communion with nature and history, and make him aware of the fact that "his ancestor, as well as the ancestor of his friend or enemy—men just like himself —acted, thought, and gestured just as he himself would or would not have done" (VI, 425). By presenting historical events on stage in such a manner, Blok hoped to contribute to making history a vital force in the lives and imaginations of men.

Blok's desire to place his talent at the service of humanity permeates the poem's first stanza: he wishes to communicate to his readers his understanding of the spiritual meaning of art (significant here is the Biblical terminology, *"uvekovechit'* " [immortalize], *"vochelovechit'* " [to embody], *"voplotit'* " [to incarnate]): to redeem from the everflowing current of time those everlasting but elusive truths which are relevant to all the ages. The challenge posed by this task fills him with a passionate desire to live.

Our present life, Blok tells us in the second stanza, is meaningless in itself; our significance lies only in the traces we leave behind. A poet's work is important only if its appeal and message outlives its own time. The belief that his poetry will prove inspiring to future generations makes the "heavy sleep" of life worth enduring to Blok.

Although in the last stanza the poet, as *persona*, recedes into the background, the limelight follows him. The "brisk and cheerful voice" of the future, acknowledging the significance of his individuality and talent, hails him as "the child of goodness and light" and "the spirit of triumphant freedom." As the poet had predicted, his countrymen accepted his self-evaluation, and, as a fitting and eloquent tribute, the last two lines of this poem were inscribed on his tombstone.

At this point it seems appropriate to analyze the phrase "the child of goodness and light," for the word "child" represents one of Blok's central concepts. In his works one often encounters the words "child," "childlike," "youth," "youthful." These words have a special connotation for the poet, a symbolism all their own: he associated "childhood" and "youth" with a spontaneous response to visual images and to nature, an openness to new impressions and a capacity to delight in them without needing to intellectualize them. He considered these qualities highly desirable for any artist, but he saw them expressed in painting much more often than in literature. In the passage quoted earlier from "Colors and Words," the perception of a painter was described as "childlike," that of a writer as "adult-like." Painters, in Blok's opinion, look at nature with children's eyes, simply and directly:

"painting teaches childhood," he wrote, "it teaches one to recognize red, green, and white" (V, 23). This directness of perception was also achieved, he believed, by certain writers. Blok thought that Pushkin, for example, was conscious of the liberating and inspiring power of graphic expression when he covered the margins of his manuscript with drawings: "Pushkin never took drawing lessons. But *he* was a child" (V, 22). Blok never failed to single out these childlike qualities whenever he encountered them. Acknowledging that Fra Beato Angelico and Bellini were his favorite artists, he hastened to add, "not for the sheer power of their art, but for its freshness and youthfulness" (VIII, 286).

"Childhood" and "youth" as metaphors are always used by Blok with discrimination; they invariably reveal a very personal attitude on the part of the poet toward his subject. For example, when he compares the city of Ravenna to "an infant sleeping in the arms of a drowsy eternity," one immediately draws a positive inference—that the traces of Ravenna's glorious youth can never be obliterated by time.

The special connotation attached by Blok to these words makes his description of himself as the "child of goodness and light" particularly impressive. He was always striving for a view of reality which would enable him to react to new experiences with childlike wonder, for he felt that the "beautiful thoughts" and radiant images which such an outlook inspired were an essential prerequisite to the creation of significant works of art.[18]

The optimism which pervades "To immortalize the past"

[18] The expression "child of goodness and light" might also be interpreted in terms of a certain naiveté and candor in Blok's personality of which he himself was aware and which many of his contemporaries regarded as being among his most outstanding traits. Throughout her biographical sketch of the poet, Zinaida Gippius emphasizes his childlike nature. Gumilev called Blok a poet "with a childlike heart" (N. Gumilev, "Pis'ma o russkoi poezii," *Apollon* VIII [1912], 61).

finds no echo in the other poems inspired by Venice, in which it seems that a sense of weariness and futility is driving the poet away from everyday reality to seek refuge in the nebulous realms of the imagination, where his creative will can reign unobstructed by the laws of logic, and where he can give life to the ghosts which haunt his mystical consciousness.

VENICE

I

With her I sailed the seas,
With her I left the shores behind,
With her I traveled far away,
With her I forgot those near and dear to me . . .

    Oh red sail
    In the green distance!
    Black spangles
    On a dark shawl!

[He] comes from a somber Mass,
There is no [more] blood in [his] heart . . .
Christ, tired of bearing his cross . . .

    To my Adriatic love—
    To my last one—
    Farewell, farewell!

A cursory glance at "Venice I" reveals a short poem of distinctive metrical structure [19] which depicts an intimate ex-

[19] Robin Kemball, in his book on Blok's versification, has singled out for comment the unusual structure of "Venice I": "The number of feet per line varies from two to four. The poem is rather of the song type, and follows no regular pattern as regards endings or rhyme scheme:

FFFF	FFFF	FFM	FFM
3333	2222	424	422
xxxx	abab	cde	dce

perience with dramatic economy: haunting memories of an ardent passion, a romantic celebration of Venice's color, a passing shadow of spiritual travail, then a sudden farewell. These motifs are handled discretely; it is possible that Blok intended the poem to be a succession of impressionistic scenes. The fact that he submitted only the second stanza for publication in his early edition of poems also suggests this was his original plan. There is no doubt, however, that "Venice 1" gains in meaning as well as complexity when each part is viewed in its relation to the whole.

The apparent theme of the poem seems to be that of love and parting—a common theme in popular songs. This induced the Soviet critic Aleksandr Kovalenkov to suspect the direct influence of an Italian tune: "Four lines without rhyme [followed by] a refrain, than a *terzina*, then a three-line stanza. Where does such a form come from? Somewhere, Blok heard the song of Italian gondoliers, transposed its sounds into Russian harmonies, and thus freed himself from the shackles of academic stanzaic standards." [20]

Although Blok may have subconsciously adopted the melodious pattern of a simple Italian song, he certainly did not intend here merely to tell a simple tale. For all its brevity and uncomplicated diction, "Venice 1" is rich in implications and is far wider in scope than a first reading reveals. After the straightforward narrative in the first stanza, the poem progresses with increasing emotional intensity and complexity towards a kind of esoteric symbolism that reveals more about the poet than about the subject itself.

There are six cases of combined ('trochaic') substitution—four in the first verse (in the first foot of each line) and one each in the first foot, lines seven and twelve" (*Aleksandr Blok, A Study in Rhythm and Metre* [The Hague: Mouton, 1965], p. 353).

[20] A. Kovalenkov, *Praktika sovremennogo stikhoslozheniia* (Moscow, 1960), p. 80.

When Belyi visited Venice in 1910, he recognized an affinity between Blok's reactions to the city and his own.[21] In his chapter on Venice in *Travel Notes*, he chose to include several quotes from Blok's "Venice 1." By borrowing his friend's poetic images to illustrate his own impressions, Belyi inadvertently provided a clue to the possible meaning of these images:

All Venice is the murmuring of Adriatic currents, a red sail in the green distance; it is the thin, transparent texture of the lace embroidery of her buildings, which have turned black with the swift passage of the centuries; sitting in the gondolas, we [Belyi and his wife] were talking:

"The land in [Venice] is nonexistent. Sailors' thoughts of land gave birth to the dream of a land for sailors—Venice.

"The dream took shape: at first with green distances and red sails; then the sails folded together to form the contours of brightly-colored palazzos.

"Look! At sunset the reflections cast by the door posts on the walls look just like sails. . . .

"And that black palazzo glitters like a black spray of spangles on a fluttering shawl."[22]

In this passage one can easily recognize the imagery of "Venice 1." Belyi's brilliant prose, with its suggestive pictorial and rhythmic effects, captures the shimmering elusive quality of Venice. It reveals the pre-eminently aesthetic perceptivity of this writer. Blok's poem, less intricate in form and far more concise, carries the reader beyond the reality of

[21] Since Belyi and Blok had reconciled their differences by 1910 and resumed their friendship it is quite possible that Blok discussed with Belyi his impressions of Italy. It seems reasonable, therefore, in seeking further clarification of Blok's text, to turn to Belyi's *Putevye Zametki* (Travel Notes), I (Moscow, 1922), which contain many direct and indirect references to the first two poems of the Venetian cycle.

[22] Ibid., p. 23.

Venice. It begins with a simple, even hackneyed phrase: "With her I sailed the seas," but one should not be deceived by the light superficial tone of the first lines. The theme here is not adventure: the poem, as usual, is all about Blok.

The rhythmic and thematic changes from one stanza to another are particularly striking in such a short lyric, and a whole gamut of emotions is condensed into a few pictorial images. A subtle ambiguity pervades the entire poem. Who is the speaker, a Venetian sailor bidding good-bye to his beloved, or Blok himself as he reluctantly departs from Venice? Who is the unidentified "her," a real woman or the city personified? Even such a straightforward descriptive stanza as the second suggests at least two possible interpretations. Is it diurnal and nocturnal Venice that are portrayed here, or meaningful moments in a personal experience? The vivid red sail against the green waters may indeed represent Venice by day; the dark shawl with its glittering black spangles may stand for Venice at night. One has only to envision the lighted gondolas sailing along the dark waters of the canals, or the palazzo which, according to Belyi, "glitters like a black spray of spangles on a fluttering shawl," to perceive in the last two lines of this stanza a possible metaphor of nocturnal Venice. This stanza, however, evokes different associations when viewed in relation to what is apparently a central theme in the poem: the awareness of the contradictory and transient quality of human experience. The "red sail in the green distance" may then be seen as a symbol of man's longing for freedom (noteworthy is the implied longing in the exclamation "Oh"), while the glittering spangles on the dark shawl—a metonymy for the Venetian women who traditionally wear this garment—may denote those ties that bind men to their homeland.[23]

[23] Obviously Blok meant to suggest more than one meaning when he changed the original version of the last two lines of stanza two

The third stanza appears thematically unrelated to the others, yet it is this stanza which casts a new and solemn light on the entire poem. Unexpectedly the image of Christ is introduced. The interpretation of this image requires a brief discussion of the significance which the figure of Christ had for Blok.

We have already noted Blok's tendency to broaden his frame of reference through the use of religious symbolism. Often this symbolism strikes a peculiarly strident note, as when he identifies himself with the image of Christ. Orlov, in his essay "The Eternal Conflict," discusses this identification. After citing the following lines from a poem dedicated by Blok to his wife,

> You are my native Galilee
> For me—the unresurrected Christ.
>
> .   .   .   .   .
>
> The Son of Man does not know
> Where to lay his head.

he observes that "the Son of Man . . . is at one and the same time the lyrical 'I' of the poet and a generalized picture of man—suffering, ostracized, and hunted from place to place—an image associated with the evangelical Christ who came into the world to redeem through suffering the sins of men." [24]

Although Blok frequently expressed sceptical views about the divinity of Christ, it was only the concept of Christ as an awesome and inaccessible God that he rejected. "What is Christ to you," he wrote his friend Evgenii Ivanov, a deeply

---

from "Venetian girls in black shawls," to "black spangles on a dark shawl!" and accentuated the emotional character of the stanza by exclamation points, which had been absent in the original (A. Blok, *Polnoe sobranie sochinenii v dvukh tomakh* [Moscow, 1946], II, 458).

[24] Vladimir Orlov, *Puti i sud'by* (Moscow-Leningrad, 1963), p. 387.

religious man, "to me is *not* Christ" (VIII, 130); and to Belyi, "I never did feel Christ; neither do I feel Him now; He is walking somewhere far away" (VIII, 103). Despite these seemingly agnostic statements, Blok was not an unbeliever. His attitude was not unlike that of Giovanni, a character in Merezhkovskii's *Leonardo da Vinci*, who drew a distinction between the two countenances of the Lord: "One as near as that of one's own kin, a face filled with human weakness— the face of Him who, on the Mount of Olives, sorrowed until bloody sweat appeared, and who prayed in a childlike way for a miracle; the other face is—superhumanly calm; wise, strange. and frightening." [25] Blok also discerned two aspects of Christ—the human and the divine—but was able to understand and relate to only the former.

The image of Christ as a symbol of suffering had an especially poignant meaning for Blok. He associated it with the agony of contemporary civilization, with the haunting sadness of the Russian steppes, with man's thwarted aspirations, and more personally, with premonitions of his own doom. The more acute his own spiritual sufferings, the better he felt he understood those of Christ—even to the point of identifying with Him:

> Christ! Sorrowful are the wide expanses of my native land,
> I am growing weary on the cross. (II, 263)

With reference to the poem in which these lines appear, the émigré philosopher and critic Georgii Fedotov has this to say:

Christ loses the last vestiges of divinity and turns into the poet's double. His humiliated countenance becomes pitiful and the crucifixion something hopeless. Blok, enticed by the idea of his own

[25] Dmitri Merezhkovskii, *Leonardo da Vinci*, Book 9, Ch. XIV.

identity with Christ, could experience Him religiously only as the Son of Man. He knew that his Christ was "unresurrected."[26]

The allusion to Christ in "Venice 1" seems more puzzling and less justifiable in terms of its context than similar allusions in Blok's other poems. The absence of logical ties between the third stanza and the others and the seemingly intentional syntactical ambiguity (the first two lines of the third stanza lack a subject) allow more than one interpretation by the critical reader. It seems plausible, however, to contend that here once again Blok chose to reveal his own forlorn and dejected state by identifying himself with Christ. It is a human, suffering God with whom he empathizes, one who like himself is a weary and lonely wanderer through life. Tired of the burden of his cross, overwhelmed by the contradictions inherent in mortality and art, Blok pauses here to seek respite in lyrical reveries.[27]

After the complexity and emotional tension of the third stanza, the fourth is anticlimactic in its simplicity. Whether its speaker is Blok or some imaginary figure, the essential thought of the poem has now crystallized: one who is driven by spiritual unrest cannot pause for long, for his only real gratification lies in the search itself, and momentary everyday pleasures cannot begin to satisfy his restless mind and heart. The poet evidently does not seek a quiet, sheltered harbor; directly or indirectly, he seems to reject the very idea that a state of permanent happiness and peace is desirable. For him

[26] G. P. Fedotov, *Novyi grad* (New York: Chekhov Publishing House, 1952), pp. 289–290.

[27] In his frequent visits to museums, Blok could not have failed to notice the many representations of Christ's passion, a subject which had great appeal for the artists of the Renaissance. Throughout his Italian poems one can often sense the inspiration and influence, albeit at times subconscious, of the art of painting.

such a condition would represent total stagnation and be incompatible, as well, with his romantic view of life. Blok may
have felt, like his favorite poet Lermontov, that "only in
storms is there peace" (from the poem "The Sail").

The reluctance and relief with which the speaker abandons
his "Adriatic love" are suggestively rendered by the ambiguity of "prosti," which means both *farewell* and *forgive*. And
on this farewell note Blok takes leave of daytime Venice with
its red sails and green distances in order to focus in the next
poem of the cycle on the mysteries which the Venetian night
guards so jealously.

VENICE

2

A cold wind off the lagoon.
The silent coffins of the gondolas.
And I, on this night—young and ill—
[Am lying] stretched out beside the lion's column.

On the tower, with iron song,
Giants beat out the midnight hour.
Mark has drowned its lacework portals
In the moonlit lagoon.

In the shadow of the palace arcade,
In the moon's faint light,
Stealthily Salome passes by
With my bloody head.

All is asleep—palaces, canals, people,
Only the gliding footstep of the phantom,
Only the head on the black platter
Gazes with anguish into the surrounding gloom.

In the comments of Russian critics on "Venice 2," one finds a rather unexpected emphasis on landscape. Orlov, who admired the "pictorial precision of all the visual images" in the Italian poems, particularly appreciated the image of "the silent coffins of the gondolas." [28] Nikitina and Shuvalov, in their detailed study of Blok's prosody, assigned the second Venetian poem (together with the majority of the poems in the Italian cycle) to a category which they labeled "lyrical landscape." They maintained that "the basic theme of such poems is the landscape," presented "from an emotional and subjective point of view." [29] Such an emphasis on landscape in a poem which is pre-eminently symbolic may be somewhat misleading, however. What stands out as the basic theme of "Venice 2" is not the scenic background but the poet's tragic awareness of his own doom, a realization which he again expressed by identifying himself with a Biblical figure—on this occasion, John the Baptist. The landscape, therefore, is only a setting, picturesque in itself and especially remarkable because of its unrelatedness to the Biblical account. Here we have another typical example of Blok's disregard for historical authenticity and of his belief that the true meaning of history lies in its relevance to the present.

The first known draft of "Venice 2" is dated July 1909, indicating that the poem was written two months after Blok's visit to Venice. The final version was completed in October of that same year. "Venice 2" was partly inspired by a painting Blok saw in the Uffizi Gallery in Florence. On May 25th the poet made the following entry in his notebook: "Carlo Dolci—also 17th century! Salome with the head of John the Baptist. Of course, no longer bright, forceful (17th cen-

[28] Vladimir Orlov, *Aleksandr Blok*, p. 153.
[29] Cf. E. Nikitina and S. Shuvalov, *Poeticheskoe iskusstvo Bloka* (Moscow, 1926), p. 45.

2. Carlo Dolci. Salome with the Head of John the Baptist (seven-
teenth century).   (Courtesy Uffizi Gallery, Florence).

tury), or young" (*Notebooks*, 140).[30] But while recognizing
its defects, Blok singled out this particular depiction of John

[30] "Salome with the head of John the Baptist" is considered one of
the least successful of Dolci's paintings and has even been removed
from the Uffizi Gallery since Blok's lifetime.

the Baptist from several similar paintings by post-Renaissance artists. It is also noteworthy that he chose Venice rather than Florence as the background to his poem. Perhaps he chose Venice because of his special feeling of affinity for its ancient past; or perhaps the mystery and solemnity of St. Mark's Square inspired him to select it as the most appropriate backdrop for a strange and solemn apparition.

In "Venice 2" the city is immersed in silence and darkness. A mood of hopelessness hangs over it, and one is reminded of Viacheslav Ivanov's poem "The Lagoon," in which the lagoon is described as a "pale shroud" and the Venetian shore as "the shores of despair." [31] It was no accident, therefore, that Blok sent his poem to V. Ivanov for comment. He accepted his fellow-poet's suggestion that he eliminate the last two stanzas (originally it had been a six-stanza poem)—a concession such as he seldom made to other critics or friends.

In the four stanzas that constitute the poem's final version, an allegorical design emerges, disclosing the duality of the *persona:* he is in fact both the spectator and the participant in the action—the observant-participant who is "young and ill," and the decapitated prophet.

In 1906 Blok had written in his *Notebook:* "Every poem is a tentcloth stretched over the spear points of a few words. These words shine like stars. And it is these words which make the poem live" (*Notebooks,* 84). The "spear points" of the second Venetian poem are associated with the poet's premonitions of doom: phrases like the "cold wind," the coffin-like gondolas, "young and ill," the "bloody head," and the "surrounding gloom," or the action of "striking" and "drowning."

The first lines with their emphasis on coldness and death

[31] Viacheslav Ivanov, "Laguna," *Kormchie Zvezdy* (St. Petersburg, 1903), p. 193.

already strike the note which marks the mood of the whole poem. The lonely figure of the poet silhouetted against the majestic ancient column, a monument symbolizing power and immortality, suggests the insignificance and frailty of human life.[32] The concise diction, the austere precision of the imagery, and the absence of active verbs (in the Russian the only verb in the entire first stanza is a past participle) combine to produce a semantic structure in keeping with the listless immobility of the dominant mood.

As an effective contrast to the first quatrain, the second exhibits both movement and sound. The tolling of the midnight hour intrudes upon the silence of the night, signaling a mystic ritual: the "drowning" in the sky of the cathedral's ornate portals. Sergei Makovskii, to whom the poem was sent for publication, failed fully to appreciate the import of the stanza's imagery and criticized its lack of verisimilitude. In reply, the poet stated:

You write: "This is incorrect. The lagoon is far from St. Mark's." Thus you suspect me of a double sin: ignorance of Venetian topography, and also decadent bad taste (for to call a lagoon illuminated by the moon a 'moonlit lagoon' would be a third-rate Balmontism). I assure you that I am speaking [here] simply of heavenly lagoons—namely, those in which Mark bathes his 'iconostasis' (in this case the portals) on moonlit nights.

Blok concluded his letter with a categorical refusal to compromise: "With these poems (as well as with 'Florence 2'), however they may be, I am satisfied; I am ready to publish them, but I cannot and will not change or correct them, because I value them highly just as they are" (VIII, 300).

[32] A similar contrast is presented by Briusov in his poem "Lev sviatogo Marka," in which the Lion's column is seen towering "over the crowds, the centuries,/ Indifferent to the world and to fate" (*Stikhotvoreniia i poemy*, [1961], p. 226).

However plausible Blok's explanation may have sounded, Makovskii, always a stickler for grammar, could not condone a catachresis like "drowned portals." For, while these portals or presumably in this case their reflection can be drowned figuratively in the lagoon, this image is clearly absurd if, as Blok asserts here, the lagoon *is* the sky. Evidently Blok did not think it necessary to supply realistic details for the literal-minded reader; indeed, he insistently ignored realism and logic: for example, when he referred to the Cathedral of St. Mark simply as Mark.[33] This unexpected and irreverent personification accentuates the irrationality of the metaphorical action of drowning, and gives it a connotation of violence and sacrilege.

The violence in the heavens which is depicted in the second stanza acquires in the third an earthly analogue in the surrealistic image of the decapitated head carried by Salome, to which the *persona* refers unexpectedly as "my bloody head."

After midnight, as things animate and inanimate merge in sleep, Venice again sinks into silence. Only specters from the remote Biblical past remain on the deserted square to haunt the poet's imagination.

"My bloody head" is a direct clue to the identification of the lyrical "I." The Biblical account of John the Baptist had for Blok a special symbolic significance, quite apart from its religious connotation. He regarded the image of the head on the platter, carried by the impious and frivolous Salome, as a uniquely appropriate means of expressing his conception of

[33] It could be argued that the issue here might have been simply one of an extra syllable. The fact that the choice of "Mark" instead of "St. Mark" was dictated by considerations other than requirements of versification is corroborated by Blok's reference to the cathedral in another version of the poem as *"svetlyi Mark"* (radiant Mark) (III, 530).

the writer's need to sacrifice himself in the service of art. Direct and indirect references to this image appear throughout his works. In "Letters on Poetry," for example, he writes:

Only the work that amounts to a confession, only a creative work in which the writer has *burnt himself to ashes,* whether to be reborn in order to create new things or to die—only that kind of work can be truly great. If this charred soul, presented on a platter as a beautiful work of art to the surfeited and disdainful crowd—to Herodias—is a mighty one, it will stir more than one generation, one nation, or one century. But even if it is not great, it must sooner or later arouse at least its own contemporaries, and not because of its excellence or novelty, but because of *the sincerity of its self-immolation.* (V, 278)

In this passage there is an implied analogy between the prophet's destiny and that of the writer. Like the Biblical prophet, the writer suffers death as the consequence of his dedication, but unlike the prophet, he takes his own life, so to speak, by "burning himself to ashes," and he does this not just once, but every time he is touched by the sacred fire of inspiration. Just as the self-indulgent Herodias was the final arbiter of the Baptist's fate, so too it is the "surfeited and disdainful crowd" that ultimately has the power either to bestow immortality upon the poet or to relegate him to oblivion.

The "infant in the charred soul"—the heart of the metaphor—reappears also in Blok's famous lecture in 1910 on Russian Symbolism. For readers of Blok this is no longer an esoteric symbol: it represents the vital, perennially youthful creative spirit, this poet's version of the phoenix rising from the ashes of the artist's soul.[34]

[34] Pavel Gromov has provided an interpretation *sui generis* of Blok's metaphor. In his detailed discussion of the relation between this lecture ("O sovremennom sostoianii russkogo simvolizma") and the Italian poems, he superimposes his own sociological interpretation

In "Venice 2," Blok's treatment of the decapitation theme is more concrete and personal than in his prose. It is not an abstract "charred soul" that Salome carries on her platter, but the poet's own bloody and still living head. In the poem Blok pictures himself as decapitated, and he does not shrink from this image in all its gruesomeness.

This mystical association with John the Baptist was surely inspired by Blok's belief in his own mission as a poet-prophet. The Biblical story assumed an even deeper personal significance for him in the light of his belief in the eternal recurrence of historical patterns. In his unswerving loyalty to his principles, in his condemnation of his own epoch and his ominous premonition of doom, Blok may indeed be compared figuratively with John the Baptist. Like the prophet, he may have seen himself standing alone, "crying in the wilderness," and like John he, too, made the ills of the world his own. But despite everything, Blok loved passionately if defiantly the very life he professed to despise. "The love and hate I bear within/ No man can endure," he declared in the poem "On death" (II, 298), and in "Retribution," he said, speaking of himself, "Affirming, he denied,/ And denying, he affirmed" (III, 323). His recognition of the prophet's inescapable fate

---

of the "infant" and the "charred soul" upon Blok's consistent and explicit symbolism. "Blok's words about the infant who still lives in the 'charred soul,'" Gromov writes, "explain why, at this difficult moment for him, he tries to hide under the aegis of symbolism. The 'charred soul' is the actual tragic consciousness of contemporary man. An undercurrent of tragic skepticism concerning the potential of the individual in present-day bourgeois society runs through Blok's lecture. . . . Symbolism is called upon to furnish a temporary 'defense' against this skepticism. The 'infant' in the contemporary soul is that living, 'human,' and natural element which has been able to survive despite the pressures of social relationships" (Pavel Gromov, *A. Blok, Ego predshestvenniki i sovremenniki* [Moscow-Leningrad, 1966], pp. 400–401).

deepened the tragic nature of Blok's vision: to be able to see through the darkness while the rest of the world sleeps unaware—is to be doomed. Significantly, in the last stanza of the poem (which he later deleted at Viacheslav Ivanov's suggestion), he had prophesied his own end:

> I shall not escape my somber destiny—
> I admit that I have fallen,
> The dancer in a transparent tunic
> Kisses my head! (III, 530)

The theme of the poet-prophet misunderstood, shamed and mocked, and then figuratively beheaded is developed further in the "Prologue" to "Retribution." Warning of an impending apocalypse, the voice of the poet thunders above the crowds:

> But yours is not the final judgment
> It will not be you who will seal my lips!
> Let the dark church be empty
> Let the pastor slumber; [35] before mass
> I will cross the boundary-line fresh with dew,
> I will turn the rusty key in the lock,
> And in the chapel, in the crimson light of dawn,
> I will serve my mass. (III, 302)

Blok's Italian poems had a profound effect on Russian readers and became standard fare for visitors to Italy. The following account supplied by the critic Vasilii Gippius testifies to their emotional impact:

In the summer of 1911, I was with V. M. Zhirmunskii in Venice. There everything reminded us of Blok and his Italian poems. I sent Blok a postcard with a view of St. Mark's Square and wrote

[35] Blok used the words "pastor," although in this context "priest" would be more appropriate.

on it two lines of verse which had been on my mind all throughout the preceding days:

> A cold wind off the lagoon.
> The silent coffins of the gondolas.

Following these lines came:

> And I, on this night—young and ill—
> [Am lying] stretched out beside the lion's column.

So persistently did these lines echo in my mind that when I
reached the lion's column, I actually wanted to act out Blok's
verses quite literally. It was not difficult at all to perform the
half-serious, half-humorous ritual. What would have been an un-
thinkable act of mischief in Petersburg could not surprise anyone
on that warm southern night. . . . When I saw Blok I told him
how, in tribute to him, I had stretched myself out beside the column. He smiled and said: "But I didn't stretch out." [36]

Blok had good reason to smile: Gippius's reaction was an in-
dication of the dramatic effectiveness of his poetry. He had
made his readers feel and see what he had felt and seen, and
accept implicitly the poetic truth of his vision.

VENICE

3

> Life's persistent din is fading,
> The tide of cares recedes,
> And a certain wind through the black velvet
> Sings about a future life.

> Shall I awaken in another homeland
> And not in this land of gloom?
> And will I in a dream some day
> Sigh over the memory of this life?

[36] V. V. Gippius, *Ot Pushkina do Bloka* (Moscow-Leningrad, 1966),
pp. 334-335.

Who will give me life? Will the descendant of a doge,
A merchant, fisherman, or priest
Share his bed in the future darkness
With my future mother?

Perhaps my future father,
Charming a Venetian maiden
With a tender *canzone*,
Already has a presentiment of me as he sings?

And can it be that in a future century
Fate will command that I, a babe,
Shall first open my quivering eyelids
Beside the lion's column?

Mother, of what do these dull chords sing?
Are you, perchance, already dreaming
Of shielding me from the wind, from the lagoon,
With your sacred shawl?

No! Only what is or has been—lives!
Reveries, visions, thoughts, begone!
The wave of the returning tide
Breaks into the velvety night!

The third poem of the Venetian cycle, "Life's persistent din is fading," was, like the second, written after Blok had left Italy. After several initial drafts, two new poems finally emerged: "Venice 3," which was one of the first Italian poems to be published, and "All this was . . . was . . . was" (III, 131), which Blok completed a year and a half later. Both these poems reflect his intense preoccupation with death and reincarnation.

Of the three Venetian poems "Venice 3" has received the least critical attention. Orlov mentions it in connection with

Blok's historical themes and concerns. "In Venice 3," he remarks, "the theme of the future . . . which the poet perceives
through the gloom of the present . . . resounds with great
intensity." [37] But Orlov's critique, focusing as it does chiefly
on the socio-historical aspect of Blok's Italian peoms, is limited in scope. A more discriminating critic, Mark Shcheglov,
in calling Orlov to task for minimizing the "immense personal
world of the artist," exposes what is in fact a general trend in
Soviet criticism on Blok:

His disregard for the "subjective" factor in Blok leads . . . Vladimir Orlov to say anything and everything, in his analysis of the
Italian cycle, that he can think up about Blok's quest for "objectivity" and his break with the "lyrical elemental world." Thus,
we find him referring to the classical features of Blok's style in
the poet's description of landscapes, to the paintings of the Renaissance, and to the typically Blokian appeal to his "purifying
centuries," that is, to the future—there is only one thing miss-
ing here: any mention of the fact that this cycle contains his most
brilliant and tragically expressive Dantesque poems—"A cold
wind off the lagoon" and "The red-hot stones burn"—which
are perhaps Blok's most "daring" poems as regards their "personal" *Weltanschauung*.[38]

Although "Venice 3" is not mentioned specifically by
Shcheglov in this passage, Blok's penchant for the metaphysical is very much in evidence in this poem.

A thoughtful, though not always sufficiently clear, analysis
of "Venice 3" is provided by F. D. Reeve in his book *Aleksandr Blok: Between Image and Idea*. Reeve discusses the
concepts of time and being and their relevance to Blok's
theory of reincarnation. Accompanying the poet on his hy-

[37] Vladimir Orlov, *Aleksandr Blok*, p. 152.
[38] Mark Shcheglov, *Literaturno-kriticheskie stat'i* (Moscow, 1965),
p. 205.

pothetical journey into the future, Reeve re-creates the pro-
cesses of his thought:

The poet wonders not only if he will be actually reincarnated (or
if, as he is, consequently, he is not a reincarnation), but also if he
will not recreate himself in his dreams, that is, if the contrary of
dreams is not the fact of metempsychosis. If there be such life, the
question then is: from what does it proceed? . . . The individual
—the poet, the "I" of the poem—has no way of knowing,
since he cannot distinguish what of the contemporary is significant. In this sense, he does not know where he is. What would
seem most significant would be prostration of himself, reduced to
his essential vitality and naiveté—himself as a child—before
the lion's column, before the symbol of that power which has
preserved culture and civilization through the ages. Should he
not begin there to study and to be the future, although his
mother may be prepared to shroud him in his own innocence?
No, because what remains of the past is the present, and that is
what is alive, whatever it may subsequently be. Wherever one
may be said to have been or to be going to be, one is here, now,
on the edge of that velvet night into which the tide, like time,
ebbs.[39]

"Venice 3" appears to be a poetic re-creation of a moment
of self-transcendence which Blok may have actually experienced in Venice. The poet's thinking emerges through his
lyricism: if "life has no beginning and no end," as he was to
state in the "Prologue" to "Retribution," and if he has a keen
awareness of his own roots going back deep into the past,
could he not also discern the dim outlines of things to come
by the same intuitive process through which he sensed his
own prior existence? But Blok's prophetic instincts proved
reliable only concerning events of a universal import, such as,

[39] F. D. Reeve, *Aleksandr Blok: Between Image and Idea* (New
York: Columbia University Press, 1962), pp. 150–151.

for example, his predictions of revolution. But when he attempts to prophesy about personal matters, his gift of clairvoyance fails him.

"Venice 3" consists of seven stanzas. The first is a symbolic point of departure from which the poet launches into the realms of the unknown; the last quatrain is the point to which he returns to seek the true meaning of the very reality he had sought to escape. The fact that the points of departure and return are one and the same is conveyed by the repetition of the images of ebbing and flowing ("the tide of cares recedes" and "the wave of the returning tide").[40]

Despite their similarities, the first and last stanzas are significantly different in tone and rhythm. The first quatrain is characterized by its slow movement, its infrequent but regular stresses, its protracted vowels and distinct interlinear pauses.[41] The poet meditates by the sea and as he watches the dark waters and listens to the song of the wind, he slips

[40] The repetition of a motif in a poem's first and last stanzas is a fairly common device in Blok's poetry and is found particularly often in his first book of verse. Iurii Tynianov gives a graphic description of this feature: "The end repeats the beginning and joins with it to form a closed circle in which the emotion fluctuates; once the emotional key has been given, the emotion builds up and then at the highest point of tension it falls back toward the beginning—in this way the end of the poem interlocks with the beginning and forms a complete unit which continues on, so to speak, beyond the ending of that poem." (Iurii Tynianov, *Problema stikhotvornogo iazyka* [Moscow, 1965], p. 257.)

[41] Boris Soloviev admires the harmonious blend of sound and meaning in this quatrain: "Here sounds arise on the crest of one and the same wave . . . almost as if they were its continuation, its echo, its reverberation; here, undoubtedly, the phonetics of the poem is indissolubly related and linked to the theme and material of the narrative . . . which it follows and 'corresponds' to faithfully; phonetics, theme and texture are inseparable" (Boris Soloviev, *Poet i ego podvig*, pp. 458–459).

imperceptibly into a dreamlike state. His thoughts drift away with the receding tide and lose themselves in the mysterious expanses beyond the "black velvet."

In contrast to the pensive, dreamy tone of the first stanza, the tone of the final one is boisterous and assertive. The poet dismisses all speculations with the colloquial *"Proch!"* (Begone!). Strong, forceful stresses enliven the lines, three successive exclamation points heighten the emotional tone and effect. The return to reality is expressed in vigorous, artless language. The "black velvet" of the first stanza is recapitulated, but in a more explicit form, as "velvety night."

In the intermediate stanzas, Blok reflects on the possibility that in some future life he might be reincarnated in Venice. But his effort to write poetry in a mystical key here fails to lend wings to his poetic inspiration. The wind in whose haunting "song" he thought he could hear prophetic sounds carries no transcendental message for him. Although he can give poetic life to a mother of the future whom he envisions only dimly, he cannot endow her with speech. With the first wave of the returning tide a vivid sensation of his physical being and his immediate surroundings fills him anew. Disdainfully he rejects "reveries" and "visions" as futile illusions which blunt our appreciation of the one and only life we can know.

"Reveries" and "visions" are familiar words to readers of Blok's poems. In the cycle *Poems about the Beautiful Lady*, these words heralded a long-desired revelation which invariably eluded the poet's grasp. Oblivious to everything around him, he awaited, trembling in ecstasy, the manifestation of Her divine favor; he even heard Her music and Her footsteps and sensed Her proximity; but then these sounds and sensations suddenly disappeared and he reawakened amid the dull surroundings of ordinary everyday reality. The feeling of hopeful expectancy in "Venice 3" recalls these earlier moods. Here wind and music have a role similar to the one they play in the "Poems about the Beautiful Lady" where Her advent was often preceded by music and Her "harmonious songs" were audible "in the vernal melodies of the wind" (VII, 346). In the Venetian poem Blok also makes the wind the harbinger of glad tidings: its sounds carry echoes of immortality. But if the youthful Blok had once been able to believe that love and faith would lead him beyond the confines of the physical world, he had by 1909 become sceptical of the validity of his intuitions. His conscious efforts to escape the "curse of abstractness" warned him against erecting poetic structures on the frail foundations of mystical visions; he now sought the support and security afforded by reality. Although Blok evaluated his poetic career as a progression from the rational to the irrational,[42] the "rational" in Blok's mature poetry is, in fact, the substructure upon which the "irrational" rests. Hence, he now realized that any attempt to construct a poem as he had done in the past, on the shifting sands of mere dreams and hypotheses, was doomed from the start. The poet apparently felt that in "Venice 3" his imagination had carried him too far from the shores of reality. This might explain the vehemence and suddenness of his return to "what has been" and "what is." Rejecting the inherent nebulousness of what might be, he concludes in peremptory fashion that "only what is or has been—lives!"

While "Venice 3" extols the present, its untitled twin "All this was . . . was . . . was . . ." (both poems, as mentioned

[42] Blok expressed this thought when, commenting on Mandelshtam's poem "Venezia," he stated: "[Mandelshtam's] poems arise out of the dreams—very original dreams—which belong only to the realms of art. Gumilev has defined [correctly] Mandelshtam's path: from the irrational to the rational (the opposite of mine)" (VII, 371).

earlier, are combined in Blok's early drafts) begins with a bold
affirmation of the past and ends on a note of confidence in
the future:

> But this I believe—all that I have loved
> So passionately, will not vanish without a trace,
> All the turmoil of our wretched life,
> All this puzzling ferment. (III, 132)

Blok's faith in life's higher meaning and his firm belief that his
spirit would never wholly die were the beacon lights that always guided him back to the shore after many a stormy
adventure. This faith made "life's din" seem less frightening
and the "tide of cares" less overwhelming; it sustained him
through emotional crises and physical hardships; it imbued
him with a passion for life that endured almost to the end of
his days, and it endowed him with sufficient spiritual strength
to withstand the many disillusioning events and experiences
which befell him.

In retrospect, the entire Venetian cycle appears as the syn-
thesis of one long, multifaceted dream. Whether one is visualizing the "red sail" and the black-spangled shawl of the first
poem, or shuddering at the eerie images of the second, or
wondering at the nocturnal voyage of the third, one is always
wholly or partially in the realm of dreams, visions, or fanta-
sies. In Venice Blok found inspiration for his poetry and an
ideal setting in which to contemplate those concepts of time,
being, and reincarnation which had always haunted him. Enriched by his first encounter with Italian art in its own milieu
and anticipating even more gratifying experiences to come
during the remainder of his Italian trip, Blok now left Venice
for Ravenna.

IV

Ravenna: A Gleam
of "New Life"

The Bloks arrived in Ravenna on May 10, 1909. A few days later the poet wrote home:

We spent two days in Ravenna. It is a dull provincial town, much duller than Venice. The little town sleeps soundly, and churches and images of the first centuries of Christianity are everywhere. Ravenna has preserved better than all the other towns its early art, that of the transition from Rome to Byzantium. And I am very happy that Briusov sent us here; we saw Dante's tomb, the ancient sarcophagi, the astonishing mosaics and Theodoric's palace. Theodoric's tomb is in a field outside Ravenna—amid roses and wisteria. In another part of the town there is a very ancient church where, right before our eyes, they dug up from beneath the ground a mosaic floor dating from the IV–VI centuries. It was damp there and smelled like a railroad tunnel; there were tombs everywhere. One tomb I discovered under an altar, in a dark stone cave with water on the ground. Light was falling on it from a little window. The tomb was covered with slabs of a soft lilac shade and also with soft green mildew. And the silence all around was frightening. The Latin inscriptions are simply amazing. (VIII, 284)

The tone of this description barely conveys the excitement and delight which the ancient town, now sunk in its "sound sleep," evoked in Blok. "I love Ravenna best of all" (VIII, 289), he remarked before leaving Italy. As a token of appre-

3. Ravenna. Palace of Theodoric the Ostrogoth on the Corso Garibaldi.   (Alinari).

ciation to Briusov for having recommended that he visit this city, he sent him several of his poems, including "Ravenna 1." Acknowledging the debt he owed to his fellow-poet on more than one count, he wrote: "The enclosed poems were inspired not only by Ravenna itself, but by your poems as well. . . .

"Ravenna has changed little since you were there. Evidently it has died a long time ago and irrevocably, and it isn't even trying to bring itself up to date with cars and trolleys like Florence. The complete absence of people and of a commercial antheap atmosphere also makes it all the more attractive" (VIII, 294). And because, at least from his standpoint, Ravenna had not changed since Dante's times, Blok felt he understood "why Dante had found a haven" in this "city of rest and peaceful death" (VIII, 294).

Ravenna is an ancient town dating back to Etruscan times. It became an important naval base during the reign of Caesar Augustus, when a port was built in Classis, three miles outside the city gates. Later the Adriatic receded, and what had once been a bustling port was, by the beginning of the twentieth century, a marshy, deserted area. Here stood the stately basilica of St. Apollinare, majestic and defiant against the background of the barren surrounding countryside, an eloquent reminder of history's inconstant fortunes.

Early in the fifth century, Ravenna attained political prominence as the center of the Roman empire under the Emperor Honorius. It is not to Honorius, however, but to his half-sister, Galla Placidia, that the city is mainly indebted for its impressive architecture, numerous vestiges of which still remain standing. This powerful and wanton empress, who had many impressive churches built in expiation of her sins, is such an integral part of Ravenna that Blok had an almost tangible sense of her ghostly presence: her image came to life, it stepped out, so to speak, from the many murals and mosaics which depict her, and her "fiery glance," still burning with unquenchable passion, was as real to him as the "caressing" and "tranquil gaze" which he detected in the eyes of the young women of Ravenna.

Galla's life and legend fascinated Blok. In his *Notebooks* he lists her as one of the "great lovers" of all time and calls her his "very own" (*Notebooks*, 153). In "Ravenna 2," the stanza dedicated to Galla is not a poet's tribute to an ancient queen, but the plea of a humble lover to his "Lady." The poem is a series of poetic paradoxes; a living poet declares his love for an almost legendary, long-dead empress; reverently, he admits the impossibility of passion, yet, impiously, he experiences it; he feels humble and insignificant, yet he boldly declares his strangely ardent feelings.

> Impossible here is passion's voice,
> There is no answer to my plea!
> Oh, how insignificant I am before you!
> I envy your fate.
> Oh, Galla!—Always I have been
> Stirred and disquieted by my passion for you!

On the strength of his "personal feelings" for Galla, Blok allowed himself the poetic license of changing her name in "Ravenna 1" from *Pacidia* to *Plakida*—a spelling he deemed more suitable. In a commentary on this poem, he apologized both for the liberty he had taken and for his feelings:

Thus I have permitted myself to give a Hellenic form to the name of Galla Placidia, whose face in certain paintings resembles that of a Greek girl. Incidentally, I hope the archeologists will forgive my personal feelings about this famous empress of the fifth century—the sister, wife and mother of Roman emperors . . . the widow of an Ostrogoth chieftain. . . . A tumultuous fate swept this passionate and power-loving woman from the ignominious chariot of a barbarian onto the throne of the Eastern Roman empire, the heart of which was then Ravenna, so magnificent in those days. The image of Galla, her face sometimes girlishly tender, at other times hard and cruel . . . has often stirred the imagination of painters, including several Russians. (III, 527–528)

Had Blok been a painter, Galla would undoubtedly have been one of his subjects, and his portrait of her would probably have been a mosaic of ethnic characteristics. In a letter to Briusov, he describes her facial type as Greek and her eyebrows as Byzantine, "arched like those of the Egyptian girl" (VIII, 294). The "Egyptian girl" whom Blok associated with his own conception of Galla, is the subject of a painting in the Archeological Museum in Florence. Her unusually large eyes, staring into space, impressed Blok so vividly that he dedicated an entire essay in "Lighting Flashes of Art" to a description of them. He wrote:

There is in them a complete indifference and a stubborn determination which transcends all conceptions of modesty, shame or impudence. All that can be said about those eyes is that they gaze at us now and always will, as they did in life. . . . There is no weariness in them, no maternal tenderness, no gaiety, no sadness and no desire. One can discern in them only a dull, insatiable hunger. . . . Neither the emperor of Rome, nor the barbaric Hyperboreans, nor the Olympian gods could ever begin to satisfy that hunger. Those eyes gaze [at us] with an awful stare, mute, agonizing—like the scent of the lotus. They gaze on, century after century, age after age. (V, 399)

"What difference does it make," asks Blok in the same essay, "who she was, a queen or a slave? Or rather, is it not obvious at first glance that this is a queen?" (V, 397–398). Blok admired in Galla not the powerful imperial figure, nor the patroness of the arts, but the passionate woman who confronted her fate with all the tragic vehemence of her impetuous nature. In her adventurous and erratic life he sensed those grand passions which in his estimation were far loftier and nobler than the dull, cautious feelings of ordinary mortals, and which raise those rare beings who experience them to cosmic and immortal levels. It is the intensity of these passions and the force of her pride and cruelty that, in "Ravenna 1," give Galla's glance the power to burn right through massive stone, and that prompted the poet to refer to her as "blessed"—an epithet he does not bestow even upon the Italian Madonnas. His own desire to live life to the full and his hopes for personal immortality account for the startling admission in "Ravenna 2": "I envy your fate."

Two other historical figures are mentioned in the "Ravenna" poems. The first of these is Theodoric the Ostrogoth, the last of Ravenna's powerful kings. His mausoleum, a decagonal stone structure with a solid stone roof, is one of the city's most remarkable monuments. The second is Dante, who spent the last four years of his life in Ravenna and is buried there. Dante's death marked the end of medieval Italy, after which, according to Blok, Ravenna fell into the fateful slumber from which it has still not awakened.

Blok was delighted with the "dead" appearance of the city—its ancient buildings and sleepy streets, its sparse population, and the unhurried pace of its life. Here was a place which had chosen to die a natural death rather than surrender to that all-conquering monster—modernity. Everything in Ravenna spoke to the poet of beauty, peace, of the ancient past he loved. Few cities in Italy contain so many impressive examples of early Christian and Byzantine art. The architectural symbolism of Ravenna's churches and mausoleums combines the ascetic spirituality of early Christianity with the ornate elegance of Byzantium. Reminders of mortality and death are everywhere: in the churches and churchyards where ancient sarcophagi are preserved; in the austere pre-Renaissance religious art whose original purpose was to turn the beholder's thoughts away from mundane things and direct them toward the life beyond. The architecture of stone and marble in the spacious bare churches communicates an overwhelming feeling of coldness, a coldness unaffected by the glow of the elaborate mosaics, which, despite the passage of so many centuries, still retain their original brilliance. A few miles from the city is the Pineta, the famous pine woods celebrated by Dante and Byron, still verdant, but showing the mournful signs of age and man's neglect.

But although the countryside and monuments of Ravenna stir a nostalgia for the past and arouse thoughts of the transience and insignificance of human life, its seemingly imperishable art speaks of permanence and meaning. Blok reacted strongly to the awe-inspiring character of the city's symbolism. The paradox of life-in-death and death-in-life inherent in Ravenna crystallized in his poetic imagination to produce one of his most masterly poems—"Ravenna 1."

RAVENNA

All that is fleeting, all that is mortal,
You have buried in the ages.
Like an infant, you sleep, Ravenna,
In the arms of a drowsing eternity.

Slaves no longer haul mosaic tiles
Through the Roman gates.
And the gilt is burning out
On the walls of cool basilicas.

From the slow kisses of the damp
The rough vaulting of the crypts has grown gentler,
Where the sarcophagi of holy monks and empresses
Have a green hue.

Silent are the burial halls,
Shadowy and cold their thresholds,
Lest, awakening, Blessed Galla's
Black glance should burn through the stone.

Of warlike affray and wrong,
The bloody trace is wiped away and forgot,
Lest the voice of Placidia resurrected
Should sing the passions of bygone years.

The sea has retreated afar,
And roses surround the rampart
To keep Theodoric, asleep in his tomb,
From dreaming of the storms of life.

But the wastes where once were vineyards,
Homes and men—all are tombs.
Only the bronze of stately Latin
Sings out trumpet-like on the slabs of graves.

Only in the intent and tranquil gaze
Of Ravenna's maidens a regret
For the unreturning sea
Sometimes shines forth timidly, then vanishes.

Only by night, bending over the valleys,
Keeping count of the future centuries,
Dante's shade with its eagle's profile,
Sings to me of a New Life.

Blok wrote the first draft of "Ravenna 1" on the day he arrived in the city. Makovskii writes that Blok had an especial
fondness for this poem and therefore made it the overture to
his Italian cycle. He, personally, however, did not share the
poet's high regard for it; he was displeased not only with the
poem's imagery, but with its inaccuracies of diction, faults
which he suspected were the consequences of Blok's careless-
ness and "insufficient knowledge" of grammar. For instance,
Makovskii could not understand how the "thresholds" of the
"burial halls" could be "shadowy" or how "the Blessed

Galla" could "awaken" and with her "black glance burn through the stone." He could not accept the inverted metaphor, the vineyards' "wastes" [1] and had difficulty in visualizing "regret shining forth" then "vanishing." He was strongly opposed to the inaccurate use of the ambiguous expression "*v rukakh*" (in the hands) instead of the more appropriate "*na rukakh*" (in the arms).[2] "The infant sleeps *in the arms* of its mother, not *in her hands*," he wrote; "the whole visual image here is false because of such 'negligence.' " [3] In his general commentary on the "Italian Poems," Makovskii offers a scathing critique of Blok as a symbolist poet; ironically, however, this critique reveals his own shortcomings as a critic rather than Blok's inadequacies as a poet: "Blok's greatest handicap is his belief that 'inspiration' alone is sufficient, that a poetic art which derives from 'otherworldly depths' needs no verification, that true poetry is a subconscious babbling and that the vague unintelligibility of this babbling is a token of symbolism." [4]

Orlov, who obviously does not share Makovskii's point of view, cites "Ravenna" as an example of Blok's "plasticity and clarity of style." "The image of an ancient culture which has retreated into the past," he writes, "is masterfully portrayed in the chiseled lines of 'Ravenna.' " [5] According to Orlov, the basic theme of this poem is the future—"the future centuries"—and a "new life" which "asserts itself despite

[1] In the translation of "Ravenna 1," "Vineyard deserts" was replaced by "wastes where once were vineyards" for the sake of greater clarity and smoothness.

[2] "*Ruka*" in Russian means both "hand" and "arm."

[3] Sergei Makovskii, *Na Parnase "Serebrianogo veka"* (Munich, 1962), p. 153.

[4] Ibid., p. 154–155.

[5] Vladimir Orlov, *Aleksandr Blok* (Moscow, 1956), p. 151–152.

the centuries-old lethargy of an ancient culture, and a 'drowsing eternity'." [6]

Although Gromov's critique is generally similar to Orlov's, it merits attention as one of the lengthiest and most quoted analyses of this poem in Soviet criticism. Gromov regards "Ravenna 1" as the key to the entire Italian cycle; he also emphasizes its relevance for an understanding of Blok's *Weltanschauung*. He sees "Ravenna" as the lyrical expression of a concept which he considers fundamental to Blok's philosophy: the belief that there exists an "inner logic which links together all the various stages of history." [7] For Gromov, the theme of "Ravenna" is "life, temporarily curtailed and dormant, but gathering its strength for a new outburst," and the most important aspect of this theme is "the tragic paradox of history, the record of which Ravenna has so vividly preserved." [8] "What is tragic," he goes on to explain, "is that the Latin inscriptions tell us more about life than does contemporary life itself." [9] According to the critic, Blok regarded as a paradox the fact that the life of Ravenna, once so intense and dynamic, could have come to such a complete standstill. This irony of history is as much a part of the theme of "Ravenna" as it is of the Italian poems in general. But it is not so much the chasm between the old and the new that Blok chooses to lyricize but the continuity which binds them. It is in this vein, that Gromov interprets the seventh stanza of the poem: "In the gaze of 'Ravenna's maidens' one sees 'regret for the unreturning sea,' and the shade of Dante 'sings of a

[6] Ibid., p. 152.

[7] Pavel Gromov, *Ego predshestvenniki i sovremenniki* (Moscow–Leningrad, 1966), p. 371. Gromov frequently refers to this concept as "Blok's historical perspective."

[8] Ibid., p. 367.   [9] Ibid.

New Life'—all this means that the past and the future are linked together inwardly, that history has penetrated into the people's soul and that the successive stages of time are related to one another in complex and tragic ways." [10] The critic who discerns in Blok's thought a point of view which can be traced back to Hegelian philosophy (significantly, Gromov avoids any specific mention of Hegel) feels that he must find some way to justify the poet's dialectic, which is so unmistakably idealistic and not entirely in harmony with his own critical analysis of his poetry. He therefore declares that Blok was at this time going through an especially "difficult, controversial stage in his development." Since Blok lacked faith in the existing social order and doubted the rationality of the historical process, he had no other alternative, according to Gromov, but "to search for that one thread which binds together the various stages of history, and he tried to find this thread in men's hearts." [11]

One of the best articles on "Ravenna" in contemporary Soviet criticism is Etkind's "The Shadow of Dante" which concentrates primarily on the language and structure of "Ravenna." After a meticulous analysis, Etkind arrives at the following conclusion: "The content of the poem, as Blok sees it, is the oneness of death and life, of [human] frailty and immortality, of non-being and time, of past and future . . . and this unity is expressed in his highly complex thought about

[10] Ibid., p. 372.

[11] Ibid. In the same chapter Gromov compares Blok's perception of history as expressed in "Ravenna" with that of Briusov in the poem "Zamknutye" ("The Secluded Ones"). Briusov, in Gromov's estimation, had a narrow, fragmented view of history; he saw it in self-contained cycles, instead of dialectically and in perspective. Gromov's interpretation of the Italian poems is discussed at greater length in Chapter V.

Time, whose flow supplies the inspiration and the structure of "Ravenna." [12]

Although all these critiques offer interesting insights into the poem, they all tend to attach little importance to what Shcheglov has called the "immense personal world of the artist," those emotional and subjective elements which play such a dominant role in Blok's poetry.

The epigraph chosen by Blok for his Italian poems was taken from an inscription in the Church of Santa Maria Novella in Florence. The four-line stanza has the solemn tone of a Biblical saying: it speaks of the ephemeral nature of life, the irretrievable passage of time, and the inevitability of death. There seems to be a direct relationship between these verses and "Ravenna 1," which immediately follows it. Indeed, what other Italian city illustrates more dramatically the meaning of this epigraph than does this town which "died a long time ago and irrevocably"? All the more striking, therefore, is the comparison in the first stanza of the ancient town to a sleeping infant. Thus, what emerges from the very beginning is not the "paradox of history" but the ambiguous nature of the poet's perception of the city. Although the simile of the infant seems to suggest that Ravenna's life is only now beginning, one soon realizes that this was not what Blok intended. Ravenna has no future and no present, only a past; and whatever life still lingers there does so only because it is rooted in that past.

Blok's "Ravenna" is populated by shadows from bygone times—throngs of nameless slaves, monks and queens—all are equal in status now, for all have been sentenced to an equal oblivion. Even inanimate objects cannot defy time's merciless laws: the gilt on the cathedral walls has faded away

---

[12] E. Etkind, "Ten' Danta . . . ," *Voprosy literatury*, XI (1970), 99.

and the sepulchral vaults have lost their sharp contours. The power of time, nevertheless, has its limitations; it can exert its tyranny only over what is material and mortal. Beneath the "cold thresholds" of the burial chambers an ancient life stirs, the eternal spirit of Ravenna symbolized by Galla and Theodoric, over which time has no dominion. Only the conspiracy of nature's elements prevents Galla from singing of the "passions of bygone years" and Theodoric from cherishing dreams of storming his way through another mortal life on earth. After this journey into a romanticized past, Blok returns reluctantly to the desolate present.

The contrast between Ravenna's former life and the present is introduced by the unobtrusive Russian conjunction "*a*"—to be understood here in the sense of "but" rather than "and." For Blok twentieth-century Ravenna is a graveyard. The only sound that he hears—the mute speech of tombstone inscriptions—comes from the past; the only noteworthy present-day sight that he sees is the shadow of "regret for the unreturning sea" which he divines in the gaze of the young women of Ravenna.

In the concluding stanza, Blok turns from the sights and sounds of day to those of night. Dante's majestic figure looming above the horizon sings to him of a "New Life." The conventional "Dante with [his] eagle's profile" [13] is followed by an unusual image of the poet "keeping count of the future centuries" (*vediá vekám griadúshchim schét*). In Blok's bold imagination, Dante becomes the accountant of eternity. The

---

[13] Iurii Tynianov remarks that "Blok is not afraid to use as an image a banal commonplace such as 'the shadow of Dante with its eagle's profile.'" The formalist critic believed that Blok intentionally resorted to stereotyped images whenever he felt that a familiar association would strengthen the emotional impact of his thought (*Problema stikhotvornogo iazyka* [Moscow, 1965], p. 55).

prosaic connotation of the verb "to keep count" suggests that Dante's prophecy of a "New Life" is based not on intuition alone, but on some innate and inexorable logic of the historical process. The sound structure of this line is significant. The repetition of "*v*," "*d*" and "*ch*" and the choppy rhythm of the short, distinctly-accented syllables give the verse a beat which could be likened to the clicking of abacus counters.[14]

The images in the last stanza are linked to those of the first: in the last, a poet whose fame is immortal—in the first, eternity; in the last, the New Life—in the first, the infant. The complex of thoughts and feelings which inspires "Ravenna" is not unlike that which inspired "Venice 3." Both poems dramatize Blok's unceasing concern with life, death, and immortality. They seem to be psychological embankments erected to ward off the specter of personal extinction. But while the Venetian poem is dominated by the poet's preoccupation with his afterlife as an individual, in "Ravenna" the personal merges with the universal, and belief in the immortality of the human spirit emerges as the main theme. Life and death are juxtaposed here, but not in the conventional sense: they are the ebb and flow of time and as such they have a special connotation in Blok's artistic vision. Although "everything on earth comes to an end," as the epigraph to the Italian poems affirms, only what is commonplace and ephemeral disintegrates once it leaves this world; while those persons who through their works or deeds, their fame or infamy leave their mark on their age attain in death a new and everlasting life. This life is symbolized in "Ravenna" by the glance and voice of Galla, the dream of Theodoric and the prophetic song of Dante. Conversely, the Ravenna of

[14] It is not farfetched to assume that Blok may have had this very picture in mind. The abacus was and still is a common sight in Russia in offices and stores.

today which contributes nothing significant to modern history or culture, is only a graveyard doomed to oblivion. According to Blok, time is not simply a force that annihilates and obliterates; it may ultimately purify and revivify by conferring immortality upon deserving individuals or cultures. Traditional Christian ideology does not enter into Blok's poetic vision of the universe. His eternity does not require divine supervision. In Blok's world, it is not the pursuit of virtue which leads one to everlasting life, nor does the concept of the resurrection of the dead in the Final Judgment form part of his thinking about the afterlife.

Although the personal note is not heard so clearly in "Ravenna" as in the other Italian poems, it is unmistakably present.[15] Its impact can be felt suddenly in the last line of the poem where it is expressed by a single inflected word, "mne" (to me). It is at this point, when Blok and Dante meet face to face, so to speak, that the reader becomes aware of the identity of the persona in the poem and recognizes one of the stances often assumed by the poet himself—that of the prophet of a new era. Through its relation to the last quatrain, the tone of the first acquires a new solemnity, and the whole apostrophe to Ravenna becomes a personal pronouncement expressing Blok's faith in the perennial renewal of all life.

The promise of a "New Life" does not mean literally that the "drowsing" town is destined to emerge as a great power at some future time. For Blok, Ravenna is merely a symbol. Struck by the notion that a "dead" town could preserve un-

---

[15] Although I hold in high esteem the late Sir Maurice Bowra's essay on Blok, I obviously cannot agree with his contention that "Ravenna" contains no profound personal note and is in fact only a by-product of travel (C. M. Bowra, *The Heritage of Symbolism* [New York, 1961], p. 153).

touched in its splendid monuments and works of art the memory of an era of wholeness and harmony, Blok makes Ravenna the symbol of his utopia—life eternally renewing and perfecting itself on earth.

Nowhere in Blok's works is there a specific definition of what such a "New Life" meant to him, although he frequently refers to the future of Russia in these terms.[16] "A completely new world is coming," Kniazhnin recalls Blok saying in 1918, "there will be an entirely new life." [17] In his poem "The Twelve," inspired by the Revolution, Blok depicts Christ marching at the head of twelve Red soldiers. Christ's Second Coming is symbolic of the new era which Russia is about to enter ahead of all the other nations. In the essay "The Intelligentsia and the Revolution" (1918), Blok tries unsuccessfully to provide a rational foundation for his premonitions and predictions. Despite all his efforts at "realism" he had remained a dreamer who needed at all costs to believe in the possibility of a better life in Russia, but who had not the slightest notion as to how this goal could be achieved in reality. His only suggestion was that one must "remake everything, fashion everything anew so that our

[16] In the concluding chapter of his monograph on Blok, Kniazhnin describes an artist's conception of an ideal world, evidently with Blok in mind: "To every golden day in eternity, to every era, to every nation there 'corresponds' its own art-expression. And in organic epochs when the life of a given people is a whole and harmonious Pantheon ornamented with filigree, or a Holy Sophia of Novgorod, or a marvel in the Romanesque style, the task of the artist is simple indeed. In fulfilling it he does not feel isolated from the wisdom of his people, which is his wisdom, nor from their art, nor their heroic deeds. Scorched by the fires of Hell like Dante, the artist sees and welcomes the world in its beauty and joy in being, and hails this world as 'Vita Nuova'" (V. N. Kniazhnin, *A. A. Blok* [Petersburg, 1922], p. 135).

[17] Ibid., p. 120.

false, foul, boring, and hideous life will become a just, pure, happy, and beautiful one" (VI, 12).

Needless to say, Blok's "Vita Nuova" had nothing in common with Dante's. It was in Ravenna, where he felt the presence of Dante's spirit most keenly, that he had a momentary vision of a "New Life," but his vision soon faded away in Florence, a city which the Russian poet, like Dante himself some six hundred years earlier, was to denounce as sacrilegious, and which he excoriated as the nadir of modern civilization.

V

Florence: The
Smoldering Iris

I

Pavel Muratov, in his introduction to *Images of Italy*, remarks that:

> If there was one common trait shared by all the Russian men of letters who wrote about Italy in this latest, fourth period in Russian literature, it was their love for Florence . . . Florence did not exist for our literature in Pushkin's, or even in Gogol's time. . . . It became an artistic shrine for our generation first and foremost as Leonardo's native city . . . One finds the first description of Florence in Merezhkovskii. . . . Florence will always remain the birthplace of humanism and of the religious cult of those values created by man's artistic genius.[1]

There is one notable exception to Muratov's statement about the love inspired in Russian writers by Florence—Aleksandr Blok. Blok is unique among Russians in his outspoken repudiation of modern Florence—a city which symbolized for him the decadence of twentieth-century Italy and, ultimately, of Western civilization as a whole.

Blok spent in Florence two of the seven weeks of his stay in Italy. He dedicated seven poems and one essay to this city and his impressions of it are set down in his letters home as well as in his diary and notes. The average visitor to Florence

---

[1] P. Muratov, *Obrazy Italii* (Moscow, 1912), I, 13.

4. Florence. The Venerable Company of the Misericordia leaving the chapel. The Misericordia is a charitable organization founded in the thirteenth century and still operating today.   (Alinari).

would not be likely to recognize his own reactions in Blok's; and someone who has never been there could not possibly visualize the city just from Blok's vague and fragmentary descriptions. And yet the poet captured something very important, although not readily apparent about Florence, and a knowledge of his poems and essay undoubtedly adds a new dimension to our perception of this city.

The unique atmosphere of Florence did not impress Blok. The classic elegance of its palaces and *piazzas*, the genius which animates its statues and monuments, the splendor of its churches and the quaint charm of its ancient streets and bridges left him unmoved. Writing home he declared spitefully: "All that is left are a few palaces, churches, and museums, some distant outlying areas, and Boboli—and as for the rest, I shake off its dust and I hope it shares the fate of Messina" (VIII, 286). The reason for his willful blindness to the beauties of Florence soon becomes apparent: "I curse Florence, not only on account of its heat and mosquitoes, but because it has betrayed itself and surrendered to Europe's rottenness: it has turned into a noisy, highfalutin town and has disfigured almost all its houses and streets" (VIII, 286). But then his anger unexpectedly subsides and the letter ends on a jocular note:

In our *pensione* there is a very clumsy waiter. The owner, taking into consideration his awkwardness, announces the majority of the dishes himself: crème renverseé, fraise écraseé, boeuf braisé, etc. We have had enough to eat, although [*sic*] on one side of us there sits an Englishwoman, an artist, with the back [of her dress] unbuttoned, while on the other side, Mme. von Lebedeff practices her English and French, on the third an Englishman sits grunting loudly, and on the fourth there is an imposing German family. My nose has gotten terribly short; most of it has been eaten away by mosquitoes. . . . One of our windows looks out onto a garden which the owner has planted for his four cats; through the other window we can see the painters who, in their hurry to finish work on an elegant villa in time for the arrival of the King of England, are trying to outdo one another in covering my bed with dust. The Arno has dried up, so that we wash in black coffee instead of water, and the ice cream is delivered only once a month from Stockholm.
[Of course] all this is a bit exaggerated. (VIII, 286–287)

To the reader these facetious exaggerations are revealing, for they show that Blok was not always totally absorbed in dreams or sunk in gloom, and that his stay in Florence had its lighter moments despite the poet's reluctance to recognize them for what they were. At times he may even have been tempted to abandon himself, like a *bona fide* tourist to the enjoyment of his impressions. But his ever active social conscience did not allow him to do so. Committed as he was to warning mankind of the approaching apocalypse, Blok did not lose sight of his mission in a place where he saw only too clearly the inevitability of doom. Ever since he had abandoned the sheltered world of Shakhmatovo for the harsh realities of urban life, he had heaped diatribes upon the modern cosmopolitan city. He deplored it especially when cities with a rich historical past "betrayed" their finest traditions by slavishly adopting modern ways. He felt this all the more strongly in Florence.

Blok's reaction to Florence was foreshadowed some years earlier in "Times out of Joint" (*Bezvremen'e*). Here he expressed his pessimistic views on civilization and drew his own symbolic picture of the modern city—the epitome of all the evils of the present age: "An enormous, clinging spider has made its dwelling in the holy and serene place which had been the symbol of the Golden Age. Pure morals, gentle smiles, peaceful evenings—everything has been woven into the spider's web and time itself has come to a standstill. Joy has grown cold, the flame of the hearth has gone out. . . . The doors are open onto a square where a snowstorm is raging" (V, 70). A deserted square lashed by a blizzard in the heart of Petersburg symbolizes the spiritual emptiness which lies at the core of modern civilization and penetrates into people's souls. In this square streetlamps glimmer dimly, drunken voices are carried along by the wind, strange women with flushed faces and wearing red clothes dash past. Outwardly their appearance is gay, but there is something morbid about their gaiety. In their heavily made-up eyes one sees the reflection of the city—"a drunken corpse dancing the jig." In the distance, Death's laughter echoes like an ominous drumbeat. Blok perceives the city as an extended metaphor of our lives: "Thus, everything that we live by and look upon as giving meaning to our lives whirls past us in a frenzied, hysterical fashion. Set afire from all sides, we spin in the air like the miserable masks caught unawares by Edgar Allen Poe's revengeful jester. But, because we are children of our age, we struggle against this dizzying pace. A certain kind of diabolic vitality helps us to burn without burning out!" (V, 71).

Evidently Blok viewed Poe's phantasmagoric tale "Hop Frog" as an apt allegory of the inanity and insanity of his own age. "Hop Frog" is the tale of an angry court jester, a crippled dwarf who sought to avenge the injustices and cruelties which the king and his courtiers had inflicted on him and on the girl he loved. The opportunity to do so presented itself at a court masquerade ball. After persuading the king and his seven ministers to dress up in the costumes of orangutangs who had escaped from their keepers, in order to give the royal guests a "scare," the jester then cunningly lured the king and his entourage into the center of the ballroom and managed to hook the collar worn by each member of the group to a heavy chain hanging from the ceiling. Suddenly the chain was pulled upwards, and the king and his ministers found themselves dangling in midair. Pretending that he was about to reveal their royal identity so as to reassure the frightened guests, the dwarf approached them with a lighted torch, but instead he suddenly set them ablaze. Triumphantly he watched their bodies burn, nor did he leave the scene until they were reduced to an unrecognizable mass of charred flesh.

Poe's vivid imagery aroused Blok's interest, perhaps because he recognized in it his own pattern of conventional metaphorical association: the masquerade suggested to him the deceptions and pretensions of modern life; the orangutang costumes reminded him of man's brutish impulses; the jester's revenge of fate's inevitable retribution; and, finally the fire itself of the inevitable end of the existing civilization.

Blok's literary impressions of Florence are punctuated with images reminiscent of *"Bezvremen'e"* and of Poe's tale. As soon as the poet realized that ancient Florence was not slumbering like ancient Ravenna, but bustling with activity and tourist traffic, he no longer saw the city as it really was. In its place, the specter of the "spider town" with its lights, its masks, and deserted streets, its spurious gaiety and all its symptoms of incurable disease, loomed up before him. Blok felt stifled by the mild May heat and by the smoke which, in his poetic imagination he saw rising everywhere. If Ravenna had struck him as a "dead" city, Florence was still very much alive, "burning," perhaps, but not "burning out."

The critic Abram Derman, after reading Blok's verses, voiced a contemporary's response to them: "Anyone who has lived in Florence will probably be surprised when he reads Blok's poems dedicated to the city. That [purely] external hustle and bustle, that layer of modernity which are so uncharacteristic of Florence and merely incidental to it and which detract so little from its sacred charm, set Blok against it irreconcilably."[2]

Despite the poet's outright rejection of Florence in the first poem of the Florentine cycle, one cannot regard his reactions as totally negative. Even a superficial reading of this cycle will disclose an ambivalence which prompts him in one poem to denounce Florence as "Judas" and utter the harshest im-

[2] A. Derman, "Ob Aleksandre Bloke," *Russkaia mysl'* VII (1913), 61–62.

precations against it, while in another he addresses the city as a "gentle iris" and envelops it in a poetic aura of blue. Blok's "spiritual maximalism" can be more readily detected in these poems than in others from the Italian cycle. His peculiar incapacity to react impassively whenever reality collided with his dreams stemmed, to cite Zhirmunskii, from his "sense of the infinity of the human soul, and of its inability to be satisfied with anything finite and limited." [3] Blok could not condone the intrusion of the temporal into the temple of the immortal. "Modern life is blasphemy before art," he proclaimed, "modern art is blasphemy before life" (*Notebooks*, 132).

So unrelentingly harsh were Blok's denunciations of Florence that it is hard to believe that he was capable of appreciating any of its aspects. However, in the private recesses of his mind, he was not insensitive to the quiet, time-laden enchantment of the city; one may note, for example, the color associations which prevail in his poetic images. Since Blok uses color symbolism in a fairly consistent manner, one can deduce with relative accuracy his attitude to a particular theme or object by observing the colors with which he identifies or surrounds it.[4]

[3] V. Zhirmunskii, "Poeziia Aleksandra Bloka," *Voprosy teorii literatury*, (The Hague: Mouton, 1962), p. 209.

[4] Cf. Andrei Belyi, "A. A. Blok," *Poeziia slova* (Petersburg, 1922), pp. 27–34. "The colors of . . . nature are not really colors but the reflection of something which lies below the surface and any analysis of how poets see nature is always an analysis of the subconscious, unknown forces which lie below the threshold of the poet's consciousness" (p. 29). In his essay "On the Present State of Russian Symbolism" (V, 425–436), Blok paints a chromatic picture of his spiritual life. His emotional states and the various stages in his poetic development are defined both chronologically and in terms of gradations of color. Thus, the color blue is prominent in the description of his early poetic period. Blue is succeeded by purple, whose various shades symbolize the gradual loss of innocence. See also Chapter II above.

In *"Bezvremen'e,"* for example, the reader's attention is constantly arrested by the symbolic use of "red": "red" is the color of everyday reality, an impudent "red sings on the dresses, cheeks, and lips of women of the streets," "red flags" are waved. A "blood-red sunset" lingers over the town at dusk. Florence, on the other hand, evokes associations with "blue." "The evening heat rises like light-blue smoke," the irises in the Cascine [5] are like "blue flames," at night the mountains hide the city "in their light blue dusk," and, as the poet's thoughts drift into daydreams, he experiences the sensation of being transported into the distance by a "blue wave." So compelling and pervasive is this symbolism of color that Florence is identified as the town where "Beato dreamed his blue dream." [6]

The association of Florence with blue, a color evocative of infinity and eternity, and one with which Blok had often surrounded his Beautiful Lady, is obviously inconsistent with the poet's avowed disgust with and contempt for this city. In order to evaluate his impressions, therefore, one must look below the surface of his words at those of his feelings and attitudes which evoked conflicting reactions throughout his stay and which elude clear-cut definitions.

II

Repelled by modern, cosmopolitan Florence and its hurried pace, Blok sought refuge from the city's sights and sounds in art galleries and museums. In the "Preface" to his "Lightning Flashes of Art," he inveighs bitterly against the soulless, insensitive attitude of the masses who seem to multiply in numbers with "every turn of a screw" and "each new

[5] A park in Florence.
[6] Blok is referring here to Fra Giovanni da Fiesole (1387–1455), better known as "Fra Beato Angelico."

technical achievement." He goes on to justify his escape into the static and still inviolate world of art: "Suffocating from anger, depression, and consternation, we are drawn to past greatness and that is why, for example, we wander through art galleries" (V, 386). But even here one cannot escape completely from the absurd ferment of modern life; the ubiquitous crowds profane the dignity of these sanctuaries with their noisy and boorish behaviour. Irritated and "humiliated," yet not discouraged, Blok admits: "At the cost of numerous wasted hours, of spiritual mortifications experienced in eighteenth-century rooms and many nightmares, I succeeded in capturing something from the Old World" (V, 387).

The entries in Blok's *Notebook* dating from May 15 to May 25, 1909, consist chiefly of notes on some of the paintings he saw in the museums of Florence. Sometimes only the artists' names are mentioned; in other places their names are followed by comments ranging from brief identifications to elaborate descriptions of those details that had most impressed the poet. As has been noted previously, Blok's judgments were not based on conventional criteria. He either failed to mention or paid little heed to many of the outstanding art treasures in the Florentine museums. Nowhere in Blok's writings is there any allusion to Michelangelo's famous sculptures or to Tintoretto's paintings. Such masters as Botticelli, Rubens, and Rembrandt are spoken of in the same breath as artists of considerably lesser stature. Vladimir Alfonsov, who has analyzed in depth the role of art in Blok's life, maintains that the poet's criteria for arriving at judgments were predetermined by earlier readings on the subject. Blok came to Italy with a prepared list, "knowing where to look and at what." [7] He did, however, develop certain definite preferences during

[7] Vladimir Alfonsov, "V mire obrazov vozrozhdeniia," *Slova i kraski* (Moscow–Leningrad, 1966), p. 64.

his stay. "Bellini, Fra Beato and several less prolific painters
—of the Venetian and Umbrian schools—have now become my favorite artists. And, by the way, so have [certain
artists] of the Florentine and Sienese schools" (VIII,
293–294). In his last letter from Italy, Blok summarizes, in
his usual impressionistic manner, his reaction to the art of
three great Italians:

Leonardo and everything which pertains to him (and he left
around him a vast "field" encompassing various degrees of
genius—long before his birth and after his death) disturbs me,
torments me and plunges me into gloom, into my "native chaos."
To the same extent Bellini . . . soothes and pleases me. Before
Raphael I am lost in [reverential] boredom as though before
some "wonderful" view at midday. (VIII, 289)

The paintings of Leonardo moved Blok profoundly. He
recognized in da Vinci's art the interplay of those conflicting
forces which racked his own soul. While Blok's comments do
not afford unusual insights into Leonardo's art, they do offer
a penetrating glimpse into the poet's inner world.

Blok was stirred by the audacity of Leonardo's conceptions. He writes: "Leonardo prepares a black background in
advance, so that his sketches of Demons and Madonnas will
stand out against it" (V, 434). In his *Notebook* he declares
that "Leonardo evidently understood that the air is black"
(*Notebooks*, 137). He credits Da Vinci with the irreverence
of nonconformity—"The resurrection of Christ, gloomy as
it always is in Leonardo's paintings" (*Notebooks*, 188). Leonardo and his disciples are "depraved," and yet "the divine is
accessible to them" (*Notebooks*, 147).

Blok had shown an interest in the art of Leonardo long before he had the opportunity to see the latter's original works.
He was also familiar with the extensive literature in Russian

on Renaissance art and in his critical judgments he was
guided by the Symbolists' tendency to view Leonardo as a
rebel, a seeker after mysterious and forbidden truths. It was
in this light that Merezhkovskii had depicted Da Vinci in his
famous novel. There are striking similarities between Merezhkovskii's and Blok's characterizations of this artist. In the following passages from Merezhkovskii's book, it is not difficult
to recognize one of the sources from which Blok derived his
conception of the Italian master: "Leonardo is a heretic and a
godless man. His mind is clouded by satanic pride. Through
mathematics and black magic he proposes to penetrate the
mysteries of nature." [8] Coming upon a statue of Venus, Leonardo immediately proceeds to measure and examine its every
detail. "Are you seeking divine proportions?" he is asked sar-
castically. "Would you reduce beauty to mathematics?" The
artist replies imperturbably: "In measuring proportions, I
usually divide the human face into degrees, minutes, seconds,
and thirds. Each division is a twelfth part of the previous
one." [9] Commenting on Leonardo's "Last Supper," one of the
characters in the novel exclaims: "Geometry instead of inspiration, mathematics instead of beauty! Everything has been
thought out, calculated and chewed over by the mind *ad nau-
seam;* tried and tested to the point of revulsion; weighed on
the scales, measured with a compass. Behind the reverent fa-
cade is—blasphemy!" [10] Merezhkovskii presents Leonardo
as a man who confronts both heaven and hell with equal bra-
zenness, a rebel whose bold new concepts aroused awe and
apprehension amongst his contemporaries: "Today a creature
out of hell, tomorrow a saint. A two-faced Janus: one face
turned toward Christ, the other toward the Antichrist. Try

[8] Dmitrii Merezhkovskii, *Leonardo da Vinci*, Book 1, Ch. II.
[9] Ibid., Book 1, Ch. VII.
[10] Ibid., Book 2, Ch. VII.

to make out which is his true face and which the false one. Or are they both true?" [11]

The Leonardo of the novel is impassive, free from any disturbing self-awareness, and scrupulously objective. Merezhkovskii makes him offer a pupil the following advice: "If you wish to be an artist, leave behind all your cares and sorrows and concern yourself with art alone. Let your soul be like a mirror which reflects all objects, all movements and colors, while itself remaining unmoved and clear." [12]

Various critics have remarked that Blok was impressed by the Italian master chiefly because he thought he recognized in Leonardo some of his own characteristics. But what they have failed to note was that the Leonardo with whom Blok identified was not the historical figure, but the one which Merezhkovskii had created by blending facts and fiction. Leonardo's contemporaries, as we have seen, condemned Leonardo's impiety; Blok also considered himself guilty of irreverence. In his poem "To my Muse" he speaks of his "fatal pleasure in trampling on cherished sacred things." Duality, an outstanding trait of Merezhkovskii's hero, was also shared by Blok. Since the earlier stages of his poetic career, he had sensed in himself a polarity of forces. "I fear my two-faced soul," he confessed in the poem "I love the lofty cathedrals" (I, 187). The dispassionate attitude to his subject of an artist-scientist as well as a keen perception of its intangible qualities is reflected in Blok's description of himself as "a writer, / A man who calls everything by its name, / Who robs the living

[11] Ibid., Book 6, (The Diary of Giovanni Beltraffio).
[12] Ibid., Book 1, Ch. VIII. This thought was also expressed by Briusov in his poem "*Poetu*": "Vsego bud' kholodnyi svidetel',/Na vse ustremliaia svoi vzor." ("Observe everything with your gaze/But remain a cold, impassive onlooker.")—*Stikhotvoreniia i poemy* (Leningrad, 1961) p. 287.

flower of its scent" (*sochinitel',/ Chelovek, nazyvaiushchii vse po imeni,/ Otnimaiushchii aromat u zhivogo tsvetka*) (II, 288).[13] Like the Leonardo of the novel, Blok strove to express the ineffable through the concrete, but he would hardly have agreed with the former that in the process of creation the artist's soul should remain "unmoved and clear." Blok felt that both equanimity and involvement were needed in order to foster the inner harmony that is an essential condition for fruitful creativity. But harmony required a firm contact with reality, a contact which Blok, unlike Leonardo, had difficulty in maintaining. The following passage from the essay, "Lack of Understanding or Unwillingness to Understand" (1912) shows his deep awareness of and pessimism about his own predicament: "The more deeply one loves art, the more incompatible it becomes with life; and the stronger one loves life, the more bottomless becomes the gulf between his life and art. And when one loves both life and art with equal passion—that is tragic" (V, 481). It is not surprising that in every new experience Blok sought a clue to the solution of this paradox.[14] In Leonardo's art he may have recognized conflicts similar to his own, and their successful resolution. Alfonsov, in his article "Words and Colors" on Blok and Ital-

[13] From the poem, "Kogda vy stoite na moem puti," (When you stand on my path).

[14] Boris Eikhenbaum, in "Sud'ba Bloka," views Blok's life as a melange of insoluble contradictions which doomed the poet from the outset. In the poem *"Dvenadtsat'"* (The Twelve), Eikhenbaum recognized Blok's attempt to resolve these discords through art, "to overcome, once and for all, his tragic awareness of the incompatibility of art, life, and politics; to find among them a new mystic bond." This mystic bond was Christ, in whom all contradictions are resolved. But according to Eikhenbaum, even this final attempt of the poet "to save himself from his tragic fate" proved to be a failure. (*Skvoz' literatury*, [The Hague: Mouton, 1962], pp. 227–228.)

ian art, underscores the point that "Leonardo was for Blok a dramatic *link* between life and art." [15]

After returning home from Italy, Blok jotted down some fresh reflections on art, from which it is apparent that he now considered Leonardo to have been one of those great artists who by masterfully combining form and content had succeeded in "building a cosmos" out of the "spiritual and physical phenomena of life." Blok's thoughts on this topic are succinctly expressed: "Form is art's organizing principle; it is artistic order. Content is the world: spiritual and physical phenomena. (There is no art without form, but art 'without content'—the result of the absence of the spiritual-physical world—is possible). . . . I acknowledge as a *great artist* only he who out of a given chaos (and not *in* it nor *on* it) (the data posited here are: psychology—uncanny; the soul—mad; the air—black) creates a cosmos" (*Notebooks*, 160).[16] It was something still more elemental, however, which attracted Blok to Leonardo, an affinity of spirit which he recognized long before his Italian trip, when he had studied closely and admiringly the famous "Mona Lisa." He discussed his reactions to it in an essay on the poetry of his fellow-Symbolist Viacheslav Ivanov. After quoting the following lines from the latter's poem "Transparency,"

> Transparency! With an ethereal caress
> You rest on the Gioconda's brow . . .
> Transparency! As a mask for the divine

[15] V. Alfonsov, *Slova i kraski*, p. 87.

[16] This complex and obscure notebook entry becomes clearer when read in conjunction with "O sovremennom sostoianii russkogo simvolizma." In this essay Blok delineates three different kinds of chaotic states to which the artist is subject. The "chaos" of "uncanny insight" may be applied to Leonardo, that of "soul madness" to Vrubel', while Belyi's art was associated by Blok with "air blackness" (V, 434).

> You hover in the Gioconda's smile! . . .
> Transparency! Create visions of life
> With a smiling fairy tale . . .

he proceeded to comment:

"Transparency" is a *symbol*, it is what makes "Maya's veil transparent." Behind this veil a *world—entire in itself—*is disclosed. The ubiquitous 'landscape' seen through the narrow window-frames or over the shoulders of the Renaissance "Madonnas" had just such a meaning. The "Madonna" Lisa-Gioconda of Da Vinci, in whose "smile transparency hovers" discloses to us the existence of another world beyond the ethereal veil of her eyes. This world would not be revealed were it not for her ambivalent gaze. Perhaps because of the conventions of pictorial "technique," the "landscape" is visible only on the sides of the figure: it is also supposed to shine *through her smile* and express the diversity of the *entire* world. It is not for nothing that beyond Gioconda there are waters and mountains and ravines—natural obstacles to the strivings of the soul—and the bridge—the artificial surmounting of elemental barriers: the *struggle* between the elements and the spirit unfolds first and foremost in her serpentine, ambivalent smile. (V, 16)

What impressed Blok in the "Mona Lisa" was its mystical quality; the artist's genius for expressing the metaphysical through the physical. For Blok this was the quintessence of art. He, too, strove to imbue his poetry with his perception of a higher reality; for him poetry was what he believed painting had been for Leonardo: a point of departure into the world that lies beyond.

One can draw an analogy between Blok's description of the Mona Lisa and his portrayal of the mysterious stranger in what is perhaps his best known poem, "The Unknown Lady." In both, the presence of abstract dimensions is felt just as intensely as the reality portrayed. In the poem the "natural obstacles to the strivings of the soul" are the limitations imposed by the senses and by reason. The "bridge" which "surmounts" them is "wine." In the painting, as Blok sees it, the mysteries of the landscape are reflected in Gioconda's smile, while in the poem "an enchanted shore and an enchanted distance" beckon to the poet from behind the Unknown Lady's veil.[17] A relationship between the landscape and the Lady's eyes similar to the one Blok had noted in the "Mona Lisa" can be seen in the lines, "Eyes of a fathomless blue / Bloom on a distant shore." (II, 186)

Zhirmunskii, whose article on Blok's poetry ranks as a classic, also described Blok's art primarily in terms of the poet's perception of transcendental realities: "The new and creative way of experiencing life which shaped the development and writing of Blok's poetry and also his life's journey, was his vivid awareness of the presence in the world of the infinite, the divine and the miraculous. This consciousness colors all his poetic experience, giving it a new meaning, a kind of new dimension and an unusual, irrational and mysterious depth." [18]

Blok's own aspirations to transcend through the experience of art the realm of the finite enhanced his appreciation of Renaissance religious painting. He was particularly impressed by the works of those artists who had turned away from mundane concerns to dedicate their lives and talents to the glorification of their simple and passionate Christian faith. Their work revealed to Blok that, unlike him, they had never faltered or strayed from their chosen path. Blok, as we have noted earlier, regarded his estrangement from the idealistic

[17] "I strannoi blizost'iu zakovannyi, / Smotriu za temnuiu vual', / I vizhu bereg ocharovannyi i ocharovannuiu dal' " ("And strangely spellbound by her nearness, / I look beyond her dark veil, / And see an enchanted shore / And an enchanted distance") II, 186.

[18] V. Zhirmunskii, op. cit., pp. 190–191.

philosophy of Vladimir Soloviev and his subsequent involvement with the world of the senses as sinful, a "fall" which had had a detrimental effect on his art. Indeed, he viewed any transition from the religious to the secular, on whatever plane—historical, personal, or artistic—as a "fall." Such attitudes would account for his unusual and largely negative reactions to the art of the late Renaissance in which he discerned an unselfconscious delight in the sensual aspects of life. This would also explain why Leonardo's paintings, in which Blok detected the "profane"—the intrusion of the secular outlook into the contemplation of the divine together with a grasp of psychology verging on the superhuman— "plunged [him] into gloom, into [his own] peculiar 'native chaos' " (VIII, 289).

If in Leonardo's art Blok sensed some of his own conflicts and psychological complexities, the art of Fra Beato Angelico recalled that state of innocence and those feelings of harmony and joyous trust in life which he had experienced as a self-appointed knight of the Beautiful Lady. In Fra Beato's devout interpretation of Biblical subjects, Blok recognized those qualities which he associated with "youth." "In Florence," he states, " [Fra Beato] takes first place . . . because of the freshness and youthfulness of his art" (VIII, 286).[19] In his *Notebook*, he records with poetic pathos:

> Every evening . . .
> Every morning—quieter than water, lower than grass.
> To look at Fra Beato. (*Notebooks*, 135)

[19] Among Russians who visited Italy, Blok was not alone in his appreciation of Fra Angelico. The Acmeist poet Nikolai Gumilev also preferred him to all other Italian painters. Like Blok, he admired his "pure and bright pigments" and was moved by the simple and sincere faith which his paintings reflected. (See Gumilev's poem "Fra Beato Angelico" in *Sobranie sochinenii* [Washington: Victor Kamkin, Inc., 1962], I, 217–218.)

The spiritual elements in Fra Beato's paintings, however, did not absorb his attention to the exclusion of other aspects. He also admired their technical mastery and made detailed notes: "Fra Beato (XIV–XV). The birth of John the Baptist.[20] The mother (in green) with the infant John and five maidens, her friends (red, blue, yellow), came to the temple to the holy elder to register the child's birth. The mother's stomach is still swollen. The old man registers the infants beside the wall on a bright and cheerful plot of grass beneath a blue sky. In the background—in a dimly lit corridor, behind—a bright green ray. (Fra Beato has in a way guessed what I would have wanted). His colors, as usual, are childlike, gay, variegated" (*Notebooks*, 137–138).

Here Blok responded to the poetry of colors with particular delight. In his descriptions of Fra Angelico's paintings, color epithets abound: "The Ascension: those who are gathered round can see only the grey hems of the robes against grey clouds in a yellow numbus" (*Notebooks*, 139), or, more impressionistically, "Deep blue vaults, the green dusk of walls" (*Notebooks*, 140).

In "Colors and Words" (1905) Blok had spoken of the importance of close, precise observation: "The art of painting teaches us how to look and how to see (these are two different things which seldom coincide)" (V, 20). Now, in Italy, he translated theory into practice. Indeed this early essay was very much in his mind as he wandered through the museums of Florence. Fra Angelico's paintings alone were sufficient evidence to confirm to him the validity of his views. "Gentle and bright colors," he had noted in the article, "help the artist

---

[20] Blok refers to this painting as "The Birth of John the Baptist." It is also called "The Baptism of John the Baptist," though of course in the strict sense of the word John the Baptist was not "baptized" as an infant.

preserve his childlike perceptivity," but then he had added, not without a certain sarcasm, "but adult writers 'greedily guard the remnant of feeling in their souls' " (V, 21).[21] So long as he stood in intent concentration before the great religious paintings of the past, Blok was able, however temporarily, to shut out everyday reality and feel a spontaneous, childlike delight in forms and colors. But, outside, walking down the colorless, noisy streets of Florence, under a spring sun whose rays "burned" the pavements, he felt like the "adult writer" who had lost the capacity to respond creatively and joyously to new impressions. Then he was driven back, as though by a spiritual compulsion, away from the lights and sounds of modern Florence to the silent enclosures of her museums and churches, to the citadels of art whose walls shielded him from mendacious semblances of life and offered him instead the timeless truths of life's illusory counterpart, the "creative lie" (*tvorcheskaia lozh'*). In "Florence 6" Blok wrote:

> In the stifling heat and lethargy of Florence
> You become even poorer in feeling:
> Church steps are silent,
> Flowers bloom without joy.
>
> So guard the remnant of your feeling,
> Cherish at least the creative lie,
> For only in art's light barque
> Will you glide away from the boredom of the world.

A visit to the birthplace of Fra Angelico, a small town on a hill near Florence, inspired "Fiesole." Some ten years later,

[21] "*Zhadno beregut v dushe ostatok chuvstva.*" From Lermontov's poem "Duma."

Blok was still able to recite it from memory whenever he reminisced about his trip.[22]

FIESOLE

An ax is striking, and from the *campanili*
The ringing sound of the valley of Florence
Flows toward us: it has arrived and awakened
A golden, ancient dream . . .

Did not the ax strike just that way
Long ago in hilly Fiesole,
When first Beato's gaze
Beheld Florence from the mountain?

Perhaps the most immediate impression conveyed by "Fiesole" is of its simplicity. Its syntax is elementary; its vocabulary quite ordinary; the metric pattern traditional; the verse pattern light. All the elements blend together to produce a meaningful amalgam of sound and sense modulated to the soft and easy music of the lines.

For the critic, simplicity in poetry is often one of the most difficult qualities to analyze, and for the poet it may be one of the most difficult to achieve. "Fiesole" was not the effortless lyrical product of a moment of inspiration; one has only to compare the 1909 draft below with the final version published in 1914 to realize that the poem's simplicity is the result of deliberate and carefully pondered choices:

Zdes' vremia tkalo svoi uzor.

Vo Fiesole stuchal topor,
Kak nynche, zavtra, kak kogda-to. . .

Topor stuchal, i s kampanil
Vse tot zhe zvon. . .

[22] Cf. I. Annenkov, *Dnevnik moikh vstrech* (New York, 1966), I, 88.

Florentsiiu s vysokikh gor
Primetil detskii vzor Beato

"Here time was weaving its pattern.

In Fiesole an ax was striking
As it does now, will do tomorrow, and once did. . .

An ax was striking, and from the campanile
Always the same sound. . .

Beato's childlike gaze beheld Florence
From the high mountains. (III, 535)

When we compare the two versions of "Fiesole," it is evident that in the final one Blok gave precedence to the smooth flow of the verse rhythm, and thereby sacrificed in part the onomatopoeic effect which had been achieved in the first version through alternating monosyllables and dissyllables, deftly chosen to convey the staccato sounds of the ax-blows. The decision to divide the poem into two quatrains was also apparently arrived at later, possibly in order to underscore the time element. In the first quatrain the sounds of the ax and the church bells carry the poet's thoughts back to a distant past. Out of that past emerges the image of Fra Beato, who, for Blok, is still very much a part of the living world and whose death he perceives as only a "golden, ancient sleep." In the second quatrain, the poet conjures up a moment from the life of Fra Beato, when the artist first "beheld Florence from the mountain." Nothing seems to have changed since, only time, that elusive, mysterious element has inexorably moved on. The two stanzas in "Fiesole" have a symmetrical structure: the first two lines in each refer to the sound of the ax —while the last two refer, first indirectly (in the first stanza), then directly (in the second) to Fra Beato. One is re-minded of Blok's definition of form as "organizing principle, artistic order."

The sound structure of "Fiesole" exhibits some interesting characteristics. All the elements of euphony are present: asso-nances, alliterations, repetitions, smooth and easy rhymes and a flowing rhythm:

> "Stuchít topór, i s kampaníl
> K nam florentíinskii zvon dolínnyi
> Plyvét, doplýl i razbudíl
> Son zolotístyi i starínnyi. . .
>
> Ne ták li zhe stuchál topór
> V nagórnom Fiesole kogdá-to,
> Kogdá vpervýe vzor Beáto
> Floréntsiu primétil s gór?"

The poem begins with an onomatopoeic phrase: *"Stuchít topor."* The vowel "i" in a strong position reverberates throughout the quatrain in various combinations, but always in proximity to the letters *"t," "r,"* and *"l."* These are the dominant sounds in the quatrain, re-echoing, as it were, the blows of the striking ax and the ringing of the bells, which flow over the valley, and then fade into the distance. The rhythm of this stanza seems deliberately slow. The caesura after *"doplyl"* and *"razbudil"* and the repetition of sibilant sounds in the last line slow down the tempo of the quatrain which virtually comes to a stop with the ellipsis—the tran-sition between the objective first quatrain and subjective sec-ond.[23]

[23] Blok remarked in "Sud'ba Apollona Grigorieva" that "The spiri-tual make-up of a true poet is revealed in everything, even in his punctuation" (V, 515). Robin Kemball, in the "Introduction" to his book on Blok's prosody, discusses the close attention paid by the poet

In the second stanza the image of the striking ax reappears, but here the stressed "a's" give the iambic verse a different cadence. This stanza differs also from the first in rhyme scheme,[24] tonality, and sound structure. A light conversational tone is realized through the interrogatory intonation and the simple syntax and diction; an accelerated tempo, the product of a greater number of stresses per line, enlivens the quatrain. Here the letters "a," "o," "r," and "t" in various combinations predominate. They are distributed as follows:

ta			t - a		to-or
a-or-o			o	o - a to	
o	a	r	or	ato	
or		r		or [25]	

It is noteworthy that "or" and "ato" are common Italian syllabic clusters, often found as end-rhymes. The frequent occurrence of these sounds as well as the absence of the typically Russian sibilants enhances the quality of lightness here, and gives the stanza the intonation peculiar to Italian verse.

---

to the minutiae of punctuation and spelling. He quotes Blok's statement that "punctuation in verse composition always has an intonational significance, in addition to a strictly grammatical one" (R. Kemball, *Aleksandr Blok. A. Study in Rhythm and Metre* [The Hague: Mouton, 1965], p. 43).

Various statements by Blok's contemporaries and by more recent critics also emphasizes his use of all sorts of concealed literary devices. N. T. Panchenko, for instance, notes that, "Even the graphic image of a poem was [for Blok] a factor in his general poetic panorama" (*Russkaia Literatura*, III [1967], 198).

[24] The rhyme scheme of the first quatrain is "abab," of the second "cddc."

[25] The fact that the unaccented "o" is pronounced in Russian as either "a" or "α" is of little consequence here. I am not including in this table the palatalized "t" which occurs twice in the last line. Obviously my observations about this poem do not claim to follow any formal pattern of linguistic analysis.

Perhaps Blok was influenced to some degree by the sounds of the spoken Italian that he was then hearing all about him. One could possibly concede that a poet who was as sensitive to both imaginary and real sounds as Blok was, would, however subconsciously, capture in his poetry the echoes of those which actually surrounded him.

Much has been written about the relationship between form and content in poetry. But whether one agrees with Belyi that "instrumentation subconsciously expresses the concord of the outer form with the conceptual content of the poetry" [26] or with Eikhenbaum's theory that instrumentation has an independent function quite apart from its content and imagery,[27] one cannot deny that the delight one experiences in reading Blok's poetry stems as much from a conscious awareness of an intangible combination of formal and conceptual elements as from the verbal music of the lines and by the spiritual quality one senses within.[28]

III

Although Blok's one essay dedicated to Florence gives us a more visual account of the city than do his seven poems, it is, like the poems, intensely subjective. It does, however, provide a valuable background and introduction to the poems, which helps us to understand their distinctive symbolism and the abrupt changes of mood and sentiments between one poem and another.

"Masks on the Street" begins with a description of one of the busiest parts of Florence, the heart of the city which swarms with crowds and traffic. Here, if anywhere, the sharp

[26] Andrei Belyi, "A. Blok," *Poeziia slova* (Petersburg, 1922), p. 34.
[27] Cf. Boris Eikhenbaum, "O zvukakh v stikhe." *Skvoz' literaturu* (The Hague: Mouton, 1962), pp. 201–214.
[28] See Chapter VI for additional comments on Blok's poetry.

contrast between the elegant and imposing Renaissance structures and the drab contemporary commercial buildings
would strike one as aesthetically offensive.

Florence.

From the café on the Piazza del Duomo one can see part of the
façade of the Cathedral, part of the Baptistery, and the beginning
of that ugly Calzaioli Street which runs between them. This
street serves as the main artery of the central quarter of the city,
which has been hopelessly defiled by hotels; it connects the Piazza del Duomo with the Piazza della Signoria." (V, 388)

Even in this straightforward descriptive passage, Blok cannot
conceal his contempt for the modern city. Colloquial epithets
such as *"urodlivyi"* (ugly, hideous), *"zagazhennyi"* (defiled,
polluted) which might sound natural coming from some irate
tourist, have a strange ring in an essay by a sensitive poet.

In the daytime here, [one has to put up with] boredom, dust,
and foul smells; but in the evening, when the intense heat subsides, when the street lamps burn dimly and the outlines of the
modern buildings are engulfed by night and so are no longer a
source of irritation, one can lose oneself comfortably in the
crowd which swarms through the square, among the shouts of
cab drivers and vendors and the clanging of trolley cars. (V, 388)

Against the background of nocturnal Florence, Blok describes an unusual procession which he regards as a symbolic
expression of the city's true essence:

A man runs ahead along the street, with a hood pulled down low
over his face: the hood has no slits for the eyes, which means that
he can see nothing except the ground over which he is running.
He holds aloft a torch which flickers in the wind. Behind him
two other men whose faces are also covered drag a long, black
two-wheeled cart. The rubber tires on the wheels turn without
making a sound. All one can hear is the anxious honking of a mo-

tor-car horn. People step aside to let the procession pass. The shape of the cart is that of a human body. A thick black cloth stretched over three hoops on the cart quivers from the bouncing, and the peculiar way in which it quivers indicates that the vehicle is not empty.

The 'Brothers of Mercy'—*Misericordia*—(that is who these people are) quickly roll their cart onto a platform in front of a house on the corner of Calzaioli Street. (V, 389) [29]

Blok goes on to compare the amazing swiftness with which the procession rushes past and disappears behind the portals of a building to the "quick and tidy manner" in which the plague, "Florence's ancient guest," once used to decimate the population. To him the whole procedure seems an absurd mockery of a ritual intended to be solemn and dignified. The sardonic tone of the description emphasizing prosaic and trivial details is designed to warn the reader that appearances are deceiving, and to suggest that some sort of conspiracy may be taking place of which the public is, or pretends to be unaware:

The gates are closed. The house looks like any other, as if nothing had happened. Inside, the corpse is undoubtedly being taken out of the cart and undressed. And probably no one in the new wave of passers-by—officers, ladies, prostitutes and merchants—suspects that the wave which had swept past just before at a dancing gallop had dumped onto this platform a cart with a corpse. (V, 389)

In suggesting that he is privy to certain facts unknown to others, Blok also intimates that for him these facts have a very

[29] Blok was obviously unfamiliar with the activities of the "Misericordia," a charitable organization whose function is to provide emergency aid to the inhabitants of Florence. It was founded in the thirteenth century and is still operating today.

special significance. In the essay, however, he does not give any specific clues as to what that meaning might be. But in the *Notebook* where the procession was first described, one reads:

I am walking out of the café—the rasping of cars . . . On a cart with springs some people are carrying a corpse. In front walks a man with a torch. They carry the corpse across the Piazza del Duomo and shut the gate. Now they must have pulled it out; the dead legs are hanging down, and they are undressing it.

Such is Florence from the other side. This is its truth. No one who went by afterwards knows that behind the gate lies an unclothed corpse. The street lights blink. (*Notebooks*, 135)

The assertion that this "other side" of Florence is "its truth" supplies the key to the essay's intended meaning.

In contrast to his poetry, Blok's prose has not yet been adequately analyzed. Outside of the Soviet Union, it has not aroused much critical interest, while Soviet criticism has focused on those of his essays that deal with social issues and evidence his hostility to conditions in tsarist Russia and to European culture in general. Blok's social attitudes, antibourgeois sentiments, and dialectical modes of perception are familiar to readers of Soviet material. D. Maksimov, for instance, in his article on Blok's prose appearing in the latest eight-volume edition of the poet's works (V, 695–708) repeatedly directs the readers' attention to the "progressive elements of Blok's worldview and art." Although he concedes that Blok's prose is "subjective and lyrical," that is to say, "the reflection of a truth discovered poetically," he presents concurrently the view that Blok's artistic goals did not differ significantly from those of a realist writer. Indeed, judging from the following statement, they hardly seem to differ from those of a news reporter: "The function of a writer, Blok believed, is to be a witness to what goes on in the world. 'An artist, that is, a witness,' notes Blok in 1917 . . . and in another place, he compares the artist to eyes which . . . see, but do not pass judgment on what they see" (V, 705).[30]

But, in fact, Blok's assertions often cannot be taken at face value, for although he may have aimed at realism and objectivity, he seldom, if ever, achieved these goals. "It is the direct responsibility of the artist to show, not to prove," he declares in the first sentence of "On the Present State of Russian Symbolism." But the reader soon discovers that what Blok "shows" is not what one might logically have expected. The content of this essay is a case in point. In contrast to its unequivocal title, it is a good example of Blok's subjective approach to practical questions and of his esoteric way of presenting them. Had the essay been entitled "On the Present and Past State of Aleksandr Blok's Symbolism," it would have given the reader a more realistic impression of its content. Only those of his contemporaries who were thoroughly familiar with the Russian literary scene could by reading between the lines perceive a parallel between the history of Russian symbolism and Blok's own artistic path as described in the essay.

A passage in the Italian essay "The Specter of Rome and Monte Luca," offers a more reliable point of departure than Maksimov's for an analysis of Blok's artistic motivations. After describing a seemingly quite ordinary mountain climb, Blok discloses his reasons for recording this event:

[30] D. Maksimov's various scholarly works on Blok reveal a firsthand knowledge of the poet and of the entire Symbolist period. But like most other Soviet critics, he places his greatest emphasis on the social aspects of Blok's art. Further comments on Soviet criticism are found in Chapter VI.

Why [do I feel the need to share it with others]? It is not because I want to tell others something amusing about myself, or have them hear something about me that I consider poetic, but because of something else—an intangible "third" force that does not belong either to me or to others. It is this force which makes me see things the way I do, interpret all that happens [to me] from a particular perspective, and then describe it as only I know how. This third force is art. And I am not a free man [for I am its servant]. (V, 403)

Blok then proceeds to "show"—and not too clearly at that—the symbolic significance of the episode he has just described in this essay. But he seldom provides his readers with even this much of an interpretation. Usually he leaves many things unsaid and what *is* said is often ambiguous. "He who wishes to understand—will do so," he says with casual unconcern in "On the Present State of Russian Symbolism" (V, 426).

It is apparent from "The Specter of Rome and Monte Luca" that the force motivating Blok the prose writer was the same as that which motivated him as a poet; he did not control his art; it controlled him. Blok's prose bears the stamp both of his concrete observations of reality and of that "third force" which invariably diverted him away from such observations toward the higher meaning beyond this reality. "Until one finds the *real* connection between the temporal and the timeless, one cannot become a writer, who is needed . . . and not merely understood," he wrote in 1912 (VII, 118). As a writer, Blok lacked that dispassionate attitude which enables one to be an "impartial witness to what goes on in the world." His spiritual maximalism and his deep-rooted and passionately held convictions prevented him from attaining the objectivity to which he aspired. His essays are never free from personal value judgments, and his attitudes can always be sensed even when they are not directly stated.

"Masks on the Street" may serve as a typical example of Blok's prose style. Here he begins by assuming the tone and stance of a casual observer of the Florentine scene. One even notices a certain effort to achieve concreteness and accuracy in description. But all this is merely a "mask"; indeed the whole idea of the essay is absurd when seen from a "realistic" viewpoint. For here we find the poet in one of the most unusual and charming cities in Europe, and what does he choose to describe in his one essay on Florence but the strange, even eerie preliminaries to a burial! But to Blok as a Symbolist this was the one meaningful sight, the only thing worth recording.

Through the symbolism of a funeral procession, he caught a glimpse of Florence's other "timeless" reality. Once the center of a great cultural and artistic efflorescence, this city is now a "corpse." Performing the last rites over it are black-hooded men whose field of vision is restricted to the ground they tread on. They are the undertakers of tradition and time-tested values, soulless phantoms without vision who are fully aware of the blasphemy they are perpetrating but who choose, under the influence of their materialistic age and culture, to remain blind to everything but their own narrow interests. The seeming disregard of the passers-by for events transpiring right in front of their eyes is emblematic of the general apathy that is eroding modern society; indeed it is an ominous sign of the forthcoming downfall of civilization.

The description of the preliminaries to the funeral is followed by another equally symbolic passage: "And now a poor frightened bat, the traditional occupant of weather-beaten houses, towers, and walls, flits through the air at the same frenzied gallop. Dazed by the crisscrossing beams of the electric lights, it almost brushes against the heads of the pass-

ers-by" (V, 389). The bat has obviously been chosen to symbolize the cultural and spiritual desolation of Florence. Bat
and man are both blind. Each is hastening to his doom at his
own pace (the undertakers' rapid walk was described as a
"dancing gallop" and the bat's flight as a "frenzied gallop").
This is the last ironic note in Blok's essay which immediately
thereafter culminates in an unexpected ending. Blok admits
that not everything about Florence is as clear to him as the
meaning of the procession: "All this is a hint of the remote
past, a recollection of something that happened long ago, a
kind of enticing illusion. Masks everywhere, and masks always conceal something else. And the blue irises in the
Cascine—whose masks are they? When a chance wind
blows through a motionless belt of intense heat, all of them,
like blue flames, bend in one direction as if they wanted to fly
away" (V, 389–390). It was noted earlier that Blok regarded his own poetic method as a progression from the rational to the irrational.[31] One is also justified in applying this
definition to his prose, for there, too, he proceeds from the
concrete to the suggestive, from the object to the idea. Indeed, "Masks on the Street" begins with an attempt at realistic description and ends with utterances as ethereal as the
irises it describes. It almost seems as though the poet's
imagination, held in check in the essay by the requirements of
a logical plan of thought and by a conscious striving to convey what he saw, was gathering momentum for its flight into
other realms. Moreover in Blok the transition from the external world of reality to the inner world of the imagination can
be construed as a transition from prose to poetry. In the
course of this process, forms lose their terrestrial "masks" and
become "allusions," "reminiscences," "illusions." They turn

[31] See Chapter III.

into poetic images, which take on different shapes in accordance with the poet's inspiration and mood, or the associations he wishes to evoke. The Florence of Blok's poetry assumes many different shapes: it is an old, haggard, woman, a gypsy harlot, an enticing dream, a gentle iris or a smoldering one. The juxtapositions of selected passages of prose and poetry that follow illustrate the transformation that Blok's impressions and observations undergo in the alembic of his poetic sensibility:

The tune of a melody sung in the Piazza della Signoria:

What shall I sing to you
tonight, Signora,
What shall I sing to make
your dreams sweet.
(*Notebooks* 136)

What shall I sing to you tonight,
Signora?
What shall I sing to make your
dreams sweet?　(5) [32]

And a beautiful one passes by.
(*Notebooks* 138)

There—she is passing by, all
in frills and lace,
With a smile on her tanned
face.　(5)

. . . Here the heat can drive you
out of your mind. (VIII, 285)

The red-hot stones
Burn my feverish gaze.　(4)

I curse Florence not only on
account of its heat and mosquitoes, but because it has betrayed itself and surrendered to
Europe's rottenness: it has
turned into a noisy high falu-

In the stifling heat and lethargy
of Florence
You become even poorer in
feeling.　(6)

Die, Florence, you Judas,

[32] The numbers in parentheses in the right-hand column refer to the Florentine poems ("Florence 1" through "Florence 7").

tin town and disfigured almost all its houses and streets. All that is left are a few palaces, churches and museums, some distant outlying areas, and Boboli—and as for the rest, I shake off its dust and hope it shares the fate of Messina. (VIII, 286)

. . . a poor frightened bat . . . flits through the air . . . (V, 389)

All this is a hint of the remote past, a recollection of something that happened long ago, a kind of enticing illusion. (V, 389)

When a chance wind blows through a motionless belt of intense heat, all of them, like blue flames, bend in one direction as if they wanted to fly away. (V, 389–90)

I am sitting in an armchair— O, if I could only sleep forever!

Vanish in the darkness of ages!

. . . . .

You have betrayed yourself
For Europe's universal yellow
    dust!

. . . . .

Begone! Disappear into the
    purifying centuries!   (1)

It sweeps on and on
It hurls itself like a bat
Against the street lamp. . .   (7)

False windows against a black
    sky
And a spotlight on an ancient
    palace.   (5)

And when I surrender myself
    to the heat,
The blue evening heat
Will carry me off into the blue
On a wave of blue.   (3)

Smoky irises in flame
As if about to fly away.   (4)

In light bluish smoke
The stifling heat of the evening
    rises . . .   (7)

O, hopelessness of sorrow
I know you by heart!

I see the tiled roof tops of Florence, and the sky. There they
are—the black spots. I am not
quite sober yet—and that is
why the truth about the black
air stares me in the face. It cannot be hidden. (*Notebooks*,
136)

I stare into the black sky of
  Italy
That mirrors my black soul.
  (4)

As the foregoing passages show, there is a close relationship
here between Blok's poetic and prose expression. Although
his prose is more explicit and less ambiguous, it is the poetry
that reveals more fully his many-sided, emotional, and often
contradictory reactions to Florence. The tensions of the
poet's inner world found release in his poetry: he needed to
personify the city, the object of his love-hate, so that he
could perceive her not as an abstraction but as a tangible reality, with her decaying body and in all her moral degradation. He could then vent his impotent anger upon her with
greater conviction and mourn her loss of innocence as one
mourns the loss of youthful illusions. He needed to assuage
his loneliness and record the sweetness of those rare moments
when his awareness of self met and fused with his awareness
of the infinite.

To give expression to his inner unrest, Blok employed startling and vivid imagery—oxymoron, hyperbole, and repetition; the scent of the roses is "corpse-like," the automobiles
wheeze, Florence's "wrinkles" are "grave-rotted." "It is
sweet to recall hopelessness," he muses in one poem, while in
another he suddenly declares: "I stare into the black sky of
Italy / That mirrors my black soul!" In one poem he blames
his lack of vitality on the hot weather, but in another the
"ancient heat" invites him to "withdraw" into its gentle em-
brace. Sensations influence perceptions: the heat becomes a

hidden presence throughout the cycle. Just as the shimmering haze rising from a cobblestone pavement on a scorching summer day dims and distorts the vision, so a sensation of shimmering heat pervades Blok's imagination and shapes his poetic perception. The extraordinary discomfort which he felt in Florence and blamed on the heat was more than just a physical reaction to the weather. It is no accident that among all the momentous events of Florence's history Blok chose to single out the burning of Savonarola at the stake. In the poet's imagination, the fire that killed the "holy monk" had never stopped burning. The image of fire as depicted in various connotations of heat and smoke appears again and again in the cycle with deliberate frequency. A hypothetical fire sets the irises aflame ("4"), it makes them smolder ("7"), it turns them the color of smoke ("2," "3," "4"); it scorches the stones ("4") and singes the roses ("7"). An inner fire streams through the poet's veins ("5").

"Dust" is another prominent image in this cycle. Whether Blok is referring to actual dust or is using the image symbolically, he is sure to include it in every poem. Dust seems to permeate the air of Blok's Florence; it has settled so heavily over its spiritual soil that it stifles and crushes beneath its thick pall the lily, the ancient emblem of the city and the symbol of its noble heritage.

The poet's sensitivity to the contrast between sounds and silence is evident throughout the cycle. Only in the peaceful seclusion of the Cascine can he shut out the city's din and immerse himself in rapt recollections of a "hopelessly" longed-for, bitter-sweet past ("Florence 2"). The animation and activity of the streets, on the other hand—the wheezing noises of cars, the ringing of bicycle bells, the noisy crowds—deaden his sensibilities and create a barren inner silence. The poet invests his surroundings with this somber silence and, as a result, the "church steps are silent" and "flowers bloom without joy" ("Florence 6").

The physical features of the city are conspicuously absent in this cycle; some of the poems are completely devoid of a sense of place, others have only tenuous ties with the local scene. Yet Florence in its vernal bloom is unmistakably present with its mists, its encircling mountains, its history and art.

Each poem is a self-contained, independent entity. The cycle comprises a variety of themes, moods and meters. These apparent differences, however, enter into homogeneous symbolic design. Words which recur frequently, such as "iris," "heat," "dust," "smoke" have an extended significance and serve as crossbeams in the symbolic substructure of the cycle. The poems are either lyrical monologues or apostrophes in which the poet addresses the city in the familiar second person form. This mode of address gives a peculiarly intimate quality to the cycle. The rhythms of poetry blend with thoughts rising from the poet's subconscious and the cycle unfolds like a poetic diary which reveals even more clearly than the entries in the *Notebook* the mercurial changes of mood and the mixed emotions experienced by the poet. It discloses that duality which is characteristic of Blok's mode of perceptivity, and which Kornei Chukovskii as defined as "pathos eroded by irony, irony overcome by lyricism, derision and praise, all at once." [33] As Chukovskii saw it,

Everything was double in Blok's soul and wayward [indeed], were those [permutations and] combinations of faith and disbelief which brought him so close to the modern spirit. He believed, but did not believe that he believed, and, as he dreamed, he mocked his own dreams. . . . He had a dual personality, and all

[33] Kornei Chukovskii, *Blok kak chelovek i poet* (Petrograd, 1924), p. 89.

his themes and his works have a dual character . . . . This is why those who were looking for a single dominating feeling in his last poems were in error. In these poems there are two antithetical poles of perception and both are present at the same time.[34]

In "Florence 1" the poet's exacerbated feelings erupt in a boisterous harangue against the city. When he submitted this poem, along with several others, for publication, he was aware that it would draw severe criticism. He wrote to Makovskii: "I will begin by standing up for my first "Florence" which probably no one will approve of. But I assure you, this is not blasphemy but feelings that I have 'painfully' experienced. And therefore there is nothing I can do about it except eliminate a few of the most 'frenzied' stanzas" (VIII, 295).[35]

Two voices can be distinguished in "Florence 1." They are thematically unrelated, they come from different worlds, but they join in unison in denouncing Florence. One reasounds like an echo from Florence's distant past. It rages with the indignation and bitterness that marked Savonarola's famous diatribes. And in the same accusing tones in which that remarkable prophetic figure had thundered from his pulpit against the corruption to which Florence had fallen prey, this voice rails against the cult of material values ("You have betrayed yourself for Europe's yellow dust") and the vulgarization of taste which has led to the "disfigurement" of the city ("Your houses are hideous," "the multistoried burden of your weary boredom"). The direct and metaphorical allusions to death and decay, the contemptuous references to worldly pursuits, and the anathemas with which the poem opens and closes are

[34] Ibid., pp. 89–90.
[35] Blok refers here to the two stanzas which he eliminated in the final version.

features which one might associate with the ideology and literary technique of the Middle Ages.

The second voice in the poem has a colloquial and mocking intonation. It is the outcry of a lover who has discovered that his mistress has been unfaithful. The face of the one he had once thought beautiful now appears before him disfigured by loathsome wrinkles.[36] No longer can she deceive him with her wiles. He repudiates her once and for all: "In the hour of love I will forget you / In the hour of death I shall not be with you!"

The personification of Florence as a faithless woman was for Blok something more than an effective poetic device: it was a deeply felt experience, as he himself admitted. The anger and pain he feels whenever facts clash with his expectations are intensified by his feelings of impotence in the face of inalterable reality. Poetry comes to his rescue, but its emotional price is high and its rewards bitter-sweet.[37] The more deeply his emotions become involved, the more urgent becomes his need to purge them through art. Whenever an experience or an attitude appears in Blok's poems in the symbolic guise of a love relationship, one knows that his involvement is at its deepest (see, for instance, the personification of Russia as a "bride" or a "wife"). It is the passions aroused by love which affect the poet's art most intimately and profoundly.

The two voices in "Florence 1"—the preacher's and the

[36] One is tempted to see an association between the word "beautiful" in the sixth line of "Florence 1" and Blok's observation in his *Notebook:* "Liuba looks younger and prettier. She walks around town. They call her *signorina* and say '*Che bella*'" (*Notebooks*, 134). Blok may have associated the theme of unfaithfulness with his wife, but the context of the poem does not warrant further speculation on this score.

[37] Cf. "K muze" (III, pp. 7–8).

lover's—mingle; and as the poem progresses they merge into a single cry of pain and indignation. In keeping with the contrapuntal theme, the poem's diction is a strange blend of formal language and colloquialisms. The frequent exclamations heighten its dramatic quality. The tension mounts as the enumeration of Florence's sins proceeds. The imprecation in the first stanza is repeated in the last, but while in the first Blok still maintains a certain poetic decor by adhering to a formal literary diction, in the last he does not hesitate to damn Florence with the coarse colloquialism "sgin' " (disappear, get lost).

Characteristic of "Florence 1" is its vivid imagery. The poet's sense-impressions affect his perceptions: as he wanders figuratively about the city he sees her disfigured features, he hears the jarring sounds of her traffic and the "nasal drone" of church music, he smells the "corpselike" odor of the roses, and feels the weight of her "multistoried" contemporary buildings as an oppressive burden of loneliness.

Another insight into Blok's Florentine impressions may be gained if we compare his conception of the city with Briusov's image of Italy as revealed in the the latter's poem "Italia." On the picture postcard which Blok sent to Briusov from Florence (significantly, it depicted Savonarola),[38] he wrote: "And here . . . as I recollect your poems, they assume for me a very new and special meaning" (VIII, 285). It is not unlikely that Blok had Briusov's "Italia" in mind when he conceived "Florence 1," and one cannot exclude the possibility that this poem was an indirect rejoinder to Briusov's.[39]

[38] Briusov's *Archives*, Gosudarstvennaia biblioteka imeni Lenina, Fond 386, Karton 77, eg. khr. 37.

[39] Briusov did not admire all of Blok's Italian poems equally. Reviewing *Nochnye chasy*, which included the Italian cycle, he noted: "Least of all do we like . . . [Blok's] somewhat contrived poems about the Italian cities." (*Russkaia mysl'*, I [1912], 32).

In "Italia," a contrast is drawn between the nation's former glory and its present degradation. Inspired, perhaps, by Leopardi's renowned early poem *"All'Italia,"* in which Italy is depicted as a woman once beautiful and powerful but now enslaved and destitute, Briusov envisioned Italy as a fallen empress:

> Italy! Sacred empress!
> Where now is your sceptre and your crown
>   of laurels?
> Your golden chariot is broken,
> The portals of your palace stand open.
> Italy! You unfortunate harlot!
>   To think you have finally come to this!
> Your mantle is in rags: in an old-fashioned dress,
> Your mouth twisted in a stern, proud smile,
> You went out to sell your still beautiful body,
> And admission to your chamber is open for a fee.[40]

The similarity between Blok's and Briusov's personifications of Italy and Florence becomes even more apparent when we examine the two "frenzied" stanzas which Blok eliminated from the final version:

> By admitting a horde of clerks
> Into the Palazzo Vecchio
> You have stripped shamelessly
> Like a woman of the streets!
>
> Like her you place in your mansion
> Your evil-smelling bed,
> Erecting a house of ill-repute—a hotel—
> In front of the magnificent, multicolored Duomo!
>   (III, 533)

[40] V. Briusov, *Izbrannye stikhi* (Moscow–Leningrad, 1933), p. 260.

Unlike Blok, Briusov does not condemn or deride his fallen idol but fascinated by her corruption, he sings the glories of her fading beauty. His "Italia" is as captivating as a "melodious tune familiar to the heart," her body is still "fragrant and fresh," and her touch can heal one's spiritual wounds. In her "momentary tenderness" one feels "the unfeigned and pure caress of Mother Earth." And Briusov, a poet whose eclectic outlook allowed him to worship before many different altars, lightheartedly concedes at the end of his poem that perhaps his image of Italy is far too idealized: "So maybe it's a pretense, what of it/ Maybe it's an illusion, —that's all right with me!" But to Blok such attitudes were foreign: he could not compromise with a reality which did not conform to his ideals, nor could he worship at a desecrated shrine. Florence did not cure his spiritual wounds. Because its real-life image did not fulfill his expectations, he felt that the city had deceived him. This betrayal had apparently reopened the scars of an old wound: it proved once again that the chasm between his ideal world and real life was still as wide as it had been during the years when he had feared that his Lady would "change her countenance." Furthermore, his sensitivity to everything which he felt to be discordant and offensive had not lessened with the years: he reacted violently against everything of the sort with the same pathos of uncompromising prophetic righteousness as before. Such a maximalist attitude could only portend more disillusionment in the future.[41]

In the next two poems of the cycle, Florence is referred to as a "gentle iris." Away from the turmoil and traffic of the city streets, the poet, now oblivious to all that had aroused his indignation, yields to reverie. In the seclusion of Florence's

[41] The fear that his ideals would not withstand a confrontation with reality pursued Blok throughout his life and was a recurring motif in his writings.

ancient park, he recalls a "lingering, hopeless love," but the object of this love is lost somewhere in his memory. So mellow is his mood that even the feeling of hopelessness which he had so often and so poignantly experienced, now turns into a "sweet" remembrance.

In "Florence 3" the setting is presumably the same as in the previous poem, but here Blok moves one step further away from reality. Exhilarated by the fragrant air in the verdant park, he envisions celestial landscapes through a mirage of blue, and hears the call of the infinite. A new serenity pervades his being: all passions are at rest as his thoughts soar above the earth on "airy sails." This one-stanza poem consists of an uninterrupted flow of metaphors related to the image of "sailing." Melodious paeons, separated only by commas, follow one another in a rhythmical wavelike pattern which complements the image of the poet who is carried "into the blue on a wave of blue." [42]

After the blissful atmosphere and the celestial "blue" of "Florence 3," the poet plunges back into the inferno of city life. "The red-hot stones burn [his] feverish gaze," "irises are in flame," and with his "black soul" he can perceive only blackness surrounding him. The familiar feeling of hopelessness, no longer soothed by the glow of pleasant memories, returns to torment him with a gnawing pain.

"Florence 5" differs from the other poems in the cycle in that it depicts an actual experience. Certain details found in

[42] Noteworthy is the sound structure of Florence 3. It exhibits that characteristic of Blok's verse which Chukovskii calls the "inertia of sounds." "Blok's semantics," writes the critic, "were controlled by his phonetics. He found it difficult to hold back [the flow of words], sound waves seemed to overpower him. No sooner did some word resound within him than he felt compelled to repeat it again . . ." (p. 96). Conspicuous is the instrumentation on the letter "n" and the repetition of the diphthong "oi" in the last four lines of "Florence 3."

the *Notebook* enable one to reconstruct the circumstances in which it was written. It is after dusk, and the poet is sitting in a café in the Piazza della Signoria, drinking wine and watching the reflections in the sky of a flashing searchlight mounted on an ancient palace. A dark-complexioned *signora* passes by smiling. The plaintive strains of a love-song echo in the poet's ears, and he borrows its lines in order to ask the passing stranger in the unspoken language of his thoughts what song he can sing so as to "make [her] dreams sweet." At first reading, this little poem strikes one as nothing more than a charming vignette; but after the last note with its melancholy refrain has ended, a thoughtful rereading will disclose new levels of meaning. The "false windows" projected by the flashing searchlight against the night sky suggest the deceptive nature of the diversions which brighten man's life, such as wine or the inviting smile of an attractive *signora*. The happiness which they promise is illusory; they are but a flash of light that momentarily dispels the darkness in which people live. Is the actual realization of a dream more enjoyable than one's anticipation of it, the poet seems to ask. Apparently not, for the mere expectation of happiness may be equally satisfying. Thus the incident on the *piazza* and the poem which it inspired must remain in effect unfinished. The poet is still lonely, but he prefers the illusions of an unfulfilled dream to the disillusion which might accompany its realization.[43]

[43] It is difficult to discern in "Florence 5" the ideological significance which Gromov attributes to it. His involved analysis, complicated by his peculiar style and dubious logic, forces this small lyrical poem (defined by him as a "small drama") into the constricting bonds of a contrived interpretation. An excerpt from his critique speaks for itself: "The searchlight on an ancient palace" is like modernity 'superimposed' on history, or, rather, 'torn out,' 'cut off' from the flow of history. From contemporary life, however, [Blok] has chosen

"Florence 6" bemoans the dulling of poetic sensibility beneath the heat and aridity of city life. As we have already mentioned, the poem concludes with the pessimistic implication that tedium reigns in the modern city and that the "creative lie"—the world of art—is man's only refuge and salvation.

The last poem of the cycle, "Florence 7," combines and recapitulates moods, images, and themes already introduced in other poems; the poet's twofold conception of the city culminates in a new personification of Florence. Now she is a seductive gypsy-harlot who dances each night in the city square and delights the onlookers with her passionate song of "faithful love." Only the poet knows the deep sorrow which gives the lie to her songs and gaiety, and his soul, like hers, grieves in secret.

[those moments] which embody the grand and true poetry of life, a poetry which can also be found today in man and in his relations with his fellow-men. The 'searchlight' of contemporary art has torn [poetry] away from the stream of life, which is also at the same time the stream of history. That is why today's poetry of life simultaneously 'reenacts' the old life which has already passed into history. The last two lines are printed in italics; they are underlined and singled out as though they were spoken by someone else, not a 'traveler' or a 'passer-by'; against the background of an ancient palace an important life-situation—at once ancient and contemporary— is being 'reenacted.' History has entered into the very soul of the character, not in a negative or disparaging way, but as the affirmation of a positive poetical meaning of life, as a potential means of helping to solve present-day problems" (Pavel Gromov, *A. Blok. Ego predshestvenniki i sovremenniki* [Moscow-Leningrad, 1966], p. 359).

VI

Additional Perspectives
on the Italian Poems

The soul of a writer who listens to the voice of a single string
or worships the *one* God expresses itself in forms that are simple, sometimes *to the point of bareness*. (From the essay "Henrik Ibsen" [V, 315])

When the Italian poems first appeared, they were ac-
claimed as evidence of a new "classical" direction in Blok's
art, a clear departure from the romantic moods which had
characterized his most recent book of poetry, *Night Hours*.
A contemporary writer, Vladimir Piast, wrote that the Italian
poems "arrived with the brass sound of Latin trumpets," and
marveled at their "unprecedented classical perfection." [1]
More recently, the Soviet critic, Lidia Ginzburg, wrote with
reference to that period:

The "classicism" of the new period of Blok's art became a topic
for discussion immediately after the publication of *Night Hours;*
chiefly because of the "Italian Poems." It was, of course, the thematic content of this cycle which prompted such an interpretation. The "Italian Poems" are classical in their measured intonation and in the precision of their rhythmic and syntactical
divisions. After the urban ambience of "Unexpected Joy" and the
stormy metaphors of "Snow Mask," their symbolism may have
appeared transparent and austere.[2]

Konstantin Mochulskii, the author of a critical biography
of Blok, also chooses a musical metaphor to describe the Ital-

[1] V. Piast, *Vospominaniia o Bloke* (Petersburg, 1923), p. 17.
[2] Lidia Ginzburg. *O lirike* (Moscow, 1964), p. 311.

ian poems: "In his 'Italian Poems' Blok creates what for him is a new pictorial and plastic style: for the first time the brass trumpets of the 'solemn Latin' resound alongside the 'harps and violins' in his orchestra." [3] Orlov notes that these poems are "notable for their plasticity and stylistic lucidity, as well as for their austere and monumental structure." [4] Alfonsov's critique shows an awareness of these same elements:

Blok's creative receptivity to the traditions of classical poetry and art significantly broadened the ideological-psychological range of his mature poetry, and to a great extent determined the characteristics of his lyric style. . . . His familiarity with Italian art helped him to feel and to convey more cogently Italy's national atmosphere and the unique features of her history and culture. In this regard, one should note, the 'Renaissance' austerity and monumentality which characterize many of the Italian poems." [5]

Critics of all persuasions stress, whether directly or by implication, the classical quality of the Italian poems: such an emphasis can be misleading, however, for "classicism" suggests a kind of sensibility that is just as alien to these poems as it is to the rest of Blok's writings. In fact, their highly impressionistic treatment of themes, their lyricism modulated by tones of mysticism or irony, and their intimate, expressive style make them essentially romantic in nature. But it is a romanticism different from that of Blok's earlier works. It is more restrained, less intense—more Pushkinian, one might say. For all that, the differences in style between the Italian poems and Blok's earlier works are not sufficiently significant and fundamental to allow one to speak of the Italian cycle as a new stage in the evolution of his poetic language. The "brass

[3] K. Mochulskii, *Aleksandr Blok* (Paris, 1948), p. 261.

[4] Vladimir Orlov, *A. Blok* (Moscow, 1956), p. 151.

[5] V. Alfonsov, "Blok i zhivopis' ital'ianskogo vozrozhdeniia," *Russkaia Literatura* III (1959), pp. 176–177.

sounds of Latin trumpets" heard by Piast and Mochulskii leave no echo whatever in the reader's mind. Most puzzling and inexplicable of all are the "Renaissance austerity and monumentality" attributed to the poems by both Orlov and Alfonsov. Rather, the uniqueness of the Italian cycle consists primarily in the manner in which the poet treats the theme of travel. Since Blok had not dedicated any of his works to foreign lands before 1909 (nor did he do so subsequently), this cycle was for him a new artistic experience reflecting a new range of perceptions. Moreover, never before had he been so deeply under the influence of the plastic arts as he was now in Italy; it is not surprising, therefore, that the style and content of the Italian poems stand somewhat apart from those of his earlier works.

The traditional verse form which Blok selected—the one element in these poems that is likely to strike the reader as classical—may indicate an artistic sensitivity to his environment, as Alfonsov suggests. Again, however, one cannot describe these poems as more "classical" than Blok's earlier works, if only for the reason, often overlooked, that the poet consistently manifested a preference for conventional forms.[6]

---

[6] Robin Kemball, in his scholarly study of Blok's prosody, calls attention to the fact that "of the 766 poems under consideration . . . no less than 364, or nearly half, are written in iambics of one kind or another; of these, in turn, as many as 250 belong to the 'classical' four-foot group alone" (R. Kemball, *Aleksandr Blok. A Study in Rhythm and Metre* [The Hague: Mouton, 1965], p. 341). Further on, again discussing Blok's extensive use of the iambic tetrameter and its predominance in his poetry over other meters, Kemball remarks: "These figures [quoted percentages] effectively belie the view sometimes heard that Blok moved all his life away from the classical form of his earlier poems toward freer and less orthodox patterns. Rather the contrary, in fact. Such new metrical forms as he did introduce largely concern the *dol'niki*, the large majority of which are contained in Book I, some in Book II, and only a handful in Book III" (ibid., p. 354).

In the Italian poems, binary meters are overwhelmingly predominant. Here, as always, Blok tended to choose iambs in preference to other measures.[7] Fourteen of the poems in this cycle are in that meter; four are trochaic, four dactylic, and one anapestic. Only one poem is in free verse.

Blok's iambic and trochaic meters differ in their rhythmical pattern from more orthodox Russian binary meters because they omit or weaken the metrical stress more frequently. Statistics quoted by Boris Unbegaun concerning the distribution of stresses in iambic tetrameter in Russian poetry indicate that the most common iambic verse form is that in which the third stress is omitted.[8] Vladimir Nabokov confirms these statistics in his study of *Eugene Onegin* by pointing out that the predominant rhythmic pattern in that work is his so-called "scud III," a four-foot iambic line with an unaccented third foot.[9]

Blok's iambic tetrameter in the Italian cycle shows a definite tendency toward an even greater weakening of the stress

[7] Blok's preference for iambics is related to his "musical" perception of life. He sensed a connection between the rhythm of the iamb and the tempo of his own epoch. In his "Introduction" to the poem "Retribution," discussing the events of the year 1911, he writes: "All these facts, seemingly so unrelated, have for me a single musical meaning. I am accustomed to juxtapose facts from all spheres of life that are accessible to my vision at a given time, and I am convinced that, once combined, they invariably create a single musical impulse.

"I think that the simplest expression of the rhythm of that time when the world, preparing itself for prodigious events, was so vigorously and systematically developing its physical, political, and military muscles was the *iamb*. This is probably why I, who had for so long been driven round the world by the whips of the iamb, was induced to abandon myself to its flexible wave for prolonged periods of time" (III, 297).

[8] B. O. Unbegaun, *Russian Versification* (Oxford, 1959), p. 20.

[9] Vladimir Nabokov, *Notes on Prosody and Abram Gannibal* (Princeton University Press, 1963), p. 70.

pattern—normally two stresses per line. The following quatrain from "Ravenna" may serve as an illustration:

Vse chto minútno, vsę chto brénno,
Pokhoronila ty v vekákh,
Ty, kak mladénets, spish, Ravénna,
U sonnoi véchnosti v rukákh.

Like the iambic, Blok's trochaic meter displays a dual stress pattern. The reduction in the number of accented syllables, the evocative use of assonances and alliterations, and the felicitous simplicity of the rhymes, blend to create a fluid, melodious intonation—an outstanding characteristic of Blok's poems. Anyone who reads them cannot fail to note their extraordinary euphony. One might say of Blok that "inebriate of sound was he" (to paraphrase Emily Dickinson). In his analysis of the poet's technique, Chukovskii speaks of the hypnotic effect which the recital of Blok's verses had upon his audiences and describes his poetry as one might a musical performance:

Every poem of his was full of those recurring echoes, with inner sounds, inner rhymes and half-rhymes signalling to one another. Every sound set off in his mind a multitude of kindred echoes, now dying away, now rising again, which seemed begging to remain in the poem as long as possible. This intoxication with sounds was the main precondition of his art. His thinking was purely phonic; he could not create in any other way.[10]

Chukovskii analyzes the composition of Blok's verse tone by tone and sound by sound, searching for those elements that might reveal to him the secret of its musicality, and trying to discover sound-patterns which could be made to fit a struc-

[10] Kornei Chukovskii, *Aleksandr Blok kak chelovek i poet* (Petrograd, 1924), pp. 94–95.

tural scheme. Although Blok had no musical talent as such, he had for language a musician's gift: a natural sense of rhythm and balance and an uncanny feeling for melodious combinations of sounds. Undoubtedly, this is one reason why his verses have inspired well-known composers like Slonimskii and Shostakovich to adopt their verbal melodies to music. According to Chukovskii, Blok even created in the same way as a musician does, responding instinctively to his auditory sense:

. . . A passive receptivity to sounds: the poet lacks the strength to control these musical waves which waft him along like a blade of grass. The secret of Blok's charm lies in his passive non-resistance to sounds, in his feminine submissiveness to them. He was more controlled by sounds than he was in control of them; he was not the high priest of his art, but its victim. . . . In this uninterrupted, over-sweet melody there was something that weakened one's muscles.[11]

Blok himself was keenly aware of the crucial role which sound played in his art:

First of all I hear sounds reverberating. I hear the intonation before the meaning. Someone within me speaks passionately and convincingly, as though in a dream. The words come later. And I have only to make sure that they fit in with this intonation and in no way clash with it. And then—there it is—the moment of truth. Each poem is a sonorous point which extends outward in concentric circles. No, it is not even a point, but rather an astronomical nebula. From it, worlds are born.[12]

The poem "Fiesole" has already been discussed with reference to its sound structure. "Siena" is another example of how Blok's sensitivity to sounds affected his art:

[11] Ibid., p. 99.
[12] Quoted in Mochulskii, *Aleksandr Blok* (Paris, 1948), p. 418.

V lone plóshchadi pológoi
Probiváetsia travá.
Mesiats óstryi, krutorógii,
Bashni—svéchi bozhestvá.

O, lukávaia Siéna,
Vsiá—kolchán uprugikh strél!
Verolómstvo i izména—
Tvoi tainstvennyi udél!

Ot sosédnikh loz i páshen
Ogradiás' so vsekh storón,
Ostriá tserkvéi i báshen
Ty vonzíla v nebosklón!

I tomlén'em dukh vliublénnyi
Ispolniáiut obrazá,
Gde kovárnye madónny
Shchuriat dlínnye glazá:

Pust' grozít maladentsu búria,
Pust' grozít mladentsu vrág,
Mat' gliaditsia v mutnyi mrák,
Ochi vlázhnye soshchúria! . . .

On a gently sloping square
Grass breaks through.
The moon is sharp-pointed, like a horn,
The towers are candles to the Divine.

O cunning Siena, the whole of you—
Is a quiver of supple arrows!
Perfidy and treason—
Are your secret destiny!

Walled off on all sides
From neighboring fields and vineyards,
You have pierced the vault of the heavens
With the pointed spires of your churches
    and towers!

The enamoured spirit languishes
Before the holy images,
In which treacherous Madonnas
Narrow their elongated eyes.

What if the infant is threatened by a storm,
What if the infant is threatened by a foe,
The mother gazes into the murky gloom,
Her moist eyes asquint . . .

    The sound pattern of this poem, even when divorced from
the meaning, supports the images evoked by its words. The
slow, prolonged sounds of the first line (resulting from the
combinations of the soft "l" and "p" with the long "o") convey the serene atmosphere of the picturesque Sienese *piazza*
whose appearance has altered little since the Middle Ages.
These long, soft sounds contrast with the harsh consonant
clusters in the next lines—"*pr*," "*tr*," "*str*," and "*kr-t*,"
which, with their distinctive sharpness, fit in well with the
images of the grass which "breaks through" and of the
"sharp-pointed moon" in the shape of a "horn." The vibrant
Russian "*r*" is again repeated three times when "cunning
Siena" is compared to a "quiver of supple arrows." It recurs
in the third stanza with the mention of "spires of . . .
churches and towers" ("*str*," "*ts-rk*"). In the last stanza the
dangers threatening the infant are also emphasized by the "*r*"
sound appearing in four different combinations ("*gr*," "*vr*,"
"*mr*," "*shch-r*"). The song-like cadence of "Siena" could eas-

ily suggest to a musician a suitable score. The patterns of *piano, crescendo,* and *forte* seem to be inherent in its sound structure. The elements of repetitions, contrast, and balance contribute to the musical quality of the poem.

Each of the Italian poems presents one aspect of Blok's journey. (They provide the most sensitive record of his impressions and reflections.) The moods and states of mind which they reveal are often paradoxical and thus typically Blokian: one finds in them humor and solemnity, detachment and involvement, spirituality and irreverence, mysticism and sensuality, hope and despair. They sound the poet's characteristic notes of gloom, but also they radiate serenity and even contentment; they reveal a preoccupation with the eternal as well as a spontaneous delight in the ephemeral, a rejection of the present and yet also a trust in the future. Taken as a whole, they reflect a quiet enjoyment of his experience which Blok was either reluctant to admit or perhaps was not even aware of consciously. In the poem below, the dark and heavy clouds which overshadow most of Blok's prose about Italy part to admit a ray of Mediterranean sun:

> After I met you on the mountain pass
>   My vision became clear, and I understood
> The smoky distances of Tuscany
>   And the outlines of the mountains.
> ("Madonna da Settignano")

Also in "Here's a young girl, barely in bloom . . .":

> Here's a young girl, barely in bloom,
> Who still does not lower her eyes, nor blush,
> As I approach she gazes at me
> With her dark, impenetrable glance.
> And if I had my way,

I'd spend my whole life in Settignano,
Beside the wind-weathered stone of Septimus Severus.
I'd look at the rocks, flooded by the sun,
At the beautiful sunburnt neck and back
Of an unbeautiful woman beneath the trembling
    poplars.

Or, in "Art is a burden on our shoulders":

Art is a burden on our shoulders,
And yet how we poets cherish
Life in all its fleeting trifles!
How sweet it is to surrender to indolence,
To feel the blood rush
Singing through one's veins,
To catch behind a fleeting cloud,
The leaping, kindling flame of love,
And to dream as if life itself
Were rising up in all its champagne sparkle,
In the gently purring crackle of a cinema
With its swiftly flashing images!
And a year later—in a foreign land:
Weariness, a strange city, a crowd—
And once again on the screen
The features of that same delightful French girl! . . .

And, finally, in "Siena Cathedral," Blok tells us in light iambics, in a rhythm almost too facile for a serious theme, that:

When you are in fear of dying soon,
When your days are overcast,
Turn your weary glance
To the tombstones of Siena Cathedral.

.   .   .   .

Be still, my soul. Do not torment me, or arouse me.
Do not constrain me, do not summon me:

Some day it will come—the stark,
Crystal-clear hour of love.

Significantly, "singing" resounds throughout the entire cycle: the bronze letters of Latin inscriptions sing, the wind sings "about a future life," Dante's shadow "sings of a New Life." A Venetian lover serenades his lady; one can hear a "loud chorus" coming from an open window. "What shall I sing to you, tonight, Signora?" Blok asks the passing stranger. Faithless Florence sings a provocative "*canzone* of devoted love," the bells of Umbria sing, the angel Gabriel "sings and whispers," a rivulet sings as it runs through the steep ravines, and even blood sings as it rushes through the poet's veins.

In the Italian poems Blok at last achieved that naturalness and lucidity for which he had so long been striving, and which had a more than purely artistic significance for him: it was in fact his defense against the outer chaos of existence and against his own inner turmoil. Anyone who expects to find in these poems Blok's usual all-pervading vagueness will be surprised by the straightforward diction and the concrete of imagery. But through the disciplined simplicity of their lines a poet emerges who, torn by the enigmas of his own ambivalence, seeks ultimate answers beyond the bounds of science and reality while sensing at the same time that life's true meaning does not lie in metaphysical formulations or obscure syllogisms but in confiding oneself with childlike trust to the appreciation of beauty, to the joy of being, to a grateful acceptance of whatever life offers. As the "adult" in Blok looked into the mirror of the Italian past and the present, he saw a reflection of the "child of goodness and light." He liked this vision of himself and wanted to capture it in song.

Many years later, another great poet, Boris Pasternak, who shared Blok's artistic aspirations and whom Anna Akhmatova

Additional Perspectives   153

characterized as "endowed with a kind of eternal childhood" [13] expressed a thought that describes his own search
for meanings as much as it does Blok's:

> In the craft of great poets
> There are signs of such naturalness,
> That to discover them
> Is to end in complete silence.
>
> One with all that exists, he who trusts
> In the future and lives with it day-by-day,
> Cannot help falling, as if into heresy,
> Into an unheard-of simplicity. [14]

Soviet writers have been quoted frequently in the course of
this book and their criticism has been compared and contrasted with the opinions of this author. Although these critics unquestionably have a profound knowledge of and insight
into their subject, and the biographical references they provide are invaluable to anyone lacking direct access to the author's archives, their generally uniform and disturbingly
one-dimensional critiques are of limited interest to Western
readers. Perhaps this in part accounts for the fact that no critical Soviet works on Blok have been translated into English.
Since mystical and romantic elements predominate in the
poet's art, any analysis which concentrates too heavily on its
sociological and historical aspects can be more distracting
than illuminating. In the pages which follow I shall discuss
my personal points of agreement or disagreement with some
of the most widely held views by Soviet critics about Blok's
Italian journey and the poetry it inspired.

According to Soviet critics, especially those with a nar-
rowly Marxist orientation, Blok, although no philosopher by

[13] Anna Akhmatova, *Sochineniia*, I (Washington, 1955), p. 225.
[14] Boris Pasternak, *Stikhotvoreniia i poemy* (Moscow, 1965), p. 351.

inclination or training, instinctively evolved his own dialectics of history: he recognized, they say, the dynamic interdependence of all phenomena; he understood that contrasting historical cycles must follow one another, bringing with them radical social changes; he realized that the present civilization had now reached a fatal crossroads and was facing inevitable doom. This pronounced emphasis on Blok's "progressive" ideas, which can be tailored to fit the philosophy of historical materialism, is very important in order to project an image of the poet as a prophet of the Revolution and precursor of the Soviet man. This, it would seem, is the Rome to which so many of the roads of Soviet criticism on Blok lead. The poet's mystical conception of Italy's historical past, his personal pessimism, and the brooding introspection which pervades so much of his writing and which reveals that he was far more concerned with the transcendental world than with social or historical matters are usually glossed over or minimized. His craving for a uniquely personal ideal world which no ideology could ever wholly satisfy is not regarded as relevant to the Italian poems. A typical Soviet critical approach may be seen in the following passage by Orlov:

As is always the case with Blok, the historical theme in the Italian poems is not, on the whole, retrospective in character. It is not static, nor treated in isolation, but closely related to the theme of the present, to an acute sense of the given historical moment. And here, too, the subject of [Blok's] poetry is the lyrical hero who experiences the contradictions of contemporary life— this time, through his sad recollections of the glorious and heroic Italian past.[15]

An "acute sense of the *given* historical moment" may be an asset to a Soviet poet today, but it was hardly Blok's most

15 V. Orlov, *A. Blok* (Moscow, 1956), p. 152.

distinctive characteristic. Alfonsov, a leading Soviet art critic, also chooses to emphasize Blok's historical consciousness; his impressionistic synopsis of the Florentine cycle indicates, however, that there may be other dimensions to his understanding of Blok's poetry:

However deeply Blok may have mourned the passing of Italy's glory, however depressing he may have found its "commercial hustle," he was nevertheless able to convey throughout his poems the bitter, but sober notion that history cannot repeat itself, that epochs succeed one another in regular sequence.

In some of the poems, the past and the present are contrasted very sharply. In the Florentine cycle Blok even uses a form which was unusual for him; namely journalistic pamphleteering marked by an emphatic harshness of intonation: "Your features are disfigured with grave-rotted wrinkles." The echoes of a great past, everywhere audible, give rise to another feeling—they invite the reader to immerse himself in the "enticing illusion" of a dream about an "eternal," beautiful ideal; they summon him to renounce the prose of contemporary reality and to lyricize this detachment, even though it bears the mark of despair. These caustic strokes in pamphlet style are followed by light, impressionistic tones: "aery sails," "fragrant stream," "to drown in the skies," to be carried away into the "blue." The enticing illusion of a dream, of a resurrected past, must give way, however, to the shameful present: Florence, after all, remains for Blok a "Judas," "faithless," "in a wreath of scorched roses." Whole epochs recede into the past, just as the life of each individual passes away and is extinguished.[16]

Among recent Soviet criticism perhaps the most independent and original discussion of the Italian poems is that of Anatolii Gorelov in his book *The Storm over the Nightingale Garden*. Although Blok's "perception of history as per-

---

[16] V. Alfonsov, *Slova i kraski* (Moscow–Leningrad, 1966), pp. 65–66.

sonal biography" and his deep sense of social and moral responsibility are discussed here also, there is at least an equal emphasis given to the more intimate aspects of the poet's nature, such as his earthier side, his "craving for what is alive (*tiaga k zhiznennomy*)" as opposed to what is abstract and "dead." [17]

Gromov, the most dogmatic of Soviet critics and the one who has written most extensively on the Italian journey, holds the Italian poems in especially high regard. He has been able to discover conclusive evidence in them to support his unique interpretation of Blok's poetry. In his recent book, *Blok. His Precursors and Contemporaries,* he traces the poet's historical consciousness back to the cycle "On the Field of Kulikovo" (1908) and draws a direct connection between this cycle and the Italian poems. Having established to his own satisfaction that an ideological relationship exists between these two cycles, he proceeds to develop his theory that an acute perception of history lay at the roots of Blok's inspiration. The reader might even conclude from Gromov's writings that Blok gave to his own views of history the kind of spiritual allegiance which would normally be accorded only to the most solemn religious convictions, for Gromov clearly implies that the poet derived from them faith in man, inspiration for his life and art, and a trust in the future, both on this earth and in the world beyond.

The intimate, subjective aspects of the Italian poems do not present any special obscurities or contradictions for Gromov. His assumption that Blok was chiefly concerned with the interrelationships of history and culture apparently absolves him in his own estimation from paying much attention to unorthodox matters such as Blok's mystical tendencies or his

[17] A. Gorelov, *Groza nad solov'inym sadom* (Moscow–Leningrad, 1970), pp. 279–298.

subjectivity. He tries to prove his points by manipulating words as only an experienced Marxist dialectician can, making certain, however, that they are sufficiently involved and obscure to discourage the average reader from investigating them too carefully. The following excerpt is a "clear" example of his style and argumentation:

In his poems, in a much more direct and spontaneous way [than in his prose], Blok correlates culture with life, with the contemporary relations between people; it is more *clearly* evident now, that the cornerstone [of his poetry] was life. Furthermore, in his poems he does not confine himself only to the somewhat simple and narrow concept of "unpoetical country," but seeks out through his poetic imagination those areas and "corners of life" in which the potentialities for an emotionally intense human existence can still be found. Because of this attitude, the relationship between culture and history becomes more direct and straightforward, while on the other hand, his approach to modern life turns out to be more complex and contradictory. The problem of how history is related to the present-day world emerges *more clearly* here, and culture seems more like an intermediary, a sort of ramified and complex "metaphorical" means of stating the major problems of contemporary life. And it becomes *absolutely clear* that there is something heroic in the very fact that Blok turns to the great culture that has "burned" him in order to preserve and enrich his historical perspective as part of his artistic consciousness. He does not "escape" from the present into culture; rather he tests the present in the light of history, and takes it to task poetically on a serious scale on behalf of high culture, and indeed also on behalf of history.[18]

[18] P. Gromov, *Blok. Ego predshestvenniki i sovremenniki* (Moscow-Leningrad, 1966), pp. 355–356. One of the peculiar characteristics of Gromov's involved and repetitious style is his emphasis on how "clear" everything will appear if one follows the logic of his critique. The italics in this quotation are mine.

One of the underlying postulates of Gromov's interpretation is that the narrator in the poems is a detached and casual observer of the Italian scene. Throughout his essay, Gromov refers to him as a "passer-by," a "traveler" whose personality is that of a "character in a prose work." [19] Significantly, the form of the Italian poems is compared to that of a "travel diary." The critic is intimating of course, that Blok is essentially a realist, an artist who portrays reality with considerable emotional detachment, perceives relations logically, and draws unbiased conclusions. There is still another implication in Gromov's choice of words and images. Casual thoughts of a kind which, by definition, are neither deep-rooted nor lasting can be conveniently attributed to a "traveler," a "passerby." This device gives Gromov a plausible excuse for dismissing as incidental those facets of Blok's creativity which do not fit in with his interpretation, such as, for example, the poet's mysticism.

It requires no extraordinary degree of sensitivity on the reader's part to realize that such an interpretation of the Italian poems exhibits ideological bias. Obviously, their creator was not a philosopher, or a historian, or a social critic, or an objective observer, but rather a man for whom visions were often more real than reality itself; an introspective poet seeking to capture in his art what lies beneath the surface, a stranger in a foreign land who reacted to his surroundings with sensitivity and imagination. In 1921, in a moving speech eulogizing Blok's memory, Eikhenbaum described him as his contemporaries saw him—an "actor" who played out his own role on the stage of life:

---

[19] By "character in a prose work," Gromov possibly intends to imply that Blok is an individual whose perceptions are those of the "ordinary man." P. Gromov, op. cit., p. 358.

The knight of the Beautiful Lady—a Hamlet reflecting on non-existence and living a wild and dissipated life; a fixture at tavern bars who had abandoned himself to the charms of gypsy girls; the gloomy prophet of chaos and death—all this was for us the consistent and logical development of one tragedy, of which Blok himself was the hero. Blok's poetry became for us the emotional monologue of a tragic actor, and Blok himself was this actor made up to look like himself.[20]

In the final analysis it is the tragic actor in Blok, not the "character in a prose work," or the oracle of history, who speaks through the poems of the Italian cycle.

[20] Boris Eikhenbaum, "Sud'ba Bloka," *Skvoz' literaturu* (The Hague: Mouton, 1962), p. 218.

VII

Conclusion

Nostalgia always presupposes a desire for union, a kind of un-fulfilled sense of separation, either a breaking off [of ties] or a persistent drive for reunion; one of the greatest paradoxes confronting those who seek may be the fact that there is no greater closeness than the greatest separation and no greater sadness than the greatest happiness. (VII, 28)

Blok and his wife left Italy on June 21, 1909. The poet's last letter from Milan, the thirteenth city they had visited, reveals that from his standpoint,

the trip did not turn out to be relaxing at all. Just the opposite. We are both dead tired and our nerves are strained almost to the breaking point. . . . I cannot respond to anything now except art, the sky, and sometimes the sea. People disgust me, all of life is horrible. European life is just as loathsome as Russian life; in general, the life people are living all over the world is, in my opinion, a sort of monstrously dirty puddle. (VIII, 288)

Further on in this letter, Blok blames his fatigue on the "haste and over-eagerness" with which he had been traveling. Although this may in part explain his irritability, there were other and more fundamental reasons for his negative attitude when he wrote: "In Italy one cannot live. It is the most un-lyrical country—there is no life, there is only art and antiquity. And that is why, when one comes out of a church or a museum, one has the feeling of being in the midst of some absurd and barbarous world" (*Letters*, 268).

Blok's impressions of a "barbarous world" must seem puzzling to anyone who knows Italy. Certainly, after reading his harsh, disparaging pronouncements on Russian life, one might have thought that life in Italy would impress him as saner and more civilized than life in his homeland; yet it was not so— for the lonely poet there was no place like home, even if his thoughts about returning there were darkened by gloomy premonitions: "The only place where I can live is Russia, although it seems that life is more frightful there (according to the newspapers and my own recollections) than anywhere else. . . . It is not easy to return, and it is as though there were nowhere to return to—they'll rob you at the customs, while in the middle of Russia they'll hang you or throw you into prison; they will insult you, and what I have written won't get past the censors" (VIII, 288). Intellectually, Blok abhorred all of Russia's social injustices and evils, but emotionally, as Chukovskii has observed, "he needed to love [Russia] just as it was, destitute, oppressed, wild, chaotic, unfortunate, ill-fated, because he felt himself to be all of these things, because he always loved desperately—through his hate, self-contempt, and pain." [1]

From 1905 on, Russia as a historical presence had occupied a prominent place in Blok's poetry, and inspired some of his finest works. He claimed that the subject of his play, "The Song of Fate," was Russia (although one would not necessarily reach such a conclusion after reading it). In a letter to Stanislavskii in 1908 in reference to this play, Blok had stated: "To this theme [Russia], I consciously and irrevocably *dedicate my life.* More clearly than ever before I realize that this is a primary question, the most vital and *real* one" (VIII, 265). An idealized image of Russia and an awareness of its grim realities existed side by side in the poet's mind in a paradoxical harmony. C. M. Bowra has described Blok's Russia as follows: "In it he found a mystical being, cruel and lovable,

[1] Kornei Chukovskii, *Aleksandr Blok kak chelovek i poet* (Petrograd, 1924), p. 126.

ideal and yet perfectly real, known in the countryside which he loved, in the multitudes which he championed, in the religion which gave him his symbols of suffering and sacrifice, of guilt and redemption." [2] There is a mystical affinity between Blok's conception of Russia's fate and his view of his own destiny. According to Zhirmunskii: "It is not the political fate of his native land that troubles the poet, but the salvation of her living soul—her mission, her predestined path, her victories and defeats along this road. Similarly, the poet evaluated his own fate as a religious tragedy, as a struggle on behalf of the divine vocation of human personality." [3]

In Blok's poetry, Russia is usually personified, but her countenance varies with the poet's mood or intent: she is by turns a "bride," a "wife," a "beloved one," a "friend"; she may appear in the guise of the "drunken Rus' " or the "destitute Finnish Rus'." [4] But when she is remembered nostalgically from foreign shores, she becomes a disembodied timeless abstraction, a "Russia in dreams" (VIII, 283). Blok writes from Milan: "Russia for me is always the same—a lyrical summit but in reality she does not exist, she never has existed, and never will" (VIII, 289).

Shortly thereafter, Blok found himself recrossing the geographical barriers which separated him from his "lyrical summit." Once back on his estate, and immersed again in the dismal, humdrum realities of Russian life, he writes:

Dark leaden clouds drift across the sky, the wind is sharp. Just as before, peasants bow, the village girls fear the lady of the manor,

[2] C. M. Bowra, *The Heritage of Symbolism* (New York, 1961), p. 165.

[3] V. Zhirmunskii, *Voprosy teorii literatury* (The Hague: Mouton, 1962), p. 211.

[4] An analysis of the distinction made by Blok between Rus' and Russia can be found in G. P. Fedotov's article "Na pole Kulikovom," *Novyi grad* (New York: Chekhov Publishing House, 1952), pp. 274–301 *passim*.

Petersburg submissively allows itself to be devoured by cholera, the caretaker kisses your hand, while the World-Soul avenges itself on us on behalf of them all. "Return" . . . Everything returns to me, everything. (*Notebooks*, 153)

A strange invocation concludes this entry in Blok's diary:

There is still much more to come. But You must return, return, return—at the end of our appointed trials. We shall pray to You amidst those fears and passions which the future has in store for us. Again I shall wait—always Your slave, betraying You, but returning again and again. . . .
    Let me behold Your dawn. Return. (*Notebooks*, 154)

The object of his devotion, the mysterious "You" to whom Blok pledges his allegiance, remains unidentified, but the context of the passage suggests that it was his "Russia in dreams." Outside of Russia the poet felt uprooted; no foreign land, however bountiful or free, could sustain his spiritual life or imbue him with the oneness with creation that was an essential condition of his being. "I could pass through any forest unnoticed," Blok is reputed to have said in reference to his native land, "and blend with the rocks and the grass. I could run away, but I would never abandon Russia. It is here alone that I must live and die." [5]

Perhaps Blok's restlessness in Italy stemmed also from his secret feelings of guilt for "running away," for "betraying Her," although on the other hand one could also say that he had never left Russia, so constantly did his thoughts revert to his native land. "No doubt," he admitted in "Silent Witnesses," "I must accept part of the blame for the gloomy nature of my impressions: for Russian nightmares cannot be dissipated even under the Italian sun" (V, 392).

Blok had a special appreciation for those features of the

[5] N. Pavlovich, *Blokovskii sbornik* (Tartu, 1964), p. 496.

Italian landscape which reminded him of Russia. In a rare, and for him unusually lengthy, description of the Italian countryside (in "The Specter of Rome and Monte Luca"), he compared what he had seen with his memories of central Russia:

Approaching this mountain [Monte Luca] with the intention of climbing it, we stopped beside an old aqueduct. . . . The place was completely sheltered from gusts of wind and, thanks to the shadows cast by the mountains and the springs and bushes, it was not parched by the sun. It was a happy spot, a blessed land, like those peaceful corners of paradise, the clearings in our central regions of Russia. These clearings are covered by young shoots, by tall thickets of rose-bay, by the white and violet caps of silverberries and, closer to the edge of the old forest, by carpets of cowwheat and frankincense. As you wander through this land, your soul becomes illuminated and your body light and airy; a large multicolored butterfly of a rare species with lacy, scalloped wings flies toward you: it is the machaon butterfly. (V, 400)

Similarly, while admiring the art of the Renaissance in Venice, Blok unexpectedly thought of Chekhov. In a curious comparison, he proclaimed the latter to be "in no way inferior to Bellini" (VIII, 283). Venice reminded him of Petersburg, while "faithless" Florence, dancing in a city square and "driving" one "mad" with her song, is strangely reminiscent of the poet's personification of Russia in the poem "Accordion, accordion" (II, 280–281).

Perhaps because he wanted to have with him tangible reminders of his native land, Blok took along on his journey a volume of Pushkin's prose and Tolstoi's *War and Peace*. In the little village of Marina di Pisa, after waking up in the middle of the night to the roar of the wind and the sea, he reviewed and reassessed his life in the light of his recent experiences and impressions, and made plans for a *"vita nuova"*:

The sudden, vivid recollection of Mitia's death,[6] Tolstoi's novel, and a feeling of peace such as I had known long ago, got me to thinking that during the past three or four years I have been drawn imperceptibly into a circle of people who are completely foreign to me, into a world of intrigue, boasting, feverish tempo and shady dealings. . . .

I must alter my course completely now, while I have not yet lost my perspective, while there is still time. The way to do this is to give up trying to make a living at literature . . . and to allow art, my precious one . . . to remain art . . . without fashionable young ladies, without benefit lectures and evenings, without acting and actors, without *hysterical laughter*. One thing at least I owe to Italy, that here I have rid myself of that kind of laughter. Please God it will remain that way. (*Notebooks*, 145)

Perhaps the relation between Blok's love for Russia and his reaction to Italy can be understood better in the light of Isaiah Berlin's classification of creative personalities as either "hedgehogs" or "foxes." Inspired by an aphorism attributed to the Greek poet Archilochus—"the fox knows many things, but the hedgehog knows only one big thing"—Berlin calls "hedgehogs" those personalities who relate everything to a single central vision, one system less or more coherent or articulate, in terms of which they understand, think and feel—a single, universal, organizing principle in terms of which alone all that they are and say has significance." [7]

"Foxes," on the other hand, are,

those who pursue many ends, often unrelated and even contradictory, connected, if at all, only in some *de facto* way. . . . Their thought is scattered or diffused, moving on many levels, seizing upon the essence of a vast variety of experiences and ob-

[6] Blok's infant son.
[7] Isaiah Berlin, *The Hedgehog and the Fox* (New York: Simon and Schuster, 1966), p. 1.

jects . . . without, consciously or unconsciously, seeking to fit
them into, or exclude them from, any one unchanging, all-embracing, sometimes self-contradictory and incomplete, at times fanatical, unitary inner vision.[8]

Blok was a hedgehog *par excellence*. It was difficult if not
impossible for him to respond to any significant experience
except by first relating it, "consciously or unconsciously," to
his "unchanging, all-embracing . . . self-contradictory . . .
fanatical, unitary inner vision." His "unitary inner vision"
was the vision of a "New Life" for man and society and at its
core was Russia—the future redeemer of mankind.

In his essay on Ibsen, describing what he regarded as the
dramatist's most characteristic trait, Blok quoted a stanza
from Pushkin's famous poem, "Once there lived a poor
knight":

> He had but one vision,
> Beyond the reach of mind,
> And its impression was graven
> Deeply upon his heart. (V, 314)

His devotion to the Virgin Mary was the sole inspiration of
Pushkin's knight. By the same token, Ibsen had one overrid-
ing concern—Norway. Tormented by self-doubt, Ibsen
left his country in order to "see the sun," which, as Blok put
it, "at home he never saw." When he returned to his sunless
land, he was unchanged as an artist and his anguish was the
same, but his armor had become thicker and tougher. "His
methods, his themes, even his appearance and handwriting
were different, but Ibsen himself had not changed, that is, he
had not deviated from his path and his 'vocation,' he had not
betrayed his youth and his *first love*" (V, 313). Recognizing

[8] Ibid., pp. 1–2.

in Ibsen sentiments akin to his own, Blok, in his interpretation of the great Norwegian's motivations and artistic goals,
filtered these through the lenses of his own *Weltanschauung*.
"Perhaps," writes the poet, "behind Hilda, Hedda, Ellida,
one can discern still another visage—that of Norway
itself; not the unfortunate Norway of reality . . . but Norway, the native land, the mother, the sister, the wife; the
Norway of green fjords, rocks and snows, the homeland of
the white eagle" (V, 314).

In his perceptive analysis of Blok's poetic cycle "On the
Field of Kulikovo," Fedotov interprets Blok in much the
same spirit as Blok had interpreted Ibsen: "The theme of Russia in Blok's works begins to resound with especial force during the final period of his creative achievement. But already
the third poem of the Kulikovo cycle tells us simply and directly . . . that Russia, Blok's native land, is one of the incar-
nations of Her whose praises he had first sung in his poems
dedicated to the Beautiful Lady. Inevitably this compels us to
link the theme of Russia to Blok's basic, and essentially his
only theme." [9]

Blok repeatedly reaffirmed his loyalty to certain fundamental beliefs and modes of perception. In 1907 he wrote to
Belyi, stating about himself that "essentially [he] had never
changed" (VIII, 201). In 1910 he underlined the phrase "*I
have never contradicted myself in what is important*" (VIII,
317). And in 1918 he said again, "nothing has changed in
me," adding fatalistically "this is my tragedy" (VII, 335).
Blok's world outlook evolved out of the nucleus of ideas
which had constituted his original vision (his utopia had
begun as the expectation of a mystical revelation). His entire
artistic development was conditioned by his early beliefs,

[9] G. Fedotov, *op. cit.*, p. 281.

which continued to influence the views and goals of his mature years. When new thoughts and experiences impinged on Blok's mind and heart, he assessed them, often subconsciously it seems, against the background of these values: those that could be "fitted" into their structure he accepted, the others he excluded.

It is not surprising, therefore, that Blok's reactions to Italy were deeply affected by his prior expectations: he vehemently rejected those aspects of the country which did not harmonize with his Platonic idea of it, and accepted only those he could relate to the "immortal" and the "sublime."

Blok repudiated that Italy which had so delighted his romantic predecessors—the Italy of picturesque landscapes, gay and warm people, and a lively and bustling urban life—all of which had enchanted Gogol; he spurned the "nights of golden Italy" and the "songs of the gondoliers" of which Pushkin had dreamed on the shores of the Neva; he turned a deaf ear to the melodious Italian sounds which Batiushkov had deemed worthy of imitation. In "Silent Witnesses" Blok declared categorically: "It is impossible to live in the Italian provinces because nothing there is alive: all the air seems to have been used up by the dead, to whom it rightfully belongs. The white eyes of magnolias stare out here and there from abandoned vineyards; intense heat hangs over the squares, which are filled with chattering, short-legged simulacra of what used to be human beings" (V, 390–391). In a letter to his friend Evgenii Ivanov, Blok remarks tartly: "There is no land here; there is only sky, mountains, and fields of vines. There are no people" (VIII, 287). Yet he goes on to complain of the slovenly appearance of these "non-people," and of their indifference to beauty. "The trees are few, the vegetation is sparse, they plant hardly any flowers." Italian roads are "dusty," and "lined with ugly vines" (*Letters*, I, 269).

Significantly, the poet described his trip as a descent into the Inferno, and envisioned himself as a Dante, a living man journeying among the dead, but destined, unlike his great predecessor, to wander through the Italian towns without any celestially appointed guide. The spirits populating this Inferno are guilty of a sin which escaped even Dante's Argus-eyed scrutiny: indifference to a great historical and cultural heritage, and distortion of the melodious Latin language. "Even in Milan, Pisa and Orvieto," wrote Blok to his mother, "the attitude of the people to the Gothic [art] of the cathedrals is one of childish unconcern; they are unable to grasp its meaning" (*Letters*, I, 269). "The clear, precise Latin enunciation has disappeared and even the pronunciation of street singers with its congenital sibilance grates on one's ear," he complains in "Silent Witnesses" (V, 390).

In the silence of non-life, Blok heard the "underground voices of the dead," voices which to him were clear and intelligible, and in harmony with that secret inner music to which his soul was attuned. To the innermost sanctuary of his vision, Blok could admit only the ancient art of Italy, the language of her glorious past and her long-dead heroes. "All that is ancient is very dear to me . . ." he wrote. "Always and everywhere the Latin language, which has been so mutilated by the Italians, is as close and dear to me as my native tongue" (VIII, 289).

The gloom about which he complained in "Silent Witnesses," an essay devoted mainly to Perugia, did not prevent him from being "thoroughly delighted" with this city, the capital of Umbria and the "birthplace of St. Francis, Perugino, and Raphael" (V, 391). He found Perugia as "intoxicating as old wine," admittedly because "Perugia's life is dead and she will have no new life; but her old life sings out trumpetlike in the voices of the beasts on her portals, fountains, and coats of arms and, above all, in the voices of her distant ancestors, invisible witnesses who live their own lives beneath the earth" (V, 392). The splendid panoramic view from Perugia, towering over the countryside, does not elicit any comment from Blok, but objects which he could discern only with difficulty in the dark underground tomb of the Volumni are described in detail: "The tomb is simple. In the rocky hill, several dozens steps below the surface, the stone sun between the two dolphins, carved over the portals overgrown with green mold, does not shine. Here it smells of dampness and earth. Inside the ten small chambers of the tomb, electric lamps blink on and off, throwing a flickering light over the low gray vaults and the carved effigies of the numerous Volumni family reclining upon the lids of their sarcophagi" (V, 392–393).

The sculpted effigies of this Etruscan family come to life in Blok's graphic descriptions:

The "silent witnesses" of twenty-two centuries lie wonderfully still and peaceful. The arm of one figure leans on two stone pillows, with the hand supporting the head; on one finger of that hand there is the inevitable ring. The other hand, resting quietly on the thigh, holds the traditional shallow cup, the *patera*, with the coin for Charon. The clothing is loose and comfortable, the bodies and faces are heavy with a tendency to corpulence (V, 393).

The glow of saintliness which the Sienese painters sought to infuse into their Madonnas eluded Blok; in their eyes, which seemed to him to be directed toward earth instead of heaven, he saw only their fallible humanity:

Even in the elongated eyes of her Madonnas there is an impertinent slyness; whether they are looking at the child, or nursing him, or humbly accepting Gabriel's blessed tidings, or simply staring into empty space—a sort of sly, catlike tenderness can invariably be detected in their eyes. Whether a storm is raging in the background or the shadows of a quiet evening are falling, they go on staring with those elongated eyes which neither promise nor discourage, but simply look askance at the Guelphic antics of their lively, bustling husbands. (V, 395)

Over and over again, one sees Blok fleeing from the vulgar tumult of the living present to the repose and stately immobility of the dead past. He rejects vehemently the busy streets of Italy's modern cities and tenderly embraces her silent tombs; he appreciates the imaginary landscapes in medieval paintings more than the actual scenery around him. He scorns and vilifies Italy's living inhabitants but idealizes her dead. He discerns a burning passion for life in the glance of a dead empress and a spiritual longing for the past in the eyes of the girls of Ravenna. Old paintings of Madonnas arouse erotic thoughts in him, while the slender grace of a living Umbrian girl fills him with an almost religious reverence. So total and undiscriminating is Blok's rejection of the conventionally picturesque and gratifying that one begins to wonder whether the poet, who was aware of his own impressionability to every sort of sensual delight, was not consciously safeguarding himself against Italy's ensnaring appeal, lest he become simply one more among the thousands of artists, musicians and writers throughout history who, failing to see below the glittering surface of Italian life, had yielded to her siren song and turned into docile singers of her loveliness.

To recapitulate, Blok's journey to Italy occurred on two levels: one physical, obvious and passive—the actual trip; the other spiritual, symbolic and dynamic—the mythical

5. Spoleto. The Cathedral. Monument to Fra Filippo Lippi. It was erected by Lorenzo the Magnificent in the fifteenth century. (Alinari).

journey into the past. Although Blok condemned and berated Italy for having fallen from the awe-inspiring heights she had attained in the Renaissance to the dismal depths of her insignificant present, he felt spiritually uplifted by his Italian experience because he found in the country's historical and artistic heritage a sustaining faith, an abiding inspiration, and an earnest hope for future immortality. Amid the spiritual wasteland of contemporary Europe, art was the only pure wellspring of life. With its power to render immortal the transitory phenomena of our existence, to refine and perfect life, to transcend different epochs, nationalities and creeds, art appeared to Blok as a unifying bond between generations, the beacon illuminating humanity's road ahead. And the paintings of the great masters had a uniquely personal impact upon the poet, for they seemed to him to contain the secret of harmony, the goal of his own never-ending quest.

Blok began and ended the Italian poems with a Latin epigraph: the first, the inscription in the Church of Santa Maria Novella, he placed untranslated as an introduction to the cycle; the other, an anonymous epitaph to Fra Filippo Lippi, stands in both Latin and Russian versions as the concluding poem. The first quotation bemoans the ephemeral nature of life; the second celebrates the permanence of art. Perhaps, when all is said and done, Blok's Italian experience and the literary works which reflect it can best be understood in the light of these two inscriptions.

CONDITUS HIC EGO SUM PICTURE FAMA PHILIPPUS

NULLI IGNOTA ME GRATIA MIRA MANUS

ARTIFICIS POTUI DIGITIS ANIMARE COLORES

SPERATAQUE ANIMOS FALLERE VOCE DIU

IPSA MEIS STUPUIT NATURA EXPRESSA FIGURIS

MEQUE SUIS FASSA EST ARTIBUS ESSE PAREM

MARMOREO TUMULO MEDICES LAURENTIUS HIC ME

CONDIDIT ANTE HUMILI PULVERE TECTUS ERAM [10]

---

[10] This unsigned epitaph, which Blok attributes to Poliziano, is inscribed on the tomb of Fra Filippo Lippi in the Cathedral of Spoleto. See "The Italian Poems" for its translation into English.

PROSE SKETCHES AND POEMS
Lightning Flashes of Art
The Italian Poems

A Note on the Translations

In my translations of Blok's poetry and prose, I have tried to keep one primary consideration in mind: fidelity to the original text in conformity with English idiom and sentence structure.

It is difficult, if not impossible, to reproduce any poem in another language without robbing it of those specific qualities and that ineffable essence which make it a work of art in the original. In translating poetry, therefore, one is faced with two essentially unsatisfactory alternatives—either to convey as precisely as possible the poem's literal meaning, or to produce a freer version that would combine the general sense of the original with some of its outstanding formal features. For the most part, I have chosen the former alternative. In my literal rendering of the poems, however, I have also tried to convey something of their poetic feeling and style by preserving, if not rhythm in the strict sense of the term, at least certain patterns and cadences so that these poems would not read altogether like prose. I have not sought to reproduce either Blok's rhyme-scheme or the tonal and phonetic qualities of his poetry. The felicitous interrelation between sound and sense, the unique harmony of his lines, simply cannot be transferred into another language.

In the commentaries on the poems I have discussed some of the formal aspects of Blok's poetry, and I hope that this analysis will give the non-Russian reader some notion of the qualities of the originals. Since Blok chose his words with equal attention to sound and sense, and sometimes even placed greater emphasis on the factor of sound, I was often faced with the problem of whether to give priority to the strictly literal meaning of a particular word or to select a compromise word or phrase in the same "field" of meaning which would convey more meaningfully, if less literally, what the poet had intended to say. In such instances, the choice was determined by the relation of the word to the poem as a whole. Here I could not avoid a certain degree of subjectivity, since the connotation or "field" of meaning covered by parallel abstract or emotionally colored words differs substantially from Russian to English, and the translator's choices will at times reflect his own perception of a given poem. But perhaps my most difficult problem was that of rendering in English the studied simplicity of Blok's poetry, for what sounds fresh and lyrical in the original can often appear naive and banal in English, however much thought and labor the translator exerts.

In translating Blok's prose, I was confronted with a different set of problems. Although my primary goal of accuracy and fidelity in translation remained the same, I allowed myself more liberties than in the translations of the poetry. Blok's essays possess many of the rhythmic, impressionistic, and lyrical qualities of his poems, but lack their finely chiseled structure and elegant conciseness. Blok's chief merit as an essayist lies in his originality of thought, in his ability to see unobvious relationships, and in his profound artistic understanding and intuition. He is not a gifted prose stylist, however; his prose is not usually lucid, smooth or free-flowing. Poetic images, complex ideas, casual observations may appear in one and the same essay, and the language may range, at times abruptly, from the colloquial to the lofty.

Blok's style, even in essays of a literary-critical nature, is lyrical and marked by a profound sensitivity and an intensity of feelings that one usually associates with a typically Russian mentality. His sentences, even his paragraphs, do not follow in a strictly logical sequence; neither does Blok hesitate to pass on as indisputable facts his own questionable, unscientific opinions. He can be obscure, ambiguous, contradictory, if effect or inner artistic logic demands it. Here scrupulously literal translations could even distract from the meaning, and the meaning, not only of the passage *per se* but in its relationship to the whole was my primary consideration.

The transliteration system I have used is the Library of Congress, System II with the diacritical marks omitted (see J. Thomas Shaw, *The Transliteration of Modern Russian for English-Language Publications* [Madison, 1967]). In the spelling of proper names, I have taken the liberty of eliminating the soft sign (') or substituting an "i" so as to represent more accurately the pronunciation, and for the sake of bibliographic simplicity and convenience.

The notes at the end of each essay in "Lightning Flashes of Art" are mine. They incorporate and expand some of the notes found in Volume 8 of the Russian edition of Blok's "Collected Works."

LIGHTNING FLASHES OF ART

An Unfinished Book of
"Italian Impressions"

FOREWORD

Time rushes on, civilization advances, mankind progresses.

The nineteenth century is an age of iron. It is a long line of draft wagons rumbling along cobblestone roads, pulled by exhausted horses, which are driven on by pale, sallow-faced men. The nerves of these men are taut from hunger and want, curses stream from their open mouths, but although they can be seen lashing their whips and shaking their reins, their curses and shouts cannot be heard because the iron bars piled into the wagons raise a deafening clatter.

And the nineteenth century is all atremble, shaking and rumbling like those iron bars. It is the people—civilization's slaves—who tremble, cowed by this very civilization. Time rushes on: year by year, day by day, and hour by hour it becomes even more apparent that civilization will collapse over the heads of its builders and crush them with its own weight; but it has not yet begun to crush them and the madness lingers on: everything is premeditated and predetermined, destruction is inescapable, but slow in coming; everything must be, but as yet nothing is; everything is ready to happen, yet nothing happens. Revolutions strike, blow themselves out, then die away. People are forever trembling with fear: once they were people, but that was long ago and now they are only pretending to be people; they are really only slaves, beasts and reptiles. God has long since ceased to watch over those who once were called people; nature stopped caring for them long ago and art no longer gladdens them. And it has been a long time since those who were once called people asked for or demanded anything from God, from nature or from art.

Civilization advances. At the beginning of the century Balzac spoke of the "human comedy," and in mid-century Scherr [1] spoke of "tragicomedy." What we have now is nothing but a street farce. The hour of farce struck when the first aeroplane left the ground. The sky has been conquered. What a majestic spectacle! A wretched mannikin soared off into the clouds; a hen flapped its wings and got ready to fly. And it did fly—over a manure pile.

Do you know that every nut in a machine, every turn of a screw, each new technical achievement adds to the numbers of the rabble all over the world? No, you wouldn't know that, for you are "educated people" and "there is no vulgarity like the vulgarity of education" [2] as your goodnatured Ruskin once put it, letting the cat out of the bag. And he had even more to say:

"Now, by general misgovernment, I repeat, we have created in Europe a vast populace, and out of Europe a still vaster one, which has lost even the power and conception of reverence;—which exists only in the worship of itself—which can neither see anything beautiful around it, nor conceive anything virtuous above it; which has, towards all goodness and greatness, no other feelings than those of the lowest creatures—fear, hatred, or hunger; a populace which has sunk below your appeal in their

[1] Johannes Scherr (1817–1886). German man of letters and novelist. Wrote extensively on civilization and literature.

[2] John Ruskin, *The Complete Works of John Ruskin,* ed. E. T. Cook and Alexander Wedderburn (London, 1905), Vol. V, p. 99.

nature, as it has risen beyond your power in their multitude;—whom you can now no more charm than you can the adder, nor discipline, than you can the summer fly.[3]

What then, is the task of art? "When all is said and done, the only thing art can do is to make the brute beast less vicious," was the opinion of Flaubert. True, it may make a beast less vicious—but it can make a man more so.

Suffocating from anger, depression and consternation, we are drawn to past greatness: that is why, for example, we wander through art galleries. And by condemning ourselves to trailing cheerlessly through Europe's art galleries and submitting to their tiresome order—an order which is at best chronological, but which in many cases has been established by the "art experts," those academicians whose name is legion—we undoubtedly hope to wrest from time at least one instant of incomparable ecstasy.

The way things stand now in European society, however, we shall soon be deprived of even these transitory pleasures. If only our worries were confined to getting our tickets stamped officially and moving past the uncommunicative guards in academies and museums! But obstacles multiply as civilization advances; and it seems most unlikely that we shall see an end to its monstrous and insane growth in our own lifetime.

The tribe of English tourists, male and female alike, is notable for its truly porcine fecundity: Leonardo's "Last Supper," for instance, is already inaccessible to the serious viewer; at the entrance to the damp stable in which the picture hangs, one runs straight into a fence of flat boards: these are the backs of the English ladies who sit side by side on chairs, like

[3] Ibid., Vol. XVIII, p. 498.

roosting hens. Their tribe breeds a species of guides who throw themselves at the visitors in a hungry pack.

Thus, all the walls of living pictures are blocked by a lifeless wall of people; the halls resound with the neighing of Englishmen and the shrill voices of guides reciting the standard nonsense. It is impossible to find seclusion or to concentrate. Fruitlessly resisting the pressure of human "roast beefs" for two solid hours is an exhausting experience, which destroys all desire to try and see anything else. And yet, I did see something. At the cost of many wasted hours, of spiritual mortifications experienced in eighteenth-century rooms [4] and many nightmares, I succeeded in capturing something from the Old World.

Treasures of the Old World, treasures of fragmented art! They intoxicate, to be sure. The most courageous among us would be shocked to learn what the coming barbarians will violate, what gems of creation will disappear without a trace at the cheerfully destructive hands of the people of the future! The time is near when art too, will undergo unheard-of destruction; retribution will also descend upon art; because it was great when life was a little thing, because its [sweet] poison alienated people from life, because it was loved desperately by a select few but was hated, hounded, persecuted, belittled and despised by the crowd.

Yet so far "nothing has happened." Isn't that so? And this is why I think that you will not be perturbed by these few pages of recollections about the things I managed to see in the course of my wanderings in the world of art.

How I wish I could speak in kindly and lighthearted words! But I cannot find such words; the glare is blinding, for wherever beauty delights, ugliness is sure to follow, and

[4] Blok disliked eighteenth century art.

bring with it sadness. Still, I was not altogether unarmed as I moved through foreign cities and valleys, nor were my eyes always blinded by the multicolored world which lay open to their gaze.

My notes will be worthwhile if, in a few words and analogies, I succeed in conveying to others like myself, that vital something that I was able to discern through the faint glimmering of a dead and alien life.

Autumn 1909; April 1918

MASKS ON THE STREET

Florence.

From the café on the Piazza del Duomo one can see part of the façade of the Cathedral, part of the Baptistery, and the beginning of that ugly Calzaioli Street which runs between them. This street serves as the main artery of the central quarter of the city which has been hopelessly defiled by hotels; it connects the Piazza del Duomo with the Piazza della Signoria.

In the daytime here [one has to put up with] boredom, dust and foul smells; but in the evening when the intense heat subsides, when the street lamps burn dimly and the outlines of the modern buildings are engulfed by night and so are no longer a source of irritation, one can lose himself comfortably in the crowd which swarms through the square, among the shouts of cab drivers and vendors and the clanging of trolley cars.

And it is here and at this hour that one may witness a strange spectacle. Suddenly one's ear is jarred by a rasping noise that sounds like that of an automobile horn; and one sees a procession hurrying past the porch of Santa Maria del

6. Florence. Piazza del Duomo. In the background is the Via Calzaioli. (Alinari).

Fiore. A man runs ahead along the street with a hood pulled down low over his face: the hood has no slits for the eyes, which means that he can see nothing except the ground over which he is running. He holds aloft a torch which flickers in the wind. Behind him two other men whose faces are also covered drag a long, black two-wheeled cart. The rubber tires on the wheels turn without making a sound. All one can hear is the anxious honking of a motor-car horn. People step aside to let the procession pass. The shape of the cart is that of a human body. A thick black cloth stretched over three hoops on the cart quivers from the bouncing, and the peculiar way in which it quivers indicates that the vehicle is not empty.

The "Brothers of Mercy"—*Misericordia*—(that is who these people are) quickly roll their cart onto a platform in front of a house on the corner of Calzaioli Street. Just as quickly the gates swing open, and the whole apparition disappears into a barnlike room on the main floor, of which one catches a momentary glimpse. Everything happens so rapidly that one has no time to indulge in guesswork or to be surprised. Probably even the plague, Florence's ancient guest, could boast no greater speed and precision in selecting and dispatching [its victims].

The gates are closed. The house looks like any other, as if nothing had happened. Inside, the corpse is undoubtedly being taken out of the cart and undressed. And probably no one in the new wave of passers-by—officers, ladies, prostitutes and merchants—suspects that the wave which had swept past just before at a dancing gallop had dumped unto this platform a cart with a corpse.

And now a poor frightened bat, the traditional occupant of weather-beaten houses, towers, and walls, flits through the air at the same frenzied gallop. Dazed by the crisscrossing beams of the electric lights, it almost brushes against the heads of the passers-by.

All this is a hint of the remote past, a recollection of something that happened long ago, a kind of enticing illusion. Masks everywhere, and masks always conceal something else. And the blue irises in the Cascine—whose masks are they? When a chance wind blows through a motionless belt of intense heat, all of them, like blue flames, bend in one direction as if they wanted to fly away.

Autumn 1909; December 1912

SILENT WITNESSES

A journey through a country with a rich past but a poor present is like a descent into Dante's Inferno. From the depths of history's naked crevices emerge images of an infinite pallor, and tongues of blue flame scorch one's face. All is well if you carry with you in your soul your own Virgil who will comfort you and say: "Have no fear: at the end of the road you will see Her who sent you." History is astonishing and depressing.

One thing makes Italy tragic: the underground murmuring of its history, a history that has stormed past never to return. In this sound, the hushed voice of madness, the muttering of the ancient Sibyls, is clearly audible. Life is right to shun this whispering. But is there any life in contemporary Italy? One seldom sees here a truly human face, and one rarely hears a beautiful voice that is unmarred by the whistling pronunciation of the letter *s*—incidentally, this speech characteristic seems to be very widespread in southern Europe today. Not only has the clear, precise enunciation disappeared but even the pronunciation of street singers grates on one's ears with its congenital sibilance. The inhabitants of provincial towns never tire of pretending that they are busy with various occupations, but in reality, the only thing that seems to be of absorbing interest to them is violent political squabbling. It is here, in this domain of English hotels which are rapidly ruining the towns, of all sorts of "Corriere della Sera" and little shops full of indescribable national and international rubbish that the "murmuring of history" is most audible. It is impossible to live in the Italian provinces because nothing there is alive: all the air seems to have been used up by the dead, to whom it rightfully belongs. The white eyes of magnolias

7. Perugia. Urn in the Hypogeum of the Volumni. Dates back to
Etruscan times.   (Alinari).

stare out here and there from abandoned vineyards; intense heat hangs over the squares, which are filled with chattering, short-legged simulacra of what used to be human beings. Coolness, the dusk of twilight and Catholic reminders of the transitory nature of life can be found only in the mountains, the cathedrals, the tombs, and the galleries.

It is here that northern and central Italy summon the Russian, into the cold of their irretrievable memories. In this land there are only two or three pitiful remnants of a way of life once full of fervor and self-confidence: a young Catholic girl leaving the confessional, her eyes sparkling with laughter; a red sail in the lagoon; an ancient shawl thrown over the supple shoulders of a Venetian girl. But all this is Venice, where living people and merriment can still be found: basically, Venice is still not really Italy; it has the same relationship to Italy as Petersburg has to Russia, in other words, it does not seem to belong to it at all.

The farther south one goes, the more deserted the landscape becomes; the less life there is above ground, the more distinctly audible are the underground voices of the dead.

Modern culture listens to the voice of the ore in the very bowels of the earth. Why then, do we not hear the voice of that which lies infinitely closer to us, right under our feet— the voice of that which is buried beneath the earth or has itself miraculously sunk into it, only to make way for a second and a third layer, which in turn are fated to be engulfed and to "return to their native soil" (*revertitur in terram suam*)?

We were delighted with Perugia, the "capital" of Umbria, the birthplace of St. Francis and also of Perugino and Raphael. Here you have three of [Italy's] most illustrious names; and when one adds that the high hill of Perugia drowns in the bluish air, that it is softly irradiated by the sun and washed by cool rains and currents of a very gentle wind,

then the only thing left is to marvel at what one sees and re-
members.

Why are they so red—the garments of the angel with
the dark countenance who appears out of the deep golden
background in front of the dark-faced Virgin in the frescoes
of Giannicola Manni? Why are the cloaks of Duccio's [1] angel
musicians on the portals of the Oratory of St. Bernardino
whirled about by such a demonic wind? Why did the de-
mented family of the Baglioni, once rulers of Perugia, literally drench the city in blood so that the Cathedral had to be
washed with wine and then reconsecrated after the terrible
carnage in the square? [2] It was during this horror that the
youthful Astorre, wearing golden armor and with a falcon on
his helmet, galloped through the square like a demon. stirring
the imagination of Raphael, who was then but a small boy.
And, finally, why does a raging griffin tearing a calf to pieces
appear on Perugia's medieval coat of arms? Or was there
something else [that I failed to see], and is all this merely a
product of the gloomy imagination of a stranger from Russia
with its Azevs [3] and its executions, its "yellow eyes of wild

[1] Agostino di Duccio (1418–1498). Not to be confused with the more
famous artist Duccio di Buoninsegna (1255–1319).

[2] Blok is referring here to the internecine wars among the Baglioni,
then the rulers of Perugia, which resulted in the carnage that occurred on July 17, 1500. Raphael depicted one of the tragic moments
in this slaughter: the grief of the mother Atalanta over the body of
her young son.

[3] E. F. Azev (1869–1918). The notorious double agent and political
renegade. Between 1903 and 1908, when he was exposed, Azev was
ostensibly a leader of the Russian Socialist revolutionary party and
the head of its "combat" organization. In this capacity he was responsible for organizing several sensational acts of terror, including
the assassination of the Minister of the Interior, Plehve. But throughout this period he was, at the same time, high in the councils of the
Okhrana (the tsarist political police) and was responsible for the betrayal and arrest of a number of his revolutionary associates. His
name has become a synonym for treachery.

taverns" [4] which stare into the boundless fields through which its main roads and byways wind and crisscross, leading no one knows where.

No doubt I must accept part of the blame for the gloomy nature of my impressions: for Russian nightmares cannot be drowned even under the Italian sun. But for the most part my gloom can be explained by the fact that Perugia's life is dead and she will have no new life; but her old life sings out trumpetlike in the voices of the beasts on her portals, fountains, and coats of arms, and, above all, in the voices of her distant ancestors, invisible witnesses who live their own lives beneath the earth.

Perugia is intoxicating like old wine. Having feasted our eyes to our hearts' content on all her sights, we bypass the main square which is profaned by a hotel, the best in town, and descend the steep hill of Perugia to make our last visit —to the famous Etruscan tomb, the *hypogeum* of the Volumni (*Sepolcro dei Volumni*) which was discovered in 1840 and is located in a valley two or three miles away.

Cornfields planted with old hollow trees, a villa covered with flowers, an obliterated fresco on the wall of a farm house, a winding white highroad, a brick factory, haymowing, and peasant women giving questionable directions. Right next to the railroad crossing there is a small house; strictly speaking it is a roof over the underground dwelling of an Etruscan family. A recent tradition has it that once, while a peasant was ploughing, his ox stumbled into the sepulcher; the peasant dug down to the entrance which was blocked by a stone, and thus discovered the tomb.

The tomb is simple. In the rocky hill, several dozen steps below the surface, the stone sun between the two dolphins, carved over the portals overgrown with green mold, does not shine. Here it smells of dampness and earth. Inside the ten

[4] From Belyi's poem "*Otchaianie*" (Despair).

small chambers of the tomb, electric lamps blink on and off, throwing a flickering light over the low gray vaults and the carved effigies of the numerous Volumni family reclining upon the lids of their sarcophagi.

The "silent witnesses" [5] of twenty-two centuries ago lie wonderfully still and peaceful. The arm of one figure leans on two stone pillows, with the hand supporting the head; on one finger of that hand there is the inevitable ring. The other hand, resting quietly on the thigh, holds the traditional shallow cup, the *patera*, with the coin for Charon. The clothing is loose and comfortable, the bodies and faces are heavy with a tendency to corpulence.

All the inscriptions on the sarcophagi are in Etruscan; only on the richest tomb—the marble one which is decorated with four delicately chiseled sphinxes, one at each corner (one sphinx is broken off), and two bronze rings—is the inscription in Latin: "*P. Volumnius A. P. violens Cafatia natus*,"—"Here lies Publius Volumnius the Indomitable, born of the Cafatia gens."

The decorations in this underground "apartment" are striking: here is everything that the family of the once Indomitable One might need so as to be able to lie in prayerful repose in the slumber of death, to count the passing of the centuries on the earth above their heads, to pray as they did in life and to wait patiently for some unknown event. On the ceilings and on the tombs are the heavy, mournful heads of the Medusae: the doves on the sides of these heads are symbols of peace: two winged feminine figures, the Genii of Death, hang from the ceiling in the vestibule.[6] The small

[5] "Silent Witnesses" is an image first used by A.A. Fet in his poem "*Starye pis'ma*" (Old letters). What follows is a description of one of the tombs in the central chamber of the *hypogeum*.

[6] They are no longer in the vestibule of the tomb; when the author visited it in 1969, she was informed that they had been stolen.

stone heads of little snakes which protrude from the wall are the *guardia del sepolcro*, the guardians of the tombs.[7]

Even more striking are the bas-reliefs of the sarcophagi themselves: not all the lids are covered with carved effigies of the deceased; some are shaped like the roofs of temples (of course of the Greek type); the small sarcophagus of a child is covered with a flower turned upside down—a stone lily.

The sides of the tombs are not the finest in Italy; in a museum in Florence, and especially in the burial vaults near the ancient Clusium (now Chiusi), one can see entire mythological stories carved on sarcophagi; but the bas-reliefs of the Perugian Volumni are particularly clearcut, simple and characteristic of this city, which was once one of the twelve towns of the Etrurian confederation.

Here we see simple, well-defined designs: flowers with four or eight petals; battles and wild-boar hunts; figures sitting on bridled dolphins; a boy and a warrior with a shield; the face of a youth who is playing the flute; a curlicue which reminds one of a butterfly; another curlicue in the form of a cross; an urn over a garland of grapes with two bulls' heads on each side; two young boys holding onto the snakes of the Medusa's head; two others holding up a tall urn amid cypress trees. Finally, there is the griffin which appears in different variations. First, a griffin in the middle of four flowers; then, the likeness of a girl with a mirror astride a tempestuous horse whose dolphin's tail winds round and round three times. The animal's head here is a combination of dragon and griffin (the head of the sitting figure has been broken off, but the folds of the dress cling closely: evidently this is a female body); then there are figures battling with a griffin; finally, on some of the sarcophagi, a griffin is obviously clawing a man.

[7] The author was informed that they have recently been removed and donated to a museum. The word "sepolcro" is misspelled in the Russian text.

So this is where the griffin originated! It has always been the emblem of Perugia—not only of Renaissance Perugia but also of Augusta Perusia, as the city was named in the age of Augustus; and, at an even more remote period, it was the emblem of Perusia when the place was a fortress of the Etruscan Lucumones.[8] The city itself contains almost no traces of that period except the remains of a thick wall and of a lower layer of coarse stones, very roughly cut, over which Augustus erected a heavy Roman arch and to which the Renaissance in turn added a light, crown-shaped *loggia* at a dizzying height.[9]

In the house of the Volumni the visitor is brought back to reality only when a train thunders overhead. He comes out into the light of day blinded, as though he had just emerged from the darkness of hell, and with his suspicion confirmed that even the most radiant of all Italian towns stands under the sign of the bloodthirsty griffin. If history were to repeat itself blood would flow once more. Nothing will happen here, however, except that some new hotels will be built or, at best, [some more monuments to] Garibaldi and Victor Emmanuel,[10] in their capes and "affecting" poses—pitiful and vain imitations of a life whose echoes are heard no more.

Life will not return here. The sandy square with a view of blue Umbria now gives shelter to no one but the tourist, the

[8] Lucumones—Etruscan princes and priests.

[9] Blok is probably referring here to the Porta Marzia, but his information does not seem to be accurate. The archway and the *loggia* are the only remains dating back to Etruscan times. In the fifteenth century the Florentine architect Sangallo, in order to preserve the sculptures, in the *loggia*, had them taken down and reset above the archway (Ottorino Guerrieri, *La Rocca Paolina in Perugia* [Perugia: Azienda Autonoma di Turismo, 1963], p. 28).

[10] Perugia dedicated two imposing monuments to Garibaldi and Victor Emmanuel II respectively.

beggar and the market-woman. Work in the fields goes on peacefully and the meager chorus of an operetta troupe can be heard practicing its repertoire behind the open windows of a barn which is used as a theatre. Yes, the "silent witnesses" may sleep in peace; no one will awaken them for a long time.

October 10, 1909

AN EVENING IN SIENA

The train crawled along the edge of a hill on a narrow strip of rails between thick walls of vines, and pulled into a tunnel. Here it suddenly stopped, backed up, and then, with a few hesitant jolts, moved slowly forward again up the steep mountainside. We could see the route we had just traversed winding away in the distance below; then, on the nearby hillside, a monastery came into view. We arrived in Siena from the south, in the rosy dusk of the dying day.

An old inn: *La Toscana.* The window is open in my small room on the top floor, and I lean out to breathe the air of the cool heights, [a delightful change] after the stuffy railroad car. . . . O my God! The pink sky will soon turn completely dark. Everywhere you look, you see sharp-pointed towers —slender and light like all Italian Gothic, slender to the point of impudence and as tall as if they were aiming straight at the heart of God. Siena plays with the austere Gothic more daringly than any other city—the overgrown child! Even in the elongated eyes of her Madonnas there is an impertinent slyness; whether they are looking at the Child, or nursing him, or humbly receiving Gabriel's blessed tidings, or simply staring into empty space—a sort of sly, catlike tenderness can invariably be detected in their eyes. Whether a storm is

8. Siena. The Cathedral. Detail from the floor of the Cathedral depicting the seven ages of man. The original design by Federighi dates back to the fifteenth century.   (Alinari).

raging in the background or the shadows of a quiet evening are falling, they go on staring with those elongated eyes which neither promise nor discourage, but simply look askance at the Guelphic antics of their lively, bustling husbands. In life those husbands were always in trouble up to their ears, forever envying the Ghibellines and waging war against their neighbor, Florence. Out of envy for the Ghibellines of Florence, the Sienese erected their own *"palazzo pubblico,"* as large as the Florentine *"Palazzo Vecchio"* and very similar to it. But on their square stands not the *marzocco* [1] with a lily, but a hungry she-wolf with protruding ribs, nursing little twins who cling to her.

But in Florence *the Palazzo Vecchio* is a grim dwelling-place for bats; there, somewhere in the uppermost chambers, the anemic and lazy Eleonora di Toledo [2] once took shelter with a mischievous and cruel boy—her son, who was later strangled. And there, too, on a stormy night filled with dismal apparitions and omens, Lorenzo the Magnificent lay dying. These events left an indelible imprint which has forever enveloped in mystery that already gloomy building, one of the gloomiest in Italy. Conversely, in the *Palazzo* of Siena, although its setting is similar to that of Florence, there is nothing gloomy either outside or inside, and whereas the walls of the *Palazzo Vecchio* are empty and bare, those of the *Palazzo Pubblico* in Siena are covered with the paintings of Sodoma, the most talented and the most vulgar of Leonardo's pupils.

Against the rose-colored background of the evening sky, however, it is not only the sharp, spearlike Sienese towers which I find astonishing. The most amazing thing of all is that the most impressive of the towers is ornamented with lampions. It is Sunday evening and, of course, at nightfall a military band will play on the square.

A stream of people carries me away from the door of *La Toscana* onto the main street. A little way down the street, to the left, are several descending steps, and through a covered passageway which in Venice would be called a *sottopor-*

[1] The *marzocco*—a lion with a shield—was the coat of arms of the Republic of Florence.

[2] Eleonora de Toledo, daughter of Pedro de Toledo, viceroy of Naples. In 1539 she married Cosimo I de Medici. Although many legends relating to incest, murder and poisoning surround the Medici family, recent research has proven that many of these have no basis in fact (see "Medici," *Enciclopedia Italiana* [Rome, 1949] XI).

tico, I come out onto the square. Facing before me is the magnificent *Palazzo,* decorated with several rows of lampions. Under the she-wolf, the military band is modestly tooting away. The entire square is in the shape of a concave semicircle; here and there, the grass is breaking through. The *Palazzo* is situated at the lower end. As I stand at the highest point of the square beside the wonderful fountain of Gaia, I can see the whole of the *Palazzo,* its façade occupying almost the entire width of the square.

At one time popular assemblies used to be held here. And even today the square is full of people—indeed it swarms with them. The evening is warm and the women wear light, gaily-colored clothes. The moon shines dimly, and still more dimly the ancient lampions glow; the band is hidden behind the crowd and its music is not very sophisticated. If you do not look too closely at the faces and clothes, you could transport yourself back into the Middle Ages and relive in daydreams one of the tales of Hoffman. This impression is accentuated by the extreme naiveté of the Italian women. They come here with the obvious and unmistakable intention of showing themselves off if they are pleased with their own looks, or of looking at others if they are themselves homely. The pretty women and the plain ones enjoy themselves equally; and all of them, the rich and the poor, the beautiful and the homely, the young and the old, parade up and down. They are all wonderfully chaste, and no ulterior motives can be observed on their faces. Probably one must be born in Italy to share in such innocent gaiety.

The lampion lights go out, the band falls silent, the girls go home to sleep. How sad it is to be left standing alone in front of the she-wolf so early in the evening. Some inoffensively intoxicated young men are wandering about in a small group and singing. Behind one window a shadow passes swiftly and a light is turned off. On a steep side street, the little tavern "Three Girls" winks with its only lantern.

Autumn 1909

THE EYES OF THE EGYPTIAN GIRL

In the Egyptian section of the Archeological Museum in Florence, there is a portrait of a young girl painted on papyrus. It dates back to the Alexandrian era, and in type it is almost Greek. Some believe it to be a portrait of Queen Cleopatra. If it were so, the value of this piece of papyrus, although cracked and split in two places, would be ten times greater. Yet now, as I examine a photograph of the Egyptian girl, I do not think it is a portrait of Cleopatra.[1] But what difference does it make who she was, a queen or a slave? Or rather, is it not obvious at first glance that this is a queen? And if it is not a portrait of the treacherous "empress of emperors" in first-century B.C. Egypt, then it is of some other, even more powerful and terrible ruler.

The archeologist always has something of the poet and the lover about him; for him Caesar's bondage to love and the ignominy of Actium are his own bondage and ignominy. To conceal his own secret shame, he hides behind the shadows of the emperor and the triumvir, and tries to justify himself in the light of their destiny.

But even if the Egyptian queen herself had posed for the artist, he obviously did not intend merely to portray a historical personage. He wanted to say something more.

The "Egyptian girl" is wearing a simple necklace of dark

[1] This photograph is included in the album of postcards and reproductions which Blok collected while abroad. Blok wrote this essay a few months after his return from Italy.

9. Portrait of a Young Woman Painted on Wood. Displayed in the
Archeological Museum in Florence.   (Alinari).

stones shaped like tetrahedrons around her slender neck. Pendants, apparently heavy ones, hang from her ears. Black hair in fine curls covers her ears and part of her forehead, framing her face in a wide halo; on top, the hair is arranged in braids fastened with four clasps, linked by a jewelled chain probably made of gold; and on the lower chain, above the middle of her forehead, there shines a precious stone. Those are the ornaments she is wearing and for all their richness they are astonishingly simple; her undergarments seem to be very light, one might even say transparent, and narrow black ribbons hold her outer garments to her shoulders.

None of the Egyptian girl's features conform to any conventional "canon" of beauty, her forehead seems too large; she had good reason, then, for covering it with her hair. In the oval shape of her cheeks there is something Mongolian, something of that quality, perhaps, that made Pushkin "lose himself in passionate reveries" in a "nomad's tent," [2] or prompted him to cover the manuscripts of his poems with profiles drawn while he was daydreaming. The nose of the Egyptian girl is regular but unfortunately somewhat fleshy; the entire lower portion of her face is surprisingly unformed; the chin is undefined, and her narrow lips are of an ungraceful shape. Her eyebrows are extraordinarily wide and long, and grow thick together over the bridge of her nose.

Her eyes are her most irregular feature. "I never saw eyes of such an unusual size," anyone would say at first glance. But that is not quite correct—eyes of such size do occur, although only rarely; here it is only the sockets of the eyes that are so extraordinarily large; the eyelashes are very long

[2] From Pushkin's poem, *"Kalmychke"* (To the Kalmuk Girl). Blok misquotes Pushkin. In the poem the line reads: *"Zabytsia prazdnoiu dushoi"* (to lose oneself, an idle soul).

and soft, the eyelids are heavy. But what strikes one is actually not the size but the expression of those eyes.

The eyes dominate the whole of her face and also, it would seem, her body and everything around her. There is in them a complete indifference and a stubborn determination which transcends all conceptions of modesty, shame or impudence. All that can be said about those eyes is that they gaze at us now and always will, as they did in life. It is simply impossible to imagine them closed, partly closed or sleepy. There is no weariness in them, no maternal tenderness, no gaiety, no sadness and no desire. One can discern in them only a dull, insatiable hunger, the kind of hunger that lasts all through life right up to the grave and beyond. Neither the emperor of Rome, nor a barbaric Hyperborean, nor an Olympian god could ever begin to satisfy that hunger. Those eyes gaze with an awful stare, mute, agonizing—like the scent of the lotus. They gaze on, century after century, age after age.

Dark circles surround these eyes. One eye (the left one, as is usually the case) is noticeably smaller than the other. This is a physiological peculiarity of all passionate natures, which results from constant tension, from a vain longing to find and to see what does not exist on earth.[3]

Autumn 1909

[3] This essay is a splendid example of Blok's subjectivity as a writer. As one can see, his description is meticulously accurate, but there is much that Blok reads into the painting that the painting itself does not warrant. It is also noteworthy that Blok does not hesitate making statements which are not corroborated by any scientific evidence (as in the last paragraph) as long as they fit into his own lyrical plan or romantic view of his subject. This subjectivity may detract sometimes from the general content and style, as it does, perhaps, in this piece, but in other essays such as "Silent Witnesses," "An Evening in Siena," or "Wirballen"—to cite the best in this series—it introduces a very special note which delights with its freshness and originality.

THE SPECTER OF ROME AND
MONTE LUCA

We left the Umbrian town of Spoleto through the main gate where all visitors must undergo an inspection and pay duty. In such a hot and dusty midday hour one loses the power to concentrate and no longer wants to look at or think about anything at all. Suddenly a man came up to us and offered to show us the ruins of a Roman bridge. When we agreed, he unexpectedly went down on his knees in the dust and opened a small trapdoor. Then he lit the stub of a candle, descended some steps, and invited us to follow him.

Once inside the trapdoor, one could smell the dampness and hear the gurgling of water nearby. About eleven feet below the surface, in the dim light shed by the candle-end, I saw in front of me, as though I had dreamed of it rather than actually seen it, a slime-covered block from a stone vault— the base of the arch of a bridge. This apparition has remained just that way in my memory—as that of the specter of Rome.

There was something extraordinary in that sight, something that was not in keeping with its seeming insignificance. I do not know what astonished me most: was it our unexpected confrontation with the bridge, or the difference in temperature between the underground passage and the square, or the unfamiliar proportions of the arch? Or was it the grim and strange impression produced by the thick crust of earth beneath which there lies buried that which even to this day elevates and ennobles our spirits?

And right then and there, as is usually the case after a shock, our fatigue disappeared. Wishing to experience something else new and different, we climbed again some steps and came out on the other side of the town, where the Monte Luca rises round and steep and covered with dense thickets. Its shape suggests the head of a man; indeed it has long been compared with the head of Michelangelo.

Approaching this mountain with the intention of climbing it, we stopped by an old aqueduct which extends along a bridge across a hollow. The place was completely sheltered from gusts of wind and, thanks to the shadows cast by the mountains and the springs and bushes, it was not parched by the sun. It was a happy spot, a blessed land, like those peaceful corners of paradise—the clearings in our central regions of Russia. These clearings are covered by young shoots, by tall thickets of rose-bay, by the white and violet caps of silverberries and, closer to the edge of the old forest, by carpets of cowwheat and frankincense. As you wander through this land, your soul becomes illuminated and your body light and airy; a large, multicolored butterfly of a rare species with lacy, scalloped wings flies toward you: it is the machaon butterfly.

And so, as we stood beside the old aqueduct before starting our climb, we too had a feeling of spiritual illumination and bodily lightness. We rapidly ascended the steep grassy slope amid low, leafy groves of alder trees. These trees opened before us a vista of other enticing shady slopes, while at the same time hiding from us that part of the path we had already traversed; they also hid what was still distant from us, so that we were able to concentrate without any distractions on our immediate goal and were not tempted to waste our energy admiring the breathtaking, panoramic view. Our goal was modest and within easy reach; and, being still full of fresh energy, we pushed on towards it and within a short time, about a half an hour, we had already reached quite a high altitude, and for the first time we felt like taking a short rest.

When we looked up at the sky through the thinning alder trees, we saw a storm cloud approaching. Right away we were conscious of something new. We had only to take a quick look down at the unusually steep slope losing itself in the dense scrub thickets below through which we had been obliged to scramble since there were no roads, to realize how high up we were already. In order to stand firmly in place without swaying back and forth, we found it more convenient to hold on to a tree. All of this, coming at once, made us slightly dizzy for the first time, and we therefore decided to continue our ascent without further delay.

Another half-hour passed; the grass was no longer so thick and fresh and the bushes were more gnarled and tougher. We came across some undergrowth that was simply too thick to allow us to force our way through it: we had to circle round it in our search for a way through. Nowhere could we see any trace of human beings. We began to come upon larger stones sticking out of the ground. A little farther on, a rocky ridge taller than my own height loomed up before me. My companion kept to the left while I went to the right looking for a gap in the ridge. Suddenly I found myself standing right above a rocky precipice. There were no shrubs nearby. I looked around, my heart sank, and I almost went hurtling down.

Suddenly I caught sight of boundless horizons stretching into the distance before me: the town of Spoleto lay far below, quite tiny; a church, standing in a field about a mile from town, looked like a dot on a map. I grabbed for some roots that clung to the rock; but my companion was already standing on a stone ledge above me and holding out her hand to me. I felt so drawn toward the precipice that I had to make an effort, not just of the arm muscles but also of the will, to force myself to reach for the roots and the sharp edges of the rocks as I scrambled up to her rescuing hand.

A moment later—for the first time on this mountain—we were walking along a well-trodden rocky path. Almost at once we found ourselves in front of a mountain monastery, as though in a ballad. This little cloister was glued to the mountainside like a theatrical prop; a gray wall of sorts, two or three windows that seemed to be there just to demonstrate the kind of windows there can be. I think it was right beside this wall that I saw the Dominican monk. He stood there silently, like everything else around us; indeed we had heard no sounds since the start of our climb. We had only experienced various visual impressions, and this latest one was quite unexpected, somewhat literary and not especially desirable; it was undesirable because at that moment the sight of that monk was for me an esthetic experience, and esthetics have little meaning for a man who finds himself standing on a high point after having almost fallen into an abyss. Such was the idle and probably sinful thought that flashed through my mind then—a frivolous, boyish fancy, no doubt.

For that reason we did not linger near this small Catholic cloister, but made for a slope we saw right behind it, leading upward through the middle of a grove of alder trees, fresher and shadier than the ones which had covered the rocky zone of the mountain.

Although my clothes were torn in places and soaked right through from the heat, I seemed to have grown stronger. My body felt as agile as a cat's, and my soul had completely disappeared, as it were,—it had plunged into the valley of Umbria along with my recent dizziness and fear of the abyss.

Half an hour more, and the alder grove had come to an end. We were at the very top of Monte Luca, in an upland meadow. Everything around us was new and we, too, felt renewed. At the edge of the deep blue sky, in which there seemed to be no trace of the recent storm, a snow-white tower of clouds had taken shape. Almost on a level with us we saw the shining, snow-covered peaks of the Apennines. Never before had I breathed in bright sunlight such cool, intoxicating air. We drank our fill from an ice-cold spring and washed our hands and faces in it. It was already well on in the afternoon.

A flock of sheep was grazing in the mountain meadow. A young shepherd approached us and said *"Buona Seire"* [1] in Italian, in a particularly melodious voice. When he found out where we came from, he began to sigh for the town lying below in the same melodious manner as he might have done about a wonderful dream: "Spoleito, Spoleito . . ."

We discovered that a path had been laid out for the tourists on the other side of the mountain. We used it to climb down, but even here the descent was so steep in some spots that it was easier to run than to walk. We were already at the foot of the mountain when the storm which had passed over us in the afternoon returned. It lashed us with some heavy drops of rain before we could get to the darkened hall of our hotel. The life of the town had already come to a standstill; the peaceful twilight helped to stamp on my memory the incomparable view of the mountain.

I could stop right at this point. I dare say that by doing so I could more easily preserve inviolate the fresh, strong impression of nature. Let it rest undisturbed in my soul and fade with the years; still it will continue to give off a delicate scent, like a heap of rose petals lying in a closed drawer, where, as they lose their color, they acquire a very special, delicate aroma, a blend of roses and time. It would be better

[1] The misspelling of *"sera"* and "Spoleto" below may have been intentional on Blok's part, and intended to convey the dialect drawl of the shepherd.

still for me if I did not set down my recollections of this episode at all, but shared it only with my companion—she
who experienced it with me; then it would not be covered
with the dust of third-hand knowledge. But I did record it,
and I feel the need to share it with others. Why? It is not because I want to tell others something amusing about myself or
have them hear something about me that I consider poetic,
but because of something else—an intangible "third force"
that does not belong either to me or to others. It is this force
which makes me see things the way I do and interpret all that
happens [to me] from a particular perspective, and then describe it as only I know how. This third force is art. And I
am not a free man, and although I am in the government service, my position is an illegal one, because I am not free; I
serve art, that third force which from the world of outer reality brings me to another world, all its own—the world of
art. Therefore, speaking as an artist I must inform you without attempting in any way to thrust my views on you (for in
the world of art there is no such thing as pressure) that the
descent underground and the mountain climb which I described have many features in common, if not with the process of creation, then at least with one of the modes of com-
prehending a work of art.

The best preparation for attaining such understanding is to
experience the sort of feeling which arises in the wanderer
who suddenly finds himself in a forest clearing, in the land of
the machaon butterflies, or beside an aqueduct at the foot of a
mountain. I am not saying that this is the only method; there
are others that are equally reliable: for example, to suffer
great misfortunes or wrongs in life, or to experience the deep
physical fatigue that accompanies prolonged mental idleness.
But these are extreme alternatives, so to speak, and the first
way is for me the most natural and the most dependable. One

can achieve this through repeated efforts or through one's own merits. But to work consistently at such an unusual task is not easy for anyone in the rush of our civilization. Everyone is in such a hurry nowadays . . .

Autumn 1909; April 1920

WIRBALLEN [1]

Late at night, in the huge, dark hall of the Wirballen customs house, reeking with carbolic acid, passengers from the German train were lined up along a dirty counter, and the customs inspection began. It went on for a long time; stacks of somebody's books were taken to some police station or other in an amiable and courteous manner. When the inspection was over, it seemed as though the passengers had passed a final examination: everyone felt relieved.

When I awoke in the morning, I looked out of the window of the railway carriage. It was drizzling, the plowed fields were slushy, the bushes were drooping. A lonely watchman with a gun slung over his shoulder was trotting along on his nag. I had a sudden, blinding sense of where I was: back in my ill-starred Russia befouled by the spittle of government clerks—dirty, downtrodden, dribbling, the laughingstock of the whole world. Hail, Motherland!

The train has just left Dvinsk, and the next large station will be Reghitza; Reghitza is still a long way off. Besides, what is there in Reghitza? The same platform, wet all over, gray storm clouds, two telegraph operators and a peasant woman trying to outshout the wind. This is broad daylight in Russia, after the mists of Umbria, the moist air of Lombardy

[1] This essay was included by Blok in "Lightning Flashes of Art" although it actually deals with his return to Russia.

and the transparent German Gothic mornings. Cozy, quiet, slow slush. But—"I want to live so passionately," exclaims the colonel in *The Three Sisters.*

By evening we will be in Petersburg. What is there, really, in Petersburg? Is it not another large, wet and cozy Reghitza? However much you may gad about on express trains all you will see is the "striped mileposts." What is Reghitza to you, what is Dvinsk or Petersburg? It's all the same slush.

And now feelings awaken within you of a kind you do not experience when "abroad." For example, whatever a man does in Russia, your first reaction to him is invariably one of pity. You feel sorry for a man who eats with a big appetite; or for a German, his face pockmarked with eczema, who watches in perplexity as his porter exchanges vulgar abuse with someone else's porter; you feel sorry when a customs officer who all his life has seen people travelling abroad and returning home, but has never himself been abroad, asks passengers courteously and yet condescendingly whether they have anything to declare, where they have been and where they are going . . .

All these are poor devils and pathetic people, and there is no use expecting anything of them; all one can do is to feel sorry for them and to shed a tear over each wet Reghitza. Peasant woman, whom are you shouting at—it's no use, you cannot outshout the wind! Muzhik, why are you trying to enter a second-class carriage—it's no use, they won't let you in. Gendarme, why do you insist on peeping through the window—there will always be someone you will miss. You cannot count them all—the peasant women, the muzhiks, the gendarmes, the criminals; nor can you count up all the places where they spend their lives; they all look the same, as one sentry box is just like another, or as the barracks of a local garrison always resemble a dog's kennel. Everywhere it is raining, everywhere there is a wooden church, a telegraph operator, and a gendarme!

Autumn 1909

THE ITALIAN POEMS

*The Russian texts with
English translations
on facing pages*

РАВЕННА

Всё, что минутно, всё, что бренно,
Похоронила ты в веках.
Ты, как младенец, спишь, Равенна,
У сонной вечности в руках.

Рабы сквозь римские ворота
Уже не ввозят мозаик.
И догорает позолота
В стенах прохладных базилик.

От медленных лобзаний влаги
Нежнее грубый свод гробниц,
Где зеленеют саркофаги
Святых монахов и цариц.

Безмолвны гробовые залы,
Тенист и хладен их порог,

[1]   RAVENNA

All that is fleeting, all that is mortal,
You have buried in the ages.
Like an infant, you sleep, Ravenna,
In the arms of a drowsing eternity.

Slaves no longer haul mosaic tiles
Through the Roman gates.
And the gilt is burning out
On the walls of cool basilicas.

From the slow kisses of the damp
The rough vaulting of the crypts has grown gentler,
Where the sarcophagi of holy monks and empresses
Have a green hue.

Silent are the burial halls,
Shadowy and cold their thresholds,

Чтоб черный взор блаженной Галлы,
Проснувшись, камня не прожег.

Военной брани и обиды
Забыт и стерт кровавый след,
Чтобы воскресший глас Плакиды
Не пел страстей протекших лет.

Далёко отступило море,
И розы оцепили вал,
Чтоб спящий в гробе Теодорих
О буре жизни не мечтал.

А виноградные пустыни,
Дома и люди — всё гроба.
Лишь медь торжественной латыни
Поет на плитах, как труба.

Лишь в пристальном и тихом взоре
Равеннских девушек, порой,
Печаль о невозвратном море
Проходит робкой чередой.

Лишь по ночам, склонясь к долинам,
Ведя векам грядущим счет,
Тень Данта с профилем орлиным
О Новой Жизни мне поет.

Май — июнь 1909

Lest, awakening, Blessed Galla's
Black glance should burn through the stone.

Of warlike affray and wrong,
The bloody trace is wiped away and forgot,
Lest the voice of Placidia resurrected
Should sing the passions of bygone years.

The sea has retreated afar,
And roses surround the rampart,
To keep Theodoric, asleep in his tomb,
From dreaming of the storms of life.

And the wastes where once were vineyards,
Homes and men—all are tombs.
Only the bronze of stately Latin
Sings out trumpet-like on the slabs of graves.

Only in the intent and tranquil gaze
Of Ravenna's maidens a sadness
For the unreturning sea
Sometimes shines forth timidly, then vanishes.

Only by night, bending over the valleys,
Keeping count of the future centuries,
Dante's shade with its eagle profile,
Sings to me of a New Life.

May–June 1909

Почиет в мире Теодорих,
И Дант не встанет с ложа сна.
Где прежде бушевало море,
Там — виноград и тишина.
В ласкающем и тихом взоре
Равеннских девушек — весна.

Здесь голос страсти невозможен,
Ответа нет моей мольбе!
О, как я пред тобой ничтожен!
Завидую твоей судьбе,
О, Галла! — страстию к тебе
Всегда взволнован и встревожен!

Июнь 1909

[2]

Theodoric rests in peace,
Nor will Dante rise from his bed of sleep.
There, where the sea once raged,
Are vineyards and silence.
In the caressing and tranquil gaze
Of Ravenna's girls—it is spring.

Impossible here is passion's voice,
There is no answer to my plea!
Oh, how insignificant I am before you!
I envy your fate,
Oh Galla!—Always I have been
Stirred and disquieted by my passion for you!

June 1909

ДЕВУШКА ИЗ SPOLETO

Строен твой стан, как церковные свечи.
Взор твой — мечами пронзающий взор.
Дева, не жду ослепительной встречи —
Дай, как монаху, взойти на костер!

Счастья не требую. Ласки не надо.
Лаской ли грубой тебя оскорблю?
Лишь, как художник, смотрю за ограду,
Где ты срываешь цветы, — и люблю!

Мимо, всё мимо — ты ветром гонима —
Солнцем палима — Мария! Позволь
Взору — прозреть над тобой херувима,
Сердцу — изведать сладчайшую боль!

Тихо я в темные кудри вплетаю
Тайных стихов драгоценный алмаз.
Жадно влюбленное сердце бросаю
В темный источник сияющих глаз.

3 июня 1909

THE GIRL FROM SPOLETO

Shapely your form as church candles.
Your glance—a glance that pierces like swords.
Maiden, I expect no startling encounter—
Let me like a monk ascend the pyre!

I do not ask for happiness. I do not need caresses.
Would I offend you with a rude caress?
Only, as an artist, I look beyond the fence
Where you are gathering flowers—and I love!

Past, always past—you are driven by the wind—
Burned by the sun—Maria! Let my eyes
Discern a cherub above you,
And my heart—taste the sweetest pain!

Quietly into your dark curls I weave
The precious diamond of secret verses.
Greedily I cast my loving heart
Into the dark well of your glowing eyes.

June 3, 1909

ВЕНЕЦИЯ

1

С ней уходил я в море,
С ней покидал я берег,
С нею я был далёко,
С нею забыл я близких...

О, красный парус
В зеленой да́ли!
Черный стеклярус
На темной шали!

Идет от сумрачной обедни,
Нет в сердце крови...
Христос, уставший крест нести...

Адриатической любови —
Моей последней —
Прости, прости!

9 мая 1909

2

Евг. Иванову

Холодный ветер от лагуны.
Гондол безмолвные гроба.
Я в эту ночь — больной и юный —
Простерт у львиного столба.

224

4

VENICE

1

With her I sailed the seas,
With her I left the shores behind,
With her I traveled far away,
With her I forgot those near and dear to me . . .

> Oh red sail
> In the green distance!
> Black glass beads
> On a dark shawl!

[He] comes from a somber Mass,
There is no [more] blood in [his] heart . . .
Christ, tired of bearing his cross . . .

> To my Adriatic love—
> To my last one—
> Farewell, farewell!

May 9, 1909

[5]   2

To Evgenii Ivanov

A cold wind off the lagoon.
The silent coffins of the gondolas.
And I, on this night—young and ill—
[Am lying] stretched out beside the lion's column.

На башне, с песнию чугунной,
Гиганты бьют полночный час.
Марк утопил в лагуне лунной
Узорный свой иконостас.

В тени дворцовой галлереи,
Чуть озаренная луной,
Таясь, проходит Саломея
С моей кровавой головой.

Всё спит — дворцы, каналы, люди,
Лишь призрака скользящий шаг,
Лишь голова на черном блюде
Глядит с тоской в окрестный мрак.

Август 1909

3

Слабеет жизни гул упорный.
Уходит вспять прилив забот.
И некий ветр сквозь бархат черный
О жизни будущей поет.

Очнусь ли я в другой отчизне,
Не в этой сумрачной стране?
И памятью об этой жизни
Вздохну ль когда-нибудь во сне?

Кто даст мне жизнь? Потомок дожа,
Купец, рыбак, иль иерей
В грядущем мраке делит ложе
С грядущей матерью моей?

Быть может, венецейской девы
Канцоной нежной слух пленя,
Отец грядущий сквозь напевы
Уже предчувствует меня?

И неужель в грядущем веке
Младенцу мне — велит судьба

On the tower, with iron song,
Giants beat out the midnight hour.
Mark has drowned its lacework portals
In the moonlit lagoon.

In the shadow of the palace arcade,
In the moon's faint light,
Stealthily Salome passes by
With my bloody head.

All is asleep—palaces, canals, people,
Only the gliding footstep of the phantom,
Only the head on the black platter
Gazes with anguish into the surrounding gloom.

August 1909

[6]   3

Life's persistent din is fading,
The tide of cares recedes.
And a certain wind through the black velvet
Sings about a future life.

Shall I awaken in another homeland
And not in this land of gloom?
And will I in a dream some day
Sigh over the memory of this life?

Who will give me life? Will the descendant
    of a doge,
A merchant, fisherman, or priest
Share his bed in the future darkness
With my future mother?

Perhaps my future father,
Charming a Venetian maiden
With a tender *canzone*,
Already has a presentiment of me as he sings?

And can it be that in a future century
Fate will command that I, a babe,

Впервые дрогнувшие веки
Открыть у львиного столба?

Мать, чтó поют глухие струны?
Уж ты мечтаешь, может быть,
Меня от ветра, от лагуны
Священной шалью оградить?

Нет! Всё, что есть, что было, — живо!
Мечты, виденья, думы — прочь!
Волна возвратного прилива
Бросает в бархатную ночь!

26 августа 1909

Shall first open my quivering eyelids
Beside the lion's column?

Mother, of what do these dull chords sing?
Are you, perchance, already dreaming
Of shielding me from the wind, from the lagoon,
With your sacred shawl?

No! Only what is or has been—lives!
Reveries, visions, thoughts, begone!
The wave of the returning tide
Breaks into the velvety night!

August 26, 1909

ПЕРУДЖИЯ

День полувеселый, полустрадный,
Голубая даль от Умбрских гор.
Вдруг — минутный ливень, ветр прохладный,
За окном открытым — громкий хор.

Там — в окне, под фреской Перуджино,
Черный глаз смеется, дышит грудь:
Кто-то смуглою рукой корзину
Хочет и не смеет дотянуть...

На корзине — белая записка:
«Questa sera... монастырь Франциска...»

Июнь 1909

7

PERUGIA

A day half joyful, half laden with toil,
The faraway blue of the Umbrian hills.
Suddenly—a brief downpour, a cool wind,
And through an open window—a loud chorus.

There in the window, under a fresco by Perugino,
Laughing black eyes, a heaving breast:
Someone's dark hand reaches for a basket,
Wants to pull it in, yet does not dare . . .

And on the basket—a white note
"Questa sera . . . The Franciscan monastery . . ."

June 1909

ФЛОРЕНЦИЯ

1

Умри, Флоренция, Иуда,
Исчезни в сумрак вековой!
Я в час любви тебя забуду,
В час смерти буду не с тобой!

О, Bella, смейся над собою,
Уж не прекрасна больше ты!
Гнилой морщиной гробовою
Искажены твои черты!

Хрипят твои автомобили,
Твои уродливы дома,
Всеевропейской желтой пыли
Ты предала себя сама!

Звенят в пыли велосипеды
Там, где святой монах сожжен,
Где Леонардо сумрак ведал,
Беато снился синий сон!

Ты пышных Ме́дичей тревожишь,
Ты топчешь лили́и свои,
Но воскресить себя не можешь
В пыли торговой толчеи!

8

FLORENCE

I

Die, Florence, you Judas,
Vanish in the darkness of ages!
In the hour of love I will forget you,
In the hour of death I shall not be with you!

Oh, Bella, laugh at yourself,
You are no longer beautiful!
Your features are disfigured
With grave-rotted wrinkles!

Your automobiles wheeze
Your houses are hideous,
You have betrayed yourself
For Europe's yellow dust!

Bicycles jingle in the dust
There, where the holy monk was burned,
Where Leonardo beheld the dusk,
And Beato dreamed his blue dream!

You are disturbing the magnificent Medici,
You are trampling on your own lilies,
But you cannot resurrect yourself
In the dust of jostling trade!

Гнусавой мессы стон протяжный
И трупный запах роз в церквах —
Весь груз тоски многоэтажный —
Сгинь в очистительных веках!

Май — июнь 1909

2

Флоренция, ты ирис нежный;
По ком томился я один
Любовью длинной, безнадежной,
Весь день в пыли твоих Кашин?

О, сладко вспомнить безнадежность:
Мечтать и жить в твоей глуши;
Уйти в твой древний зной и в нежность
Своей стареющей души...

Но суждено нам разлучиться,
И через дальние края
Твой дымный ирис будет сниться,
Как юность ранняя моя.

Июнь 1909

3

Страстью длинной, безмятежной
Занялась душа моя,
Ирис дымный, ирис нежный,
Благовония струя,
Переплыть велит все реки
На воздушных парусах,
Утонуть велит навеки
В тех вечерних небесах,
И когда предамся зною,
Голубой вечерний зной
В голубое голубою
Унесет меня волной...

Июнь 1909

The long-drawn drone of a nasal mass
And the corpse-like smell of roses in your churches—
The whole multistoried burden of your weary boredom—
Begone! Disappear into the purifying centuries!

May–June 1909

[9]   2

Florence, you are a delicate iris;
For whom was I pining in solitude
With a lingering, hopeless love,
All day long in the dust of your *Cascine?*

O, it is sweet to recall hopelessness:
To dream and live in your rustic seclusion;
To withdraw into your ancient heat
And into the gentleness of one's own aging soul . . .

But it is our destiny to part,
And from faraway lands
I'll see in dreams your smoky iris,
Like my early youth.

June 1909

[10]   3

A lingering, tranquil passion
Has awakened in my soul.
The smoky, delicate iris,
A fragrant stream, bids me
Sail across all rivers
On aery sails,
And drown forever
In those evening skies.
And when I surrender myself to the heat,
The blue evening heat
Will carry me off into the blue
On a wave of blue . . .

June 1909

4

Жгут раскаленные камни
Мой лихорадочный взгляд.
Дымные ирисы в пламени,
Словно сейчас улетят.
О, безысходность печали,
Знаю тебя наизусть!
В черное небо Италии
Черной душою гляжусь.

Июнь 1909

5

Окна ложные нá небе черном,
И прожектор на древнем дворце.
Вот проходит она — вся в узорном
И с улыбкой на смуглом лице.

А вино уж мутит мои взоры
И по жилам огнем разлилось...
Что мне спеть в этот вечер, синьора?
Что мне спеть, чтоб вам сладко спалось?

Июнь 1909

6

Под зноем флорентийской лени
Еще беднее чувством ты:
Молчат церковные ступени,
Цветут нерадостно цветы.

Так береги остаток чувства,
Храни хоть творческую ложь:
Лишь в легком челноке искусства
От скуки мира уплывешь.

11 мая 1909

4

The red-hot stones
Burn my feverish gaze.
Smoky irises in flame,
As if about to fly away.
Oh, hopelessness of sorrow,
I know you by heart!
I stare into the black sky of Italy
That mirrors my black soul.

June 1909

5

False windows against a black sky
And a spotlight on an ancient palace.
There—she is passing by, all in frills and lace,
With a smile on her tanned face.

But already the wine clouds my vision
And streams through my veins like fire . . .
What shall I sing to you tonight, Signora?
What shall I sing to make your dreams sweet?

June 1909

13

6

In the stifling heat and lethargy of Florence
You become even poorer in feeling:
Church steps are silent,
Flowers bloom without joy.

So guard the remnant of your feeling,
Cherish at least the creative lie.
For only in art's light barque,
Will you glide away from the boredom of the world.

May 17, 1909

Голубоватым дымом
Вечерний зной возносится,
Долин тосканских царь...

Он мимо, мимо, мимо
Летучей мышью бросится
Под уличный фонарь...

И вот уже в долинах
Несметный сонм огней,
И вот уже в витринах
Ответный блеск камней,
И город скрыли горы
В свой сумрак голубой,
И тешатся синьоры
Канцоной площадной.

Дымится пыльный ирис,
И легкой пеной пенится
Бокал Христовых Слез...

Пляши и пой на пире,
Флоренция, изменница,
В венке спаленных роз!..

Сведи с ума канцоной
О преданной любви,
И сделай ночь бессонной,
И струны оборви,
И бей в свой бубен гулкий,
Рыдания тая!
В пустынном переулке
Скорбит душа твоя...

Август 1909

In light bluish smoke
The stifling heat of the evening rises,
The king of the Tuscan valleys . . .

It sweeps on and on
It hurls itself like a bat
Against the street lamps . . .

And over in the valleys
Lights already shine in countless throng,
And from the shop windows comes
The answering gleam of precious stones.

And the mountains have hidden the city
In their light blue twilight,
And the *signori* are amused
By a ribald *canzone.*

The dusty iris smolders,
And a goblet of Christ's Tears
Foams with light froth.

Dance and sing at the banquet,
Faithless Florence,
In a wreath of scorched roses!

Drive me mad with a *canzone*
Of devoted love,
Make the night sleepless,
And tear the strings,
And beat your hollow tambourine
Hiding your sobs!
In a deserted alleyway
Your soul mourns . . .

August 1909

* * *

Вот девушка, едва развившись,
Еще не потупляясь, не краснея,
Непостижимо черным взглядом
Смотрит мне навстречу.
Была бы на то моя воля,
Просидел бы я всю жизнь в Сеттиньяно,
У выветрившегося камня Септимия Севе́ра.
Смотрел бы я на камни, залитые солнцем,
На красивую загорелую шею и спину
Некрасивой женщины под дрожащими
                                         тополями.

15 мая 1909
Settignano

Here's a young girl, barely in bloom,
Who still does not lower her eyes, nor blush,
As I approach she gazes at me
With her dark impenetrable glance.
And if I had my way, I'd spend my whole life in Set-
    tignano,
Beside the wind-weathered stone of Septimus Severus.
I'd look at the rocks, flooded by the sun,
At the beautiful sunburnt neck and back
Of an unbeautiful woman beneath the trembling
    poplars.

May 15, 1909
Settignano

MADONNA DA SETTIGNANO

Встретив на горном тебя перевале,
    Мой прояснившийся взор
Понял тосканские дымные дали
    И очертания гор.

Желтый платок твой разубран цветами —
    Сонный то маковый цвет.
Смотришь большими, как небо, глазами
    Бедному страннику вслед.

Дашь ли запреты забыть вековые
    Вечному путнику — мне?
Страстно твердить твое имя, Мария,
    Здесь, на чужой стороне?

3 июня 1909

16

MADONNA DA SETTIGNANO

After I met you on the mountain pass
 My vision became clear, and I understood
The smoky distances of Tuscany
 And the outlines of the mountains.

Your yellow kerchief is adorned with flowers
 Of a somnolent, poppy-colored shade.
Your eyes as large as the sky
 Follow the poor wayfarer as he walks on by.

Will you grant to me—an eternal wanderer
 Permission to forget age-old prohibitions?
And may I passionately proclaim your name, Maria,
 Here, in a strange land?

June 3, 1909

ФЬЕЗОЛЕ

Стучит топор, и с кампанил
К нам флорентийский звон долинный
Плывет, доплыл и разбудил
Сон золотистый и старинный...

Не так же ли стучал топор
В нагорном Фьézоле когда-то,
Когда впервые взор Беато
Флоренцию приметил с гор?

Июнь 1909

17

FIESOLE

An ax is striking, and from the *campanili*
The ringing sound of the valley of Florence
Flows toward us; it has arrived and awakened
A golden, ancient dream . . .

Did not the ax strike just that way
Long ago in hilly Fiesole,
When first Beato's gaze
Caught sight of Florence from the mountain?

June 1909

СИЕНА

В лоне площади пологой
Пробивается трава.
Месяц острый, круторогий,
Башни — свечи божества.

О, лукавая Сиена,
Вся — колчан упругих стрел!
Вероломство и измена —
Твой таинственный удел!

От соседних лоз и пашен
Оградясь со всех сторон,
Острия церквей и башен
Ты вонзила в небосклон!

И томленьем дух влюбленный
Исполняют образа,
Где коварные мадонны
Щурят длинные глаза:

Пусть грозит младенцу буря,
Пусть грозит младенцу враг,
Мать глядится в мутный мрак,
Очи влажные сощуря!..

7 июня 1909

18

SIENA

On a gently sloping square
Grass breaks through.
The moon is sharp-pointed, like a horn,
The towers are candles to the Divine.

O cunning Siena, the whole of you—
A quiver of supple arrows!
Perfidy and treason—
Are your secret destiny!

Walled off on all sides
From neighboring fields and vineyards,
You have pierced the vault of the heavens
With the pointed spires of your churches and towers!

The enamoured spirit languishes
Before the holy images,
In which treacherous Madonnas
Narrow their elongated eyes.

What if the infant is threatened by a storm,
What if the infant is threatened by a foe,
The mother gazes into the murky gloom,
Her moist eyes asquint! . . .

June 7, 1909

СИЕНСКИЙ СОБОР

Когда страшишься смерти скорой,
Когда твои неярки дни, —
К плитам Сиенского собора
Свой натруженный взор склони.

Скажи, где место вечной ночи?
Вот здесь — Сивиллины уста
В безумном трепете пророчат
О воскресении Христа.

Свершай свое земное дело,
Довольный возрастом своим.
Здесь под резцом оцепенело
Всё то, над чем мы ворожим.

Вот — мальчик над цветком и с птицей,
Вот — муж с пергаментом в руках,
Вот — дряхлый старец над гробницей
Склоняется на двух клюках.

Молчи, душа. Не мучь, не трогай,
Не понуждай и не зови:
Когда-нибудь придет он, строгий,
Кристально-ясный час любви.

Июнь 1909

19

THE SIENA CATHEDRAL

When you are in fear of dying soon,
When your days are overcast,
Turn your weary glance
To the tombstones of Siena Cathedral.

Tell me, where is the place of eternal night?
It is here—the lips of the Sibyls
In senseless frenzy prophesy
The Resurrection of Christ.

Fulfill your earthly task,
Be satisfied with your allotted span.
Here beneath the chisel, all our fortunetelling,
Our incantations have turned to stone.

Here a boy with a bird stands over a flower,
Here is a man with a parchment in his hands,
Here—a decrepit old man
Bends on his two crutches over a tomb.

Be still, my soul. Do not torment me or arouse me,
Do not constrain me, do not summon me:
Someday it will come—the stark,
Crystal-clear hour of love.

June 1909

Искусство — ноша на плечах,
Зато как мы, поэты, ценим
Жизнь в мимолетных мелочах!
Как сладостно предаться лени,
Почувствовать, как в жилах кровь
Переливается певуче,
Бросающую в жар любовь
Поймать за тучкою летучей,
И грезить, будто жизнь сама
Встает во всем шампанском блеске
В мурлыкающем нежно треске
Мигающего cinéma!
А через год — в чужой стране:
Усталость, город неизвестный,
Толпа, — и вновь на полотне
Черты француженки прелестной!..

Июнь 1909
Foligno

20

Art is a burden on our shoulders,
And yet how we poets cherish
Life in all its fleeting trifles!
How sweet it is to surrender to indolence,
To feel the blood rush
Singing through one's veins,
To catch behind a fleeting cloud,
The leaping, kindling flame of love,
And to dream as if life itself
Were rising up in all its champagne sparkle,
In the gently purring crackle of a cinema
With its swiftly flashing images!
And a year later—in a foreign land:
Weariness, a strange city, a crowd—
And once again on the screen
The features of that same delightful French
    girl! . . .

June 1909
Foligno

* * *

Глаза, опущенные скромно,
Плечо, закрытое фатой...
Ты многим кажешься святой,
Но ты, Мария, вероломна...

Быть с девой — быть во власти ночи,
Качаться на морских волнах...
И не напрасно эти очи
К мирянам ревновал монах:

Он в нише сумрачной церковной
Поставил с братией ее —
Подальше от мечты греховной,
В молитвенное забытье...

Однако, братьям надоело
. . . .
. . . .
. . . .

Конец преданьям и туманам!
Теперь — во всех церквах она
Равно — монахам и мирянам
На поруганье предана...

Но есть один вздыхатель тайный
Красы божественной — поэт...
Он видит твой необычайный,
Немеркнущий, Мария, свет!

21

Eyes that are modestly lowered,
A shoulder covered with a veil . . .
To many you seem holy,
But, Mary, you are faithless . . .

To be with the virgin is to be in night's power,
It is to ride over the waves of the sea . . .
Small wonder that those eyes
Made the monk jealous of the layman.

He and his brethren placed her
In a somber niche in the church,
Away from sinful dreams
In prayerful oblivion . . .

But the brethren grew tired
. . . .
. . . .
. . . .

But so much for legends and things obscure!
Now, in all the churches,
She is being profaned
By monks and laymen alike . . .

But there is one secret admirer
Of her divine beauty—the poet . . .
He sees, o Mary, your singular
And unfading light!

Он на коленях в нише темной
Замолит страстные грехи,
Замолит свой восторг нескромный,
Свои греховные стихи!

И ты, чье сердце благосклонно,
Не гневайся и не дивись,
Что взглянет он порой влюбленно
В твою ласкающую высь!

12 июня 1909

On his knees in your dark niche
He'll seek forgiveness for his sins of passion,
He'll seek forgiveness for his immodest raptures,
His sinful verses!

And you, whose heart is compassionate,
Be not angered or astonished
That now and again he gazes lovingly
Up to your realm of gentleness!

June 12, 1909

БЛАГОВЕЩЕНИЕ

С детских лет — видения и грезы,
Умбрии ласкающая мгла.
На оградах вспыхивают розы,
Тонкие, поют колокола.

Слишком резвы милые подруги,
Слишком дерзок их открытый взор.
Лишь она одна в предвечном круге
Ткет и ткет свой шелковый узор.

Робкие томят ее надежды,
Грезятся несбыточные сны.
И внезапно — красные одежды
Дрогнули на золоте стены.

Всем лицом склонилась над шелками,
Но везде — сквозь золото ресниц —
Вихрь ли с многоцветными крылами,
Или ангел, распростертый ниц...

Темноликий ангел с дерзкой ветвью
Молвит: «Здравствуй! Ты полна красы!»
И она дрожит пред страстной вестью,
С плеч упали тяжких две косы...

Он поет и шепчет — ближе, ближе,
Уж над ней — шумящих крыл шатер...
И она без сил склоняет ниже
Потемневший, помутневший взор...

ANNUNCIATION

Since childhood years—visions and daydreams,
Umbria's caressing mists.
Roses burst into flame on the fences,
The thin bells sing.

Her dear girl friends are too playful,
Their frank look is too bold.
She alone in an eternal circle
Weaves and weaves her silken design.

Her timid hopes weary her,
She dreams impossible dreams.
And suddenly—red garments
Quiver against the gold of the wall.

She bows her head low over her silks,
But everywhere—through the gold of her lashes—
Is it a whirlwind with many-colored wings,
Or an angel prostrate before her . . .

The dark-faced angel with a bold branch
Speaks: "Hail! Thou art full of beauty!"
And she trembles at his passionate tidings,
Her two heavy braids fall from her shoulders . . .

He sings and whispers—closer and closer,
He is above her now—a tent of rustling wings . . .
And she, bereft of strength, lowers still more
Her dimmed and darkened gaze . . .

Трепеща, не верит: «Я ли, я ли?»
И рукою закрывает грудь...
Но чернеют пламенные дали —
Не уйти, не встать и не вздохнуть...

И тогда — незнаемою болью
Озарился светлый круг лица...
А над ними — символ своеволья —
Перуджийский гриф когтит тельца.

Лишь художник, занавесью скрытый, —
Он провидит страстной муки крест
И твердит: «Profani, procul ite,
Hic amoris locus sacer est».

Май — июнь 1909
Perudgia — Spoleto

Trembling in disbelief: "Is it I, is it I?"
And covers her breast with her hand . . .
But the flaming distances turn black—
She cannot leave, nor rise, nor breathe . . .

And then—the radiant circle of her face
Is aglow with unknown pain . . .
And above them—the symbol of self-will—
Perugia's griffin—claws a calf.

Only the artist, hidden behind a curtain,—
Foresees the cross of passionate torment
And repeats: *"Profani, procul ite,*
Hic amoris locus sacer est."

May–June 1909
Perugia—Spoleto

УСПЕНИЕ

Ее спеленутое тело
Сложили в молодом лесу.
Оно от мук помолодело,
Вернув бывалую красу.

Уже не шумный и не ярый,
С волненьем, в сжатые персты
В последний раз архангел старый
Влагает белые цветы.

Златит далекие вершины
Прощальным отблеском заря,
И над туманами долины
Встают усопших три царя.

Их привела, как в дни былые,
Другая, поздняя звезда.
И пастухи, уже седые,
Как встарь, сгоняют с гор стада.

И стражей вечному покою
Долины заступила мгла.
Лишь меж звездою и зарею
Златятся нимбы без числа.

А выше, по крутым оврагам
Поет ручей, цветет миндаль,
И над открытым саркофагом
Могильный ангел смотрит в даль.

4 июня 1909
Spoleto

23

ASSUMPTION

They laid out her shrouded body
In the young forest.
From the torments it had borne
It had grown young again, its beauty restored.

No longer loud and raging,
But with feeling, an old Archangel
For the last time puts white flowers
Into her clasped hands.

The sunset gilds the far-off heights
With a parting glow of farewell,
And the three dead kings
Arise above the valley fogs.

Another belated star has brought them hither
As in the days of yore,
And the shepherds, grey-haired now,
As of old drive their flocks from the hills.

And the mist has now come forth to guard
The valley's eternal peace.
Only between the star and the dawn
Countless halos glow.

And up above, through steep ravines
There sings a brook, there blooms an almond tree,
And over the open sarcophagus
The angel of the sepulcher gazes into the distance.

June 4, 1909
Spoleto

ЭПИТАФИЯ ФРА ФИЛИППО ЛИППИ

Здесь я покоюсь, Филипп, живописец навеки
                             бессмертный,
Дивная прелесть моей кисти — у всех на устах.
Душу умел я вдохнуть искусными пальцами в краски,
Набожных души умел — голосом бога смутить.
Даже природа сама, на мои заглядевшись созданья,
Принуждена меня звать мастером равным себе.

В мраморном этом гробу меня упокоил Лаврентий
Ме́дичи, прежде чем я в низменный прах обращусь.

17 марта 1914

---

    * Эпитафия сочинена Полицианом и вырезана на могильной плите художника в Сполетском соборе по повелению Лаврентия Великолепного.

24

EPITAPH TO FRA FILIPPO LIPPI *

Here I lie at rest, I Philippus, a painter forever immortal,
The wondrous enchantment of my brush is on everyone's lips.
With my artful fingers I knew how to breathe a soul into my colors,
I knew how to confound the souls of the pious with the voice of
     God.
Even nature herself, marveling at my creations,
Could not help speaking of me as a master equal to herself.

Lorenzo de'Medici laid me to rest in this marble tomb
Before I am changed into lowly dust.

March 17, 1914

* This epitaph by Poliziano was inscribed on the tombstone of the
painter following the instructions of Lorenzo the Magnificent [A.
Blok].

Bibliography

The Works of Aleksandr Blok

Sobranie sochinenii v vos'mi tomakh. Edited by V. N. Orlov, A. A. Surkov, K. I. Chukovskii. Moscow, 1960–1965.

Zapisnye knizhki A. Bloka. Edited by P. N. Medvedev. Leningrad, 1930.

Zapisnye knizhki. 1901–1920. Edited by V. N. Orlov. Moscow, 1965.

Pis'ma Aleksandra Bloka k rodnym. 2 vols. Moscow, 1927, 1932.

Aleksandr Blok, Andrei Belyi: Perepiska. Edited by V. N. Orlov. Moscow, 1940.

Kniga o Leonide Andreeve. "Vospominaniia A. Bloka." Berlin, 1922.

Russkie pisateli o literaturnom trude. Vol. IV. Leningrad, 1956.

"Aleksandr Blok u mikrofona." *Krugozor* VII (July 1967), Record 5.

"A. Blok i zhivopis': tri neopublikobannykh pis'ma Bloka," ed. K. Rovda, *Russkaia Literatura,* II (1962), 174–176.

Soloviev, Sergei. *Pis'ma Aleksandra Bloka.* Leningrad, 1925.

Biographical and Critical Material.
Reminiscences of Contemporaries.

Abernathy, Albert. "A Vowel Fugue in Blok." *International Journal of Slavic Linguistic and Poetics* VII (1963), 88–107.

Adamovich, Georgii. "Aleksandr Blok." *Sovremennye zapiski* XLVII (1931), 283–305.

Aikhenvald, Iu. *Siluety russkikh pisatelei,* Vol. 3. Berlin, 1923, pp. 250–264.

Alfonsov, V. "Blok i zhivopic' ital'anskogo vozrozhdeniia: po motivam ital'anskikh stikhov." *Russkaia literatura* III (1959), 169–177.

——. *Slova i kraski.* Moscow–Leningrad, 1966, pp. 13–88.

Alianskii, S. M. *Vstrechi s Blokom.* Moscow, 1969.

Anichkov, E. "Rodnoe: Aleksandr Blok i Andrei Belyi." *Novaia russkaia poeziia,* 1923; rpt. The Hague: Mouton, 1969, pp. 90–108.

Annenkov, I. *Dnevnik moikh vstrech.* Vol. I. New York: Inter-Language Associates, 1966, pp. 56–96.

Antokolskii, P. A. *Poety i vremia.* Moscow, 1957, pp. 49–73.

Ashukin, N. A. *Blok v vospominaniiakh sovremennikov i ego pis'makh.* Moscow, 1924.

Asmus, V. "Filosofiia i estetika russkogo simvolizma." *Literaturnoe nasledstvo* XXVII/XXVIII, 1937.

Bazzarelli, Eridano. *Aleksandr Blok. L'armonia e il caos nel suo mondo poetico.* Milano: U. Mursia & Co., 1968.

Beketova, M. A. *Aleksandr Blok. Biograficheskii ocherk.* Petersburg, 1922.

——. *Aleksandr Blok i ego mat': vospominaniia i zametki.* Leningrad-Moscow, 1925.

Belyi, Andrei [B. N. Bugaev]. "Vospominaniia ob A. Bloke." *Epopeia* I (1922), 123–278, II (1922), 105–299, III (1922), 125–301, IV (1923), 61–305.

——. *Poeziia slova.* Petersburg, 1922, pp. 27–34.

——. *Nachalo veka.* Moscow–Leningrad, 1933, pp. 258–262, 287–347.

——. *Mezhdu dvukh revoliutsii.* Leningrad, 1934, pp. 326–336.

Berberova, Nina. *Alexandre Blok et son temps,* suivi d'un choix de poèmes. Paris, 1947.

Berg-Papendick, Wanda. "Vvedenie." *Der Mystiker Aleksandr Block im Spiegel seiner Lyrik.* Frankfurt-Mainz, 1967, pp. 6–31.

Blagoi, D. D. *Tri veka.* Moscow, 1933, pp. 269–300, 323–340.

Blokovskii sbornik. Ed. by I. Lotman. Tartu, 1964.

Bobrov, Sergei. "Simvolist Blok." *Krasnaia nov'* I (1922), 244–250.

Bonneau, Sophie. *L'univers poétique d'Alexandre Blok*. Paris, 1946.

Bowra, C. M. "The Position of Aleksandr Blok." *The Criterion* XLIV, Vol. XI (April 1932), 422–438.

——. *The Heritage of Symbolism*. London, 1943, pp. 144–179.

Briusov, V. "Aleksandr Blok." *Russkaia mysl'* I (1912), 30–32. VII (1912), 18–19.

——. *Dalekie i blizkie*. Moscow, 1912, pp. 160–162.

——. "Aleksandr Blok." *Izbrannye sochineniia v dvukh tomakh* II (Moscow, 1955), pp. 282–294.

Christa, Boris. "Metrical Innovations in Blok's Lyrical Verse." *Journal of the Australasian Universities (AUMLA)* XVII (May, 1962).

Chukovskii, K. I. *Kniga ob Aleksandre Bloke*. Petersburg, 1922.

——. *Aleksandr Blok, kak chelovek i poet*. Petrograd, 1924.

——. *Sovremenniki*. Moscow, 1962.

Chukovskii, N. "Chto ia pomniu o Bloke." *Novyi mir* II (February, 1967), 229–237.

Chulkov, Georgii, *Nashi sputniki*. Moscow, 1922, pp. 80–89.

Derman, A. "Ob Aleksandre Bloke." *Russkaia Mysl'* VII (July, 1913), 57–71.

Desnitskii, V. A. "Sotsiial'no-psikhologicheskie predposylki tvorchestva A. Bloka," in *Pis'ma Aleksandra Bloka k rodnym*, Vol. II. Moscow–Leningrad, 1932.

Dolgopolov, L. K. *Poemy Bloka i russkaia poema kontsa XIX–nachala XX vekov*. Moscow–Leningrad, 1964.

Eikhenbaum, B. *Skvoz' literaturu*. Leningrad, 1924; rpt. The Hague: Mouton, 1962, pp. 215–232.

Erenburg, I. *Portrety russkikh poetov*. Berlin, 1922, pp. 36–39.

Farber, L. M. "Perepiska iz dvukh mirov." *Neva* 8 (1971), 184–187.

Fedotov, G. P. *Novyi grad*. New York: Chekhov Publishing House, 1952, pp. 274–300.

Fookhd-Stoianova, T. "O kompozitsionnykh povtorakh u Bloka." *Dutch Contributions to the Fourth International Congress of Slavists, Moscow, Sept. 1958*. The Hague, 1958, pp. 175–203.

Ginzburg, L. Ia. *Blokovskii sbornik*. Tartu, 1964, pp. 157–171.

———. *O lirike*. Moscow–Leningrad, 1964, pp. 267–329.

Gippius, V. V. *Ot Pushkina do Bloka*. Moscow, 1966, pp. 331–340.

Gippius, Z. N. "A. Blok." *Zhivye litsa*. Prague, 1925.

Gofman, M. "A. Blok." *Kniga o russkikh poetakh poslednego desiatiletiia*. St. Petersburg, 1907, pp. 297–330.

Golitsyna, V. N. "K voprosy ob esteticheskikh vzgliadakh A. Bloka." *Voprosy russkoi i zarybezhnoi literatury*. Leningrad, 1966, pp. 101–127.

Goltsev, V. V. "Tvorcheskii put' A. Bloka." *Sobranie sochinenii A. Bloka*. Moscow, 1929.

Gordin, A. "Risuet Aleksandr Blok." *Neva* 8 (1971), 188–190.

Gorelov, A. *Groza nad solov'inym sadom. Aleksandr Blok*. Leningrad, 1970.

Gorkii, M. [A. M. Peshkov]. "A. A. Blok." *Russkii sovremennik*. Leningrad, 1924, I, 42–66.

Gromov, Pavel. *Geroi i vremia*. Leningrad, 1961, pp. 385–578.

———. *A. Blok. Ego predshestvenniki i sovremenniki*. Moscow–Leningrad, 1966.

Gumilev, N. "Pis'ma o russkoi poezii." *Apollon* VIII (1912), 60–61.

Ivanoff, Alessandro. "Blok 1909: Significato di una protesta." *Atti dell'Istituto Veneto di scienze, lettere ed arti* CXIX (1960–1961), 125–144.

———. "Realismo equivoco nella prosa di A. A. Blok." *Atti dell'Istituto Veneto di scienze, lettere ed arti* CXVIII (1959–1960), 75–92.

Ivanov, Georgii, *Peterburgskie zimy*. New York: Chekhov Publishing House, 1952.

———. "Stikhi o Rossii—Aleksandra Bloka." *Apollon* VIII–IX (1915), 96–99.

Ivanov-Razumnik, R. V. *Aleksandr Blok. Andrei Belyi*. St. Petersburg, 1919.

———. *Pamiati Aleksandra Bloka*. St. Petersburg, 1922.

———. *Vershiny*. Petrograd, 1923, pp. 16–26, 175–203.

Jakobson, Roman. "Devushka pela." *Orbis scriptus.* Munich: Wilhelm Fink Verlag, 1966, pp. 385–401.

Kemball, Robin. *Aleksandr Blok. A Study in Rhythm and Metre.* The Hague: Mouton and Co., 1965.

Khlodovskii, P. I. "Blok i Dante." *Dante i vsemirnaia literatura.* Edited by N. Balashov. Moscow, 1967, pp. 176–248.

Kisch, Sir Cecil. *Aleksandr Blok. Prophet of Revolution.* New York: Roy Publishers, 1960.

Kniazhnin, V. N. *Aleksandr Aleksandrovich Blok.* St. Petersburg, 1922.

Krasnova, L. V. "Ob odnoi osobennosti poeticheskogo sintaksisa Aleksandra Bloka." *Voprosy russkoi literatury* I (1971), 78–86.

Kruk, I. T. "Blok i Gogol." *Russkaia literatura* I (1961), 85–103.

———. *Poeziia Aleksandra Bloka.* Moscow, 1970.

———. "Obraz demona v poezii Bloka." *Russkaia literatura xx veka.* Kaluga, 1968, pp. 212–226.

Libedinskaia, L. *Zhizn' i stikhi.* Moscow, 1970.

LoGatto, E. *Russi in Italia.* Roma: Editori Riuniti, 1971, pp. 263–277.

Lunacharskii, A. V. *Klassiki russkoi literatury.* Moscow, 1937, pp. 390–423.

Makovskii, Sergei. *Na Parnase "Serebrianogo veka."* Munich, 1962, pp. 143–175.

Maksimov, D. E. "O proze Bloka." *A. Blok. Sobranie sochinenii v vos'mi tomakh,* Vol. V. Moscow–Leningrad, 1962, pp. 695–708.

———. "Lermontov i Blok." *Poeziia Lermontova.* Moscow, 1964, pp. 247–265.

Mandelshtam, Osip. *Sobranie sochinenii.* New York: Chekhov Publishing House, 1955, pp. 358–362.

Mariia, Monakhinia. "Vstrechi s Blokom." *Sovremennye zapiski* LXII (1936), 211–228.

Mashbits-Verov, I. *Russkii simvolizm i put' Aleksandra Bloka.* Kuibyshevskoe knizhnoe izdatel'stvo, 1969.

Maslenikov, Oleg. *The Frenzied Poets: Andrey Biely and the Russian Symbolists*. Berkeley: University of California Press, 1952, pp. 146–196.

Medvedev, Pavel. *Dramy i poemy A. Bloka*. Leningrad, 1928.

Mendeleeva-Blok, L. D. "Tri epizoda iz vospominanii ob Aleksandre Bloke." *Den' Poezii*. Leningrad, 1965, pp. 307–320.

Mikhailovskii, B. V. *Russkaia literatura XX veka*. Moscow, 1939, pp. 259–283.

Minskii, N. "Ot Dante k Bloku." *Sovremennye zapiski* VII (1921), 188–208.

Mochulskii, K. V. *Aleksandr Blok*. Paris, 1948.

Nelie, S. "Romanticheskaia ironiia v kritike burzhuaznogo mira. A. A. Blok." *Krasnaia nov'* X–XI (1931), 235–251.

Nikitina, E. P. and Shuvalov, S. V. *Poeticheskoe iskusstvo Bloka*. Moscow, 1926.

Novikov, Ivan. *Pisatel' i ego tvorchestvo*. Moscow, 1956, pp. 516–523.

Odoevtseva, Irina. *Na beregakh Nevy*. Washington, D.C.: Victor Kamkin, 1967, pp. 252–319.

Orlov, Vladimir. "A. Blok i A. Belyi v 1907 gody." *Literaturnoe nasledstvo* XXVII/XXVIII (1937).

——. *A. Blok*. Moscow, 1956.

——. *Literaturnye pamiatnye mesta Leningrada*. Leningrad, 1959, pp. 435–458.

——. *Puti i sud'by*. Moscow, 1963.

Pamiati Aleksandra Bloka: LXXXIII otkrytoe zasedanie Vol'noi Filosofskoi Assotsiatsii. A. Belyi, R. V. Ivanov-Razumnik, A. Z. Shteinberg. St. Petersburg, 1922.

Panchenko, N. "Aleksandr Blok za chteniem i pravkoi svoikh rannikh stikhov." *Russkaia literatura* III (1967), 198–205.

Papernyi, Z. *Poeticheskie obrazy Maiakovskogo*. Moscow, 1961.

Pascal, P. Trois poètes russes à Venise. *Venezia nelle letterature moderne*. Venice-Rome, 1961.

Pasternak, Boris. "Liudi i polozheniia." *Novyi mir* I (January, 1967), 204–236.

Paustovskii, Konstantin. *Naedine s osen'iu.* Moscow, 1967, pp. 102–109.

Pavlovich, N. A. *Dumy i vospominaniia.* Moscow, 1962.

Pereleshin, Valerii. "Solov'inyi sad Aleksandra Bloka." Grani 68 (1968), pp. 132–136.

Piast, V. A. *Vospominaniia o Bloke.* St. Petersburg, 1923.

Poggioli, Renato. *The Poets of Russia, 1890–1930.* Cambridge: Harvard University Press, 1960, pp. 179–211.

Reeve, F. D. *Aleksandr Blok: Between Image and Idea.* New York: Columbia University Press, 1962.

Remenik, G. A. *Poemy Aleksandra Bloka.* Moscow, 1957.

Ripellino, Angelo Maria. *Letteratura come itinerario nel meraviglioso.* Turin: Einaudi editore, 1968, pp. 125–178.

Rubtsov, A. B. *Dramaturgiia Aleksandra Bloka.* Minsk, 1968.

Russkaia literatura xx veka. Kaluga, 1968.

Rybnikova, M. A. *A. Blok-Gamlet.* Moscow, 1923.

Rylenkov, Nikolai. *Dusha poezii.* Moscow, 1969.

Rylskii, Maksim. *Klassiki i sovremenniki.* Moscow, 1958, pp. 308–314.

Sapogov, V. A. "Liricheskii tsikl i liricheskaia poema v tvorchestve A. Bloka." *Russkaia literatura xx veka.* Kaluga, 1968.

Shcheglov, Mark. *Literaturno-kriticheskie stat'i.* Moscow, 1965, pp. 201–206.

Smolenskii, Vladimir. "Mistika Aleksandra Bloka." *Vozrozhdenie* XXXVII (1955), 110–126, XXXVIII (1955), 91–102.

Soloviev, Boris. *Poet i ego podvig.* Moscow, 1965.

Stepun, Fedor. "Istoriosofskoe i politicheskoe mirosozertsanie Aleksandra Bloka." *Vozdushnye puti* IV (1965), 241–255.

———. *Mystische Weltschau.* Fünf Gestalten de russischen Symbolysmus. Munich: Hanser, 1964, pp. 356–427.

Struve, Gleb, "Tri sud'by." *Novyi Zhurnal* XVI (1947), 209–228.

Tarasenko, A. *Poety.* Moscow, 1956, pp. 320–359.

Terapiano, Iurii. "Aleksandr Blok." *Sovremennik* IV (1961), 54–58.

Timofeev, Leonid. "Poetika kontrasta v poezii Bloka." *Russkaia Literatura* II (1961), 98–107.

Timofeev, Leonid. *A. Blok.* Moscow, 1957.

——. *Tvorchestvo Aleksandra Bloka.* Moscow, 1963.

Trotskii, L. *Literatura i revoliutsiia.* Moscow, 1923.

Turkov, A. *A. Blok.* Moscow, 1969.

Tynianov, Iurii. *Arkhaisty i novatory.* Moscow, 1929, pp. 512–520.

Vengrov, Natan. *Put' Aleksandra Bloka.* Moscow, 1963.

Volkov, Nikolai. *A. Blok i teatr.* Moscow, 1926.

Zaitsev, Boris. *Dalekoe.* Washington: Inter-Language Associates, 1965, pp. 7–19.

Zakrzhevskii, A. A. *Religiia. Psikhologicheskie paralleli.* Kiev, 1913, pp. 407–436.

Zamiatin, Evgenii. *Litsa.* New York: Chekhov Publishing House, 1965, pp. 15–21.

Zelinskii, Kornelii. *Na rubezhe dvukh epokh.* Moscow, 1962, pp. 6–10, 150–174.

Zhirmunskii, V. M. *Voprosy teorii literatury. Stat'i 1916–1926.* Petrograd, 1922; rpt. The Hague: Mouton, 1962, pp. 190–268.

——. "Anna Akhmatova i Aleksandr Blok." *Russkaia literatura* III (1970), 57–82.

Zorgenfrei, V. A. "Aleksandr Aleksandrovich Blok. Po pamiati za 15 let, 1906–1921." *Zapiski mechtatelei* VI (1922), 123–154.

Bibliographical References

Ashukin, N. *A. Blok. Sinkhronicheskie tablitsy zhizni i tvorchestva.* Moscow, 1923.

Blium, E. and Gol'tsev, V. "Literatura o Bloke za gody revoliutsii." In Nikitina, E. F., ed. *O Bloke.* Moscow, 1929, pp. 333–381.

Kolpakova, E., Kupriianovskii, P., Maksimov, D. *Bibliografia A. Bloka.* Uchenye zapiski Vil'niusskogo gosudarstvennogo pedagogicheskogo instituta, Vol. VI (1959), 289–354.

Muratova, K. D. (ed.). *Istoriia russkoi literatury kontsa XIX-na-chala XX veka.* Moscow, 1963, 124–135.

Nikitina, E. F. and Shuvalov, S. V. "Bibliografiia." In *Poetiches-koe iskusstvo Bloka.* Moscow, 1926. Pp. 161–191.

Paiman, A. "Materialy k bibliografii Aleksandra Bloka (Za-rubezhnaia literatura)." *Blokovskii sbornik.* Tartu, 1964, 557–573.

Miscellaneous

Belyi, Andrei [B. N. Bugaev]. *Putevye zametski.* Vol. II. Moscow, 1922.

Belza, Igor. *Dante i Slaviane.* Moscow, 1965.

Berberova, Nina. *The Italics Are Mine,* tr. Philippe Radley. New York: Harcourt, Brace and World, Inc., 1969.

Berlin, Isaiah. *The Hedgehog and the Fox.* New York: Simon and Schuster, 1966.

Bobrinskii, P. "Mysli o russkom simvolizme." *Mosty* IX (1962) 171–176.

Briusov, V. *Izbrannye sochineniia.* 2 vols. Moscow, 1955.

———. *Stikhotvoreniia i poemy.* Leningrad: Biblioteka poeta. Bol'shaia seriia, 1961.

Donchin, Georgette. *The Influence of French Symbolism on Russian Poetry.* The Hague, 1958.

Ellis [Kobylinskii, L. L.]. "Itogi simvolizma." *Vesy* 7 (1909).

Engelberg, E., ed. *The Symbolist Poem.* New York: E. P. Dutton and Co., 1967.

Erlich, V. "The Concept of the Poet as a Problem of Poetics." *Poetics.* Warsaw, 1961.

———. *The Double Image: Concepts of the Poet in Slavic Litera-tures.* Baltimore: The Johns Hopkins Press, 1964.

———. *Russian Formalism.* The Hague: Mouton, 1965.

Gofman, V. "Iazyk simvolistov." *Literaturnoe nasledstvo* XXVII/XXVIII, 1937.

Grevs, I. *Turgenev i Italiia.* Leningrad, 1925.

Gumilev, N. "Pis'ma o russkoi poezii." *Apollon* VIII (1912), 60–62.

Ivask, Iu. "Epokha Bloka i Mandelshtama." *Mosty* XIII–XIV (1968), 209–235.

Ivanov, Viacheslav. *Kormchie zvezdy*. St. Petersburg, 1903.

Kauchtschischwili, Nina. *L'Italia nella vita e nell'opera di P. A. Vjazemskij*. Milan: Società editrice Vita e Pensiero, 1964.

Kovalenkov, Aleksandr. *Praktika sovremennogo stikhoslozheniia*. Moscow, 1960.

Kviatkovskii, A. *Poeticheskii slovar'*. Moscow, 1966.

Lo Gatto, E. *Il mito di Pietroburgo*. Milano: Feltrinelli, 1960.

Luporini, M. B. "Un paesaggio italiano dell'Evgenij Onegin, Charles Nodier e 'La superba lira d' Albione.'" *Studi in onore di E. Lo Gatto e Giovanni Maver*. Florence: Sansoni ed., 1962.

MacLeish, Archibald. *Poetry and Experience*. Baltimore: Penguin, 1963.

Mandelshtam, Osip. "Petr Chaadaev." *Apollon* VI–VII (1915), 57–62.

———. *Razgovor o Dante*. Moscow, 1967.

Merezhkovskii, Dmitrii. *Voskresshie bogi. Leonardo da Vinci*. Moscow, (n.d.)

———. *O prichinakh upadka i o novykh techeniiakh sovremennoi russkoi literatury*. St. Petersburg, 1893.

Muratov, N. *Ocherki Italii*. 2 vols. Moscow, 1912.

Otsup, Nikolai. "N. S. Gumilev." *Opyty* I (1953), 117–142.

Pachmuss, Temira. *Zinaida Hippius. An Intellectual Profile*. Carbondale and Edwardsville: Southern Illinois University Press, 1971.

Rozanov, Vasily. *Ital'ianskie vpechatleniia*. St. Petersburg, 1909.

Russkaia literatura kontsa XIX—nachala XX v. 1901–1907. Moscow, 1971.

Sborniki po teorii poeticheskogo iazika. Petrograd, 1916.

Shiriaev, B. *Religioznye motivy v russkoi poezii*. Brussels, 1960.

Struve, Gleb. "Ital'ianskie obrazy i motivy v poezii Osipa Mandelshtama." *Studi in onore di Ettore Lo Gatto e Giovanni Maver*. Florence, 1962.

Taranovski, Kiril. "The Sound Texture of Russian Verse in the Light of Phonemic Distinctive Features." *International Journal* of *Slavic Linguistics and Poetics* IX. The Hague: Mouton, 1965–1966.

Tomashevskii, Boris. *O stikhe*. Moscow, 1928.

——. *Teoriia literatury. Poetika*. Moscow, 1928.

Trilling, Lionel. *The Experience of Literature*. New York: Doubleday and Co., 1967.

Triomphe, R. "Etude de structure." *Cahiers de monde russe et soviétique* I (1960), 387–417.

Unbegaun, B. O. *Russian Versification*. Oxford, 1956.

Valentinov, N. *Dva goda s simvolistami*. The Hoover Institute on War, Revolution & Peace, Stanford University, 1969.

Veselovskii, A. N. "La Bella Italia i nashi severnye turisty." *Ogni*. Book I. Petrograd, 1916.

Voloshin, Maksimilian. "Konstantin Bogaevskii." *Apollon* VI (1912), 5–24.

Weidle, Vladimir. "O liubvi k stikham." *Vozdushnye puti* IV (1965), 179–191.

——. *Rim*. Paris, 1967.

Yurieff, Zoya. "Vvedenie." *Lug zelenyi*. New York: Johnson Reprint Corporation, 1967.

Zhirmunskii, V. *Kompozitsiia liricheskikh stikhotvorenii*. St. Petersburg, 1921.

——. *Rifma, ee istoriia i teoriia*. St. Petersburg, 1923.

Index